Tradition and Adaptation

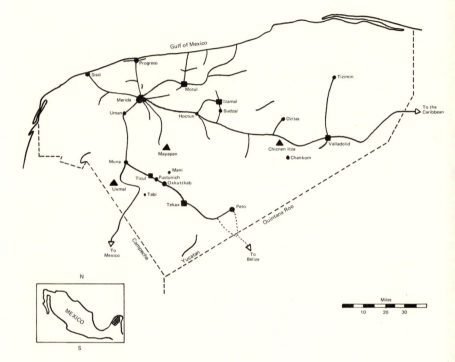

The State of Yucatan (Shaded Area on Inset) with Major Towns and
All Paved Roads as of 1963

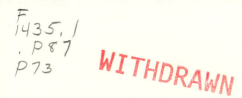

TRADITION AND ADAPTATION

Life in a Modern Yucatan Maya Village

Irwin Press

GREENWOOD PRESS

Westport, Connecticut ● London, England

Library of Congress Cataloging in Publication Data

Press, Irwin.
  Tradition and adaptation.

  Includes bibliographical references and index.
  1. Mayas—Social life and customs. 2. Pustunich,
Mexico—Social   life   and   customs.   3. Acculturation—Case
studies. I. Title.
F1435.1.P87P73   301.35′2′09726   75-71
ISBN 0-8371-7954-8

All photographs courtesy of Reginald Heron, Department of Fine Arts, Indiana University

Library of Congress Catalog Card Number: 75-71
ISBN: 0-8371-7954-8

First published in 1975

Greenwood Press, a division of Williamhouse-Regency Inc.
51 Riverside Avenue, Westport, Connecticut 06880

Printed in the United States of America

For
Al Mellick

Contents

Preface

Julian Pitt-Rivers, in his opening chapter of *Peoples of the Sierra*, admits to having selected Alcala "in the first place, among many other considerations, because I was invited into the *casino*, the club, and given a drink more promptly here than in any other place I had been."[1]

I chose Pustunich, (aside from considerations such as size, economic base, and outside-contact configuration), because I was immediately treated to a soft drink and invited to attend a communal hunt the following Saturday. It was the hunt, I think, that did it, although I was treated with kindness in every Yucatec community I visited. I had heard that Yucatecans were different from other Mexicans, but didn't really believe it until I hit the Yucatan Peninsula and stopped for the night in a Campeche hotel. In other areas of Mexico, people are generally loathe to admit to having Indian blood or cultural charactertistics. But the bellboy, upon picking up my bags, immediately said "aka' hana? . . . that means 'do you want to eat?' It's Maya. We're all Maya here." I was delighted, and the delight lasted for the next year and a half. There was not a town I visited that I would not have minded remaining in. The openness, friendliness, and lack of distrust were universal.

I returned from Pustunich to Merida and purchased a nineteenth-century double-barreled fowling piece with external hammers. Returning to Pustunich on Friday evening, I was given room to sling my hammock in the town office, and slept next to the one-armed policeman. About dawn I was awakened by sharp whistles from all parts of the village, as hunters left their houses and signaled to others to join them. Assembled at the south edge were about forty men—almost a quarter of the adult male population. They were dressed in denims and whites, with deerskin sandals. Over each shoulder hung a woven bag (with *pozole* and other edibles) and a water gourd shaped like an hourglass. We started off and spent the next seven hours tramping through the bush. I was given the best spots to wait, while the beaters came through the forest shouting ''he-le-le-le-le-le-le-huuuuuuuuuuuy'' to frighten the deer, wild goat, peccary, and bush turkey toward those of us who lay in ambush. I saw nothing, shot nothing, and returned exhausted, desiccated, and laden wth pin-head sized ticks, but had a grand time. I forgave my fellow hunters for telling jokes that were better than mine. I asked the mayor if he knew of anyone who would be willing to house me. He immediately offered the indefinite use of a fine new masonry house which he had built on the highway at the back of his property. He would not hear of my paying a rent—not then, or ever.

I have often thought that few have had more luck than I in finding their first field-work community so congenial. It was more often than not the villager who produced the first ''hello'' when passing on the street. Almost anyone I met would be willing to chat, and to appear at the door of any house was to be invited in for a cool glass of barley water (*horchata*). This had its disadvantages, in that unboiled village water was amoeba-laden. Luckily, the Maya are archetypical ''Jewish mothers.'' All I had to say was that I had just previously drunk something hot and the offer—or glass—would be hastily withdrawn. Everyone knows that to follow hot food with cold causes stomach problems.

My initial impression of Pustunich as a friendly, cheerful, contented, and virile community remained unchanged through the remainder of my stay. The many visitors we had consistently affirmed the impression. David Gutmann, a psychologist from the University of Michigan, derived similar impressions from personal observations and TAT instruments. He makes the following observation: ''Aside from the heat by day and the scorpions by night, Pustunich is one of the most comfortable places that I have ever known, and my comfort was largely based on my sense of honesty and general decency of the villagers. From the first, these people were remarkably acceptant of and generous towards the foreigners in their midst.''[2]

My wife's observations are similar to mine. She was made to feel thoroughly at home. If, when I was out of town, a nonvillage drunk would position himself outside our door (which was a bus stop), she reports that, almost imperceptibly, village men would begin to gather while one would come to the back door suggesting that she bolt the front until the undesirable had boarded his bus. If a stranger came visiting during my absence, he would be escorted to the door of our house, not merely directed. We never had to lock our doors, nor did we have to ask twice for help on any matter. We borrowed money three times, yet were ourselves borrowed from only twice. There was little drunkenness, little fighting, and little meanness.

It was clear from the first glimpse of the many shortwave radio antennas that the village was confronting, if not directly experiencing, a considerable transition. I had come to equate transition with anxiety, witchcraft, alcoholism, nativistic movements, abandonment of ancestors' skulls, and a host of other mild to drastic reactions. Pustunich matured my understanding of the process of cultural and social change.

I wish to thank Fred Strodtbeck and Fred Eggan for their advice and support, and Julian Pitt-Rivers and Robert A. Levine for their counsel. Nothing, of course, would have been possible without my wife, Gloria. Her patience, collaboration, TLC, and criticism made the whole possible. Finally, to our brothers and sisters—the people of Pustunich— we both give thanks.

Field-work in Pustunich was conducted over fourteen months of 1963 and 1964. This study, though written in the present tense, refers to the village as it was in September 1964. A short re-visit in 1968 revealed no noticeable changes. Subsequent correspondence with villagers and anthropologists who worked in Pustunich and Ticul indicates that no substantial changes have yet occurred. However, trends in village physical improvement (water, electricity) and in class mobility begun prior to 1964 are continuing (see Chapters 6 and 9).

NOTES

1. Julian Pitt-Rivers, *The People of the Sierra* (Chicago: University of Chicago Press, 1961), p. 2.

2. David Gutmann, *Field Report on Research in Pustunich* (Ann Arbor: The University of Michigan, Department of Psychology [mimeographed] 1965), p. 3.

Tradition and Adaptation

1

Introduction: The Theoretical Context

The Community

All too often we read of peasantries severely disrupted by change. Roads open, factories rise from the fields, urban centers expand into the hinterlands, and once-stable villages wither or transform more or less abruptly beneath a bombardment of unprecedented forces. Certainly this occurs. Yet, for a majority of the world's peasants, change is a less spectacular process, a perennial adjustment to both internal and external factors, to local innovation and outside policy.

This is a description of a peasant community confronting change. The confrontation, however, has been a continual one since the community was founded over 700 years ago. Our goal is two-fold: To present an accurate picture of village life today, and to phrase the description in such a way as to illuminate the processes by which a successful peasant community is created and sustained.

By any anthropological definition, Pustunich is a peasant town: it is a "part-society"[1] "subject to the demands and sanctions of [outside] power holders";[2] "the primary means of livelihood [is] cultivation of the soil";[3] it traditionally lacks "effective local leadership";[4] it is small and quite homogeneous;[5] its people speak an aboriginal tongue as well as the national language; the people marry endogamously (with respect to the village) a majority of the time; it is land-based with pointed digging-stick technology; it is shoeless and lives in thatched huts; it supports a pagan priest, two native curers, and both Catholic and field-oriented pagan ritual.

In most respects the community is no closer to an urban existence, no nearer to cultural or economic dissolution, than it was at its founding, or at the conquest of Yucatan, or during the colonial epoch, the hacienda era, the Mexican Revolution, or the world wars. Conquest, conversion to Catholicism, imposition of colonial *encomendero* and, later, municipal control over local villages merely transferred the seats of esoteric knowledge and power from one group of elite (the Maya royalty) to another. The creation of an *ejido* (government land-grant for communal use) from Pustunich's farmlands simply legitimized centuries of traditional use, and, indeed, provided for the first time legal protective clout. The growth of cash use and wage labor opportunities not related to traditional corn production provided access to income sources, the lack of which forced villagers off the land in prior times of drought or economic need. The long years of continuous "outside" contact have left other marks as well. Radios, bicycles, sewing machines, plastic hair curlers, permanent waves, enameled pots, high-heeled women's shoes, and lottery tickets are everyday items. Technicolor movies, television, autos, and trucks are available in the community. Physicians are patronized regularly. All village youngsters have gone to school and a few have attended secondary and normal schools. Some children are now being dressed in the city fashion, with shoes and dresses, and are destined to leave the community. Modern committee organization has a firm foothold. The baseball team, one of the best in Yucatan, sports full uniforms supplied by one of the state's major breweries. How, then, are we to describe this community? And what will the description tell us?

Redfield and the Folk Society

This is perhaps the first peasant community study on Yucatan published since Redfield and Villa's Chan Kom series. For this reason, it might be wise to reiterate the theoretical context generated by earlier work in the peninsula. It is easy, today, in the light of decades of criticism, evaluation, comment, and argument, to say, simply, that "*my* Yucatec village" doesn't fit Redfield's elegant, idealistic, folk-urban continuum. What more apropos criticism can be brought to bear than the demonstration that a peasant community in Yucatan itself doesn't lend itself to his model?

For example, Redfield notes that, as one moves from the folk to the urban poles, the yearly patron-saint fiesta of Yucatan changes substantially. That is, (a) it becomes a money-earning enterprise; (b) novenas fall into the hands of a few women, with little participation from municipal authorities; (c) the bullfight becomes commercial, with professionals hired and an admission fee charged; (d) attendance at folk dances falls off; (e) merchants utilize the fiesta to make a profit; (f) youth begin to enjoy modern dance. This, says Redfield, is an example of "the disorganization of culture."[6] In fact, Pustunich's fiesta *is* highly commercialized, being the principal source of town income. However, for this very reason, secular town leaders are closely involved in fiesta organization. As we will see later, Pustunich is still a highly conservative corn-farming village and can hardly be referred to as disorganized or urban-oriented. What then is the utility of Redfield's folk-urban model?

Redfield saw societies as lying along an ideal continuum from folk to urban. Folk societies exhibited such characteristics as:

isolation; cultural homogeneity; organization of conventional understandings into a "single web of interrelated meanings"; adjustment to the local environment; predominantly personal character of the relationships; relative importance of sacred sanctions as compared with secular; development of ritual expression of belief and attitude; tending for much of the behavior of the individual to involve his familial or local group.[7]

Redfield implied that, left to their own devices, folk societies would remain essentially unchanged; only outside contact with urban-influenced phenomena materially affects them. Such "lessening isolation" results in "disorganization of culture," "secularization," and "individualization," all of which are features he associated with urban society.[8] Furthermore, because folk societies constitute closed systems (one activity not following another so much as *being* another[9]), change in one sector will effect change in others. In other words, any contact with urban life will likely break down the folk community's structure.

Redfield placed the peasant community near the folk pole. Indeed, he was among the very first modern anthropologists to turn researchers' attention away from more exotic cultures. Only a handful of peasant monographs had been published when Redfield went to Mexico. Though highly informative, such studies as Durham's (on Albania, 1909) and Blackman's (Egypt, 1927) did not examine peasantries as a special type of society. Even subsequent New World studies, such as those of Parsons (1936) and Herskovits (1937), were more devoted to acculturative processes than to defining and operationalizing a conceptual model of peasantries. Redfield's early studies of Tepoztlan (1930) and Chan Kom (originally co-authored with Villa Rojas in 1934) approached peasant communities as coherent entities with generalizable life-styles.[10] At this early date, however, peasants were still to be lumped with "primitive" groups near the folk pole and to be differentiated from others on the basis of urban transformations (not merely admixture), or relative degree of "spoilage."

In terms of theory, Redfield's idea was not so new. Toennies' contrast between *Gemeinschaft* and *Gesellschaft*, Maine's contrast between personal and territorial bases for relationships, Durkheim's mechanical versus organic solidarity, and the Chicago School of Sociology's view of the city all contributed strongly to Redfield's formulation, as he himself indicates.[11] In many respects, he simply replaced the words *primitive* and *savage* with the less pejorative *folk*. Apparently the idea's "time had come," for after initial digestion of his major theoretical-empirical (the order here is intended) statement of 1941 (*The Folk Culture of Yucatan*), American anthropologists hurried to test the model, expand upon it, refute it, or simply discover peasants for themselves.[12] Studies virtually tumbled upon one another. Beals (1946), Gillin (1947, 1951), Tchopik (1947), Foster (1948), Fuente (1949), Lewis (1951), Pierson (1951), Bunzel (1952), Tax (1953), and others all published monographs on Latin-American peasants within the same short period.[13] Most of these Meso-American peasant studies comprised the first offerings of the newly inaugurated Smithsonian Institute of Social Anthropology publication series. The folk-urban continuum was an attractive and simple conceptual framework. Its ideal polar types at the very least provided bases for research and comparison. Though most paid little more than lip service to Redfield's procedural scheme, the idea that peasants constitute a special type of social system, coherent enough to lend itself to comparative analysis, was largely Redfield's and was implicit in the broadness of the studies and the similarity of the units which most scholars subsequently chose for description and analysis.

Such research, of course, weakened the folk-urban continuum. The model reflected an earlier decade when there were little data available on peasantries. The subsequent rash of studies produced more variables than could be handled by the folk model and demanded new approaches to typing and analyzing peasant society.

Toward a New Approach

Criticism of Redfield is by now old hat. The major objections involved: rigidity of the model;[14] lack of historical or functional insight;[15] lack of correspondence of the type to real communities;[16] misrepresentation and oversimplification of both the reality of the city[17] and of peasant interpersonal relationships themselves.[18]

Critical response to Redfield, however, laid the groundwork for a new understanding of peasant social structure. Redfield himself responded to others by admitting, subsequently, that the relationship between the peasant community and the city might be a very special one, and that this relationship might be stable. In a later paper, he noted that folk societies could possibly be found in a variety of situations. The village communities of classical China were folk types, he says, even though they existed in a greater society with a literate elite. Peasants, he concludes, are country people who have developed "economic and political relationships, as well as relationships of status, with the city people."[19] This important conclusion predated by a year Kroeber's use of the term *part-society* in reference to peasants.

By 1956, Redfield had almost made an about-face. No longer, he claimed, was the peasant a victim of the city, on the path to inevitable social and cultural dissolution. Peasant society, rather, was a thing in itself, a stable configuration of local and national elements. Peasants were the "rural dimension of old civilizations." Indeed, the peasant was now viewed as positively resistant to the inroads of industrial urban influence. "The more primitive man is likely to enter modern industry when it is established in his country; the landowning peasant, with a way of life already in stable adjustment to aspects of civilization, is more resistant to industrialization." More specifically,

the social structure of peasant and peasant-like societies includes, then, the relations of cultural influence and example between the elite half and the peasant half of the whole larger social system. It will not do to describe these relations only as relations of ruler and ruled or of exploiter and exploited, although these elements are likely to be present. The student will want also to describe the prestige or contempt, the feelings of superiority or inferiority, and the examples of excellence to be emulated or of baseness to be avoided that may be present in the relations between peasant and elite. . . .

In peasant societies we see a relatively *stable* and very roughly typical *adjustment* between local and national or feudal life, a developed larger social system in which there are two cultures within *one culture, one social system* composed of upper and lower halves. [Emphases mine][20]

The emphases indicate Redfield's recognition of peasant society as a stable type in its own right, a consistent social and cultural entity endowed with continuity. The "higher-lower" dichotomy is not as biased as it sounds. As we will see, peasants are well aware of most elements of their relationship with the wider society, and often have a difficult time in balancing contempt or distrust with envy or outright identification. "The peasant," concludes Redfield, "is a rustic and he knows it."[21] In short, the peasant is not merely *in* the total society, he is definitely a *part* of it.

The Part-Society

It is precisely the fact that the peasant is an interacting part of a wider social, cultural, and political system that distinguishes him from the primitive. At the same time, what distinguishes the peasant from the farmer of modern industrial society is the peasant's variance from the official sociocultural theme. It is important to recognize that such variation results from reinterpretation or modification of outside forms as much as it reflects purely local developments. This is at the heart of the part-society concept. The variance can be cultural or political in nature, or both. Fallers grants more importance to cultural variance for his definition of peasantry.[22] To Eric Wolf, the critical differential is power. Thus, concludes Wolf, "it is only when a cultivator is integrated into a society with a state—that is, when the cultivator becomes subject to the demands and sanctions of power-holders outside his social stratum—that we can appropriately speak of peasantry."[23]

Whether the differential is that of culture or power, the implication of *continuing interaction*, with some degree of symbiosis, between peasant and the wider society is clear. Such integration (in Wolf's terms above) is largely impossible between peasantry and modern, industrial, urban-oriented society. The latter's demands for extensive, variable-skill labor, for population concentration, for extensive agribusiness lands, for large-scale credit mechanisms, and for a cash-earning, product-consuming populace conflict almost totally with the "classic" peasant life-style.[24] Peasantry developed and flourished in relation to the pre-industrial society and city whose economies and social systems were themselves geared to, and dependent upon, peasant production and social forms. Even today, there is only one supermarket in Merida. The management of the city's foodstuffs is totally in the hands of small-scale marketeers who maintain buying relationships with small-scale middlemen, who in turn purchase most raw materials directly from the Yucatec peasantry. The afternoon siesta, the proximity of homes to businesses in the city, the importance of landholding to the prestige economy, the utilization of kin and ritual kin (*compadres*) in circumventing "official" bureaucratic mechanisms are all equally compatible with peasant expectations and behavior.

Peasants today are most numerous and vigorous in nonindustrial or still-developing nations where they have been able to maintain a stable, working relationship with the wider society and its cities. This relationship is sensitive and constantly shifting to meet demands from both within and without the local community. Wolf makes the point that even the more closed, corporate peasant communities "are neither simply 'survivals' nor the results of 'culture lag' . . . . They exist because their functions *are* contemporaneous."[25] The important point here is the implication of long and traditional interaction between the peasant community and the "outside." Foster refers to the process as "simmering."[26]

"Simmering" involves the blending of older, pre-peasant forms with "national," "outside," or "urban" forms as well as with unique local independent developments. The sociocultural items of "outside" origin may have entered the community at any time in its history. These items themselves are potentially subject to reinterpretation or preservation quite beyond original usage or subsequent life-span on the national level.

In Pustunich, St. Michael the Archangel has assumed parenthood of the four *balams* (gods) of the field.

The simmering process ensures that a peasant community such as Pustunich shares many aspects of the wider society with which it communicates and interacts. When we describe the average Pustunicheño as a moderately literate, Spanish-speaking Catholic, married to one woman, tracing descent through both parents, clanless, who maintains a more or less active *compadre* relationship with others, and who buys with cash a certain percentage of his goods on the open market, we are also describing the average Mexican whether he is rural or urban. This sharing has further implications. In Latin America, peasants and city dwellers alike are fully aware of, and committed to, differences in status between *indios* and *ladinos*. There are likely few *indios* or *mestizos* who are not envious of the superior position of the *ladino*. Peasants are not indifferent to the advantages of speaking better Spanish, possessing European physical features and surname, owning large amounts of land, having powerful and wealthy friends, feeling at ease or competent in bureaucratic situations, accumulating capital reserves, and sporting the material paraphernalia of a "modern" life-style. Thus "inside" and "outside" merge in the peasant context to create a unique configuration of forces for disruption and stability.

Overall, Redfield's model was weakest precisely where he failed to recognize that the line between inside and out, sacred or profane, is often impossible to draw and in some instances meaningless. "Outside" or urban phenomena hold no monopoly on disruptive consequences, nor do traditional institutions on conflictless continuity.

Perhaps Wolf's observation of the contemporaneity of peasantries comes closest to summarizing the interplay of factors that comprise peasant life. The continuing contribution of peasants to national economies,[27] to popular religious practice, food usage, and regional urban subculture,[28] are but the more outwardly directed aspects. Locally, contemporaneity is reflected in the manner in which modern political, economic, dress, social class, recreational, and other usages are present and continuously undergoing modification. Such modifications enter the local structure, become stamped with the identity of local tradition, and subsequently themselves serve as mediators and validators of yet "newer" usages. As peasants *are* susceptible to a variety of pressures from the outside, behavior directed to accommodation or thwarting of these pressures is de facto contemporary. From this point of view, such ostensibly centripedal phenomena as invidious economic leveling, witchcraft, and "limited good" value orientations are active contemporary mechanisms that function to limit or deny entry to specific contemporary socioeconomic phenomena. Action and reaction are inseparable.

With this view in mind some scholars are tending to reevaluate peasants in terms of equilibrium.[29] Equilibrium implies both change and maintenance of structural integrity. This latter means simply the maintenance of some functional relationship among roles, groups, and institutions. The disruption of existing interaction channels or expectations of role behavior creates disequilibrium. The integration of new roles, values, or interaction channels into the system recreates equilibrium. The reestablishment of equilibrium requires that the "loose-ends" (of whatever origin and form) be tied into the overall system. That the "old" social structure may have been changed thereby is immaterial. No social structure is holy.

The importance of these considerations lies in the resulting acceptance of dynamic input and output as normal. Individual social systems must not be viewed as pure entities somehow fouled through changes or acceptance of influence from without. This part-society approach to peasantries runs throughout the following anatomy of a Yucatec Maya community.

The Context of the Study

Yucatan was an ideal location for Redfield's folk-urban study. It was and remains strikingly homogeneous. The native people represent one physical and linguistic stock. Further, there is but one seat of urban influence (Merida), the peninsula having been effectively isolated by sea, jungle, and rivers from mainland Mexico and the outside world. To Redfield, differences between the communities, therefore, could be attributed only to differential access to the city. Each community study was for him a snapshot which captured a moving object on its way to an inevitable destination.

In truth, Redfield's photography was not of the best. Merida, the pre-industrial capital, is large but hardly an urban metropolis. Reed and others have further noted that Meridanos and provincial city dwellers had little direct contact with the peasants.[30] Indeed, it can be convincingly argued that the *henequen* plantation has had far more impact upon Yucatec Maya than has any city. The pre-industrial capital itself never crowded out villagers or snared farmers in debt to company stores, nor put an end to corn farming nor forced wage labor upon peasants.

Chan Kom, furthermore, was not the best choice of towns. It had barely celebrated its fiftieth birthday when Redfield began his field study. It had been founded and subsequently populated by refugees from various villages which had been decimated by the Caste War of the previous century. In other words, while conserving many general Maya features, the townspeople had experienced great trauma and had yet to develop a tight identity as a community with fixed ways and clear expectations. Every oldster could say with authority, ''in the old days it was different,'' and be right. A strong precedent for change had been built into the soul of the community.

Pustunich offers a different view of Yucatec peasant society. It is perhaps no more typical than many other communities of the peninsula, but it has ''simmered'' a great while, developed a strong identity, and has thus weathered change in a special way. We approach it here specifically as a part-society. Each peasantry is part of a distinct nation or wider society. Each peasantry has its own special history, its own special problems in maintaining its position vis-à-vis the wider society. Each exhibits its own special blend of ''inside'' and ''outside'' features. To describe one peasant community, therefore, is not to describe all. It is, rather, to add further insight into the more general problem of process— whether the process is that of continuity or of change.

We begin with the assumption that the community is part of many wider entities, that its history, world view, life cycle, class structure, and social system exhibit forces for both conservatism and change and represent a complex amalgam of forms whose origins tumble upon one another and infuse the peasant life with its special vitality.

NOTES

1. A. L. Kroeber, *Anthropology* (New York: Harcourt, Brace, 1948), p. 284. Robert Redfield, *Peasant Society and Culture* (Chicago: University of Chicago Press, 1956).

2. Eric R. Wolf, *Peasants* (Englewood Cliffs, N.J.: Prentice-Hall, 1966), p. 11.

3. Raymond Firth, *Social Change in Tikopia* (London: George Allen and Unwin, 1959), p. 503.

4. George M. Foster, "What Is a Peasant?" In Jack M. Potter, May N. Diaz, George M. Foster, eds., *Peasant Society* (Boston: Little, Brown, 1967), p. 8.

5. Robert Redfield, *The Little Community* (Chicago: University of Chicago Press, 1958), p. 4.

6. Robert Redfield, "The Folk Society." *American Journal of Sociology* 52 (1947), p. 307.

7. Robert Redfield, *The Folk Culture of Yucatan* (Chicago: University of Chicago Press, 1941), p. 343.

8. Ibid., pp. 339 and 343.

9. Robert Redfield, "The Folk Society." *American Journal of Sociology* 52 (1947): 299.

10. Edith M. Durham, *High Albania* (London: Edward Arnold, 1909). Winifred S. Blackman, *The Fellahin of Upper Egypt* (London: George G. Harrap, 1927). Elsie C. Parsons, *Mitla, Town of the Souls* (Chicago: University of Chicago Press, 1936). Melville J. Herskovits, *Life in a Haitian Valley* (New York: Knopf, 1937). Robert Redfield, *Tepoztlan, A Mexican Village* (Chicago: University of Chicago Press, 1930). Robert Redfield and Alfonso Villa Rojas, *Chan Kom: A Maya Village* (Washington: Carnegie Institution of Washington, Publication No. 448, 1934).

11. Robert Redfield, *The Folk Culture of Yucatan* (Chicago: University of Chicago Press, 1941), p. 343.

12. Ibid.

13. Ralph Beals, *Cheran: A Sierra Tarascan Village* (Washington: Smithsonian Institution, Institute of Social Anthropology, Publication #2, 1946). John Gillin, *Moche: A Peruvian Coastal Community* (Washington: Smithsonian Institution, Institute of Social Anthropology, Publication #3, 1947). John Gillin, *The Culture of Security in San Carlos* (New Orleans: Middle American Research Institution, Publication #16, 1951). Harry Tchopik, Jr., *Highland Communities of Central Peru* (Washington: Smithsonian Institution, Institute of Social Anthropology, Publication #5, 1947). George M. Foster, *Empire's Children: The People of Tzintzuntzan* (Washington: Smithsonian Institution, Institute of Social Anthropology, Publication #6, 1948). Julio de la Fuente, *Yalalag: Una Villa Zapoteca Serrana* (Mexico, D.F.: Museo Nacional de Antropologia, Serie Cientifica #1, 1949). Oscar Lewis, *Life in a Mexican Village: Tepoztlan Restudied* (Urbana: University of Illinois Press, 1951). Donald Pierson, *Cruz das Almas, A Brazilian Village* (Washington: Smithsonian Institution, Institute of Social Anthropology, Publication #12, 1951). Ruth Bunzel, *Chichicastenango* (Washington: American Ethnological Society, Pub. 22, 1951). Sol Tax, *Penny Capitalism:*

A Guatemalan Indian Economy (Washington: Smithsonian Institution, Institute of Social Anthropology, Publication #16, 1953).

14. Horace Miner, "The Folk-Urban Continuum." *American Sociological Review* 17 (1952), pp. 535-537. Melville J. Herskovits, *Man and His Works* (New York: Knopf, 1952), p. 605.

15. George P. Murdock, Review of Redfield's "The Folk Culture of Yucatan " *American Anthropologist* 14 (1943): 135.

16. Sidney Mintz, "The Folk-Urban Continuum and the Rural Proletarian Community." *American Journal of Sociology* 59 (1953): 136-143.

17. Oscar Lewis, *Life in a Mexican Village: Tepoztlan Restudied* (Urbana: University of Illinois Press, 1951), pp. 432-440. Horace Miner, *The Primitive City of Timbuctoo* (Princeton: Princeton University Press, 1953).

18. George M. Foster, "Interpersonal Relations in Peasant Society." *Human Organization* 19 (1960-61): 174-178. Edward C. Banfield, *The Moral Basis of a Backward Society* (Glencoe, Ill.: The Free Press, 1958). G. Reichel-Dolmatoff and A. Reichel-Dolmatoff, *The People of Aritama: The Cultural Personality of a Colombian Mestizo Village* (Chicago: University of Chicago Press, 1961).

19. Robert Redfield, "The Folk Society." *American Journal of Sociology* 52 (1947): 306.

20. Robert Redfield, *Peasant Society and Culture* (Chicago: University of Chicago Press, 1956), pp. 29, 59, 64, and 65.

21. Ibid., p. 64.

22. Lloyd A. Fallers, "Are African Cultivators to be Called 'Peasants'?" *Current Anthropology* 2 (1961): 108-110.

23. Eric R. Wolf, *Peasants* (Englewood Cliffs, N.J.: Prentice-Hall, 1966),: 11.

24. Cf. George Dalton, "Peasantries in Anthropology and History." *Current Anthropology* 13 (1972): 385-415.

25. Eric R. Wolf, "Closed Corporate Peasant Communities in Meso-America and Central Java." *Southwestern Journal of Anthropology* 13 (1957), p. 9.

26. George M. Foster, "What Is a Peasant?" In Jack M. Potter, May N. Diaz, George M. Foster, eds., *Peasant Society* (Boston: Little, Brown, 1967), p. 2.

27. Sol Tax, "The Indians in the Economy of Guatemala." *Social and Economic Studies* 6 (1957): 413-424.

28. Alfredo Barrera Vasquez, "El Idioma Español en Yucatan." *Enciclopedia Yucatanse* (Mexico, D.F.: Gobierno de Yucatan, Vol. 6, 1946): 341-375.

29. See June Nash, *In the Eyes of the Ancestors* (New Haven and London: Yale University Press, 1970).

30. Nelson Reed, *The Caste War of Yucatan* (Stanford: Stanford University Press, 1964).

2

The Context: Pustunich as Part of ''Wholes''

As a part-society, Pustunich reflects features of Spanish-American, Meso-American, Maya, and Yucatec origin. Along with other communities of Spanish-influenced countries, Pustunich exhibits certain common characteristics. It must use the Spanish language in all official contacts with governmental and bureaucratic bodies. It is nominally Catholic, and engages in a highly personalistic relationship with the Christian hierarchy of deities, mediated through saints' images. It baptizes its young and engages in the *compadre* relationship and celebrates a Catholic annual ritual round. It sports a mayoral form of town government (aside from any other leadership group which may be present). The town is laid out in grid pattern, with a central focal meeting place (the square) whose dominant feature is the church. It further shares with all other Spanish-influenced peasantries a body of folk concepts that explain and deal with health, illness, and other ''life crisis'' phenomena and that place heavy reliance upon folk curers. Indeed, it is this fairly homogeneous Hispanic cultural overlay that makes Latin America a useful laboratory for the study of change processes, in that a major variable—in this case the colonial cultural overlay—is largely a constant.

Pustunich is also a Middle or Meso-American community. The term *Middle America* has come to signify both more and less than a geographical area. Physically, it stretches roughly from Costa Rica to the

United States border. As a cultural area designation, Kirchoff and others prefer to speak of *Meso America*, physically somewhat more restricted than Middle America, and roughly embracing those peoples who were within the range of more immediate cultural influence from the Pre-Colombian high cultures of Mexico, Guatemala, and the Honduras.[1] Tribally, Meso America would extend from below the Yaqui on the north to the termination of Maya-related groups in the south. However, there is still much argument as to whether southern United States and Antilles groups might be profitably included.

The most important diagnostic features of Meso America include (1) at least partial dependence upon subsistence agriculture with corn as its focus; (2) dependence upon corn tortillas, beans, chili peppers, and, in many areas, rice as common diet elements; (3) division of labor along the lines of sex and age; (4) the existence of civic and religious centers with which people identify and which house patron saints' images; (5) a tendency toward village endogamy and solidarity; (6) respect for age; and (7) primacy of the nuclear family and absence of clans or other large kin-based groupings.[2]

Other suggested features are not so universal as those listed above. In fact, some of the more well-known "traits" attributed to Meso America are restricted to its most heavily researched areas—Highland Guatemala, Chiapas, and Oaxaca. Yucatec peasant communities differ in some highly important ways. Yucatan lacks a civil religious hierarchy, cargo system, strongly developed envy-witchcraft syndrome, village markets, and village specialty handicrafts. Smaller peasant towns tend to be class-homogeneous in that few if any ladinos reside in predominantly farming communities. The results of these differences are important with respect to potential for change. There is less pressure for economic conformity, more independence of religious, political, and economic institutions from one another—all of which are ostensibly permissive of novel behavior with less chance of immediate repercussion throughout the entire social systemic core.

As a community within the cultural-linguistic Maya group of Meso America and more specifically of Yucatan, Pustunich exhibits unique characteristics. The local Yucatec Maya dialect is spoken by all as a first language. It is not readily understood by speakers from other Maya areas of Mexico and Guatemala. Yucatec villagers in even wholly cash crop zones practice a ritual round devoted to rain making, to propitiation of the field (*milpa*) spirit guardians, and to harvest thanks. Certain features of milpa group composition, village and familial cooperative activities (such as hunting, town maintenance, lime-making, and house building) vary in unique ways from analogous phenomena in other areas. Dress is unique and distinguishes the Yucatec peasant from others in Meso America. Certain elements of social structure, such as preferences for minimal extension of the godparent ritual kinship bond, *compadrazgo*, appear to be Yucatec-specific.[3]

Yucatan occupies the northern portion of that peninsula which juts out from Mexico and Guatemala to form the southern and eastern borders of the Gulf of Mexico. The state is largely flat, riverless, and lakeless. The Puuc Hills, stretching roughly from east to west, form a horizontal spine which cuts off the lower quarter of the state. Southward are foothills and vast areas of uninhabited bush. Here may be found deer, wild goat, peccary, boar, armadillo, jaguar, and mischievous *alux* (the spirit helpers of forgotten sorcerers). North of the Puuc lie over 2,300 towns and settlements, the henequen plants which supply the largest share of state income, the tourists who come to visit the spectacular ruins of Uxmal and Chichen Itza, and the state capital, Merida. Most towns, however, do not lie on paved roads.

Until recently, Yucatan was all but isolated from mother Mexico. It is bounded by water on the west, north, and east, and by swamp, rivers, and jungle to the south. Paved roads and ferries to the mainland have existed for less than thirty years. The Mexico-Merida railway is less than thirty-five years old[4] and full-scale commercial air transportation is relatively new. The ship route from Yucatan to Tampa, New Orleans, or Galveston is not much longer than the sea distance to Vera Cruz on the Mexican mainland.

Yucatecans have long felt different from Mexicans. The ubiquitous influence of the homogeneous Maya cultural base, plus the shared experience of the nineteenth-century native rebellion, has forged a common and jealously guarded self-perception. Bitter, sporadic conflict with centralist government troops in the nineteenth century, government establishment of chicle price controls in the twentieth, and other disputes have resulted in discussion of secession and use of the pejorative term *huach* for mainland Mexicans—about as complementary as *gringo* for North Americans. To this day wealthy Yucatecans prefer to send their children to the United States or Europe for education and "finishing."

Because of its relative isolation, Yucatan, perhaps more than other Mexican states, is dependent upon a single center for distribution of urban, "modern," or "outside" influence. Merida, the capital, is a metropolis of 190,000 inhabitants, roughly half the state's entire population. The next largest "city" has a population of less than 25,000. As the peninsula is sparsely settled and a geographical dead-end, few non-Yucatecans make the state a regular part of sales territories. The result of a single broker-center, of long isolation, and of traditional distrust of mainland Mexico has been a strikingly autonomous political, economic, and cultural evolution upon a homogeneous Maya base. Much Maya is spoken in Merida and few are the Yucatecans who cannot understand at least a few phrases. Furthermore, few politicians, whether local or state candidates, are unable to converse more or less fluently in Maya. Most Yucatecans, regardless of background or social class, own Maya peasant clothing for the popular *jarana* dances. Though a clear class system does exist, overall there is little of the antipathy or condescension toward Indians found in other heavily native states of Mexico.

The result is a duality of factors of potential importance to change. No Yucatecan is wholly an outsider to others. Communication is easy. The cultural and social isolation of peasant communities from the larger towns, the city, and the influential classes is far from absolute. On the other hand, the very provinciality of the peninsula, coupled with the existence of only one conservative distributive center, has militated against a strong flow of innovative phenomena to the peasant hinterland.

The state itself may be viewed as containing three major economic-cultural zones. One is the vast henequen (sisal) area surrounding Merida. It is the most acculturated area of Yucatan, characterized by large plantations, wage labor, alcoholism, and loss of many Maya indigenous traits.[5] A second zone lies to the east of the henequen heartland. Valladolid is its urban center. The town of Chan Kom lies here, as does the famous temple city of Chichen Itza. It is a zone of corn and cattle, with perhaps the highest degree of Maya monolingualism.

Across the southern portion of Yucatan, just south of the henequen zone, runs the third zone, the Puuc hill range. The zone along the hills is an important one historically. Groups here were among the first to cooperate with the conquistadors. With the Puuc serving as a natural barrier, this became the "frontier" of Yucatan. Spaniards who could not qualify socially in Merida or Valladolid saw the frontier as an opportunity for achievement. As a jumping-off point for Mexico, Guatemala, and the Bay of Chetumal, the zone welcomed travelers and traders. There has been considerable contact between Spaniard and settled Indian. Both economic and Caste War displacement appear to have been less severe than in either the henequen or eastern indigenous zones. There were fewer haciendas than in the henequen zone; most that did exist produced sugar whose land requirements and, more importantly, harvest labor periods did not compete strongly with the milpa. Today the area is fed by paved highway and narrow gauge railroad. There is considerable traffic coming and going to the British Honduras. The area may be characterized as quite culturally conservative, though more familiar with outside customs than the eastern indigenous zone. In this more fluid region, on the major highway from Merida to Belize, lies Pustunich.

NOTES

1. Paul Kirchoff, "Meso America." In Sol Tax, ed., *Heritage of Conquest* (Glencoe, Ill.: The Free Press, 1952), pp. 17-30.

2. Robert Redfield and Sol Tax, "General Characteristics of Present-Day Meso-American Indian Society." In Sol Tax, ed., *Heritage of Conquest* (Glencoe, Ill.: The Free Press, 1952), pp. 31-39.

3. Alfonso Villa Rojas, *The Maya of East Central Quintana Roo* (Carnegie Institute of Washington Publication No. 559, 1945).

4. Howard F. Cline, *The United States and Mexico* (Cambridge: Harvard University Press, 1963), pp. 61-62.

5. Alfonso Villa Rojas, untitled cultural-ecological map of Yucatan prepared for the Instituto Nacional de Antropologia e Historia (Mexico, D.F., 1962).

3

The Village: Setting and Overview

Tentative hillocks create a natural southern boundary for Pustunich. Between these small ridges and the main Puuc (half a mile to the south) lies a dry plain with several privately owned milpas and a major government irrigation project in which a dozen villagers grow corn, produce, oranges, and other citrus. The Puuc rises abruptly and rockily. Hardly more than 500 feet in height at any point, it creates an effective barrier to all but the largest-wheeled carts and strongest horses.

From the top of the hills, perhaps a mile south of the village center, only the two-tiered church steeple can be seen above the town's lush trees. Beyond the church, perhaps five kilometers to the north, rises another steeple above the trees of Dzan. Between Pustunich and Dzan lie the latter's ejido and scattered, privately owned plots of Pustunich men. A sharp-eyed viewer might also be able to pick out the steeple of the old Maya capital of Mani some five kilometers to the northeast. By foot, it's half an hour's walk through bush trails to Dzan and forty minutes to Mani. Both towns can be reached by bus—Dzan through Ticul, two miles west of Pustunich, and Mani through Oxbutzkab, five miles east.

On the east, Pustunich is bordered by two henequen plantations. One is owned by a villager, the other by a Meridano who likes to spend weekends away from the city in the crumbling, yet imposing, manor on the old hacienda.

On the west, Pustunich is bordered by still another henequen plantation, that of an absentee landlord residing in Merida.

South of Pustunich the Puuc extends for several miles, decreasing in
height. In the hills themselves, farming is difficult and sparse. Almost all
of Pustunich's ejido and the majority of its milpas lie south of Puuc, in the
flat though rocky lands which never interested the Spanish entrepreneurs
or settlers. This bushland is second growth, rarely exceeding fifteen to
twenty feet in height. The frequent rock outcrops and thin topsoil prevent
plow agriculture. The area is crisscrossed with numerous paths, a few
being wide enough to allow passage of horse carts. Game is ordinarily
plentiful, providing fair to good hunting, depending upon the spring
rains. There are deer, peccary, armadillo, wild turkey, a small straight-
horned goat (*yuk*), rabbit, fox, pigeons, quail, pheasant, and a variety of
goose-like bird (*chachalaca*). Only further south in the chicle forests of
Quintana Roo can one encounter monkey, jaguar, and boar. Here, for
$160.00, fashionable Merida tourist agencies offer day-long hunting
"safaris" to wealthy American tourists.

Aside from a few haciendas, the bush is uninhabited. It is conceivable
that a Pustunicheño could walk the 400-odd miles south to Guatemala
City without encountering another soul.

Sixteen buses stop daily in Pustunich on the way to and from Merida.
The village is also linked to Merida by narrow gauge railway, in existence
since the turn of the century. Though the right-of-way passes through the
northern sector of Pustunich, one must go to the station in Ticul to board.
Fare to the capital is cheaper by half than the bus, but the trip takes three
to four hours and allows only three hours of business in Merida before
returning at two or three in the afternoon. Buses are frequent and take
only one-and-a-half hours each way.

Ticul, the largest town in the south of Yucatan, lies only a few miles up
the road from Pustunich. At between 12,000 and 18,000 inhabitants, the
state government lists it as a city. It is the seat, or *cabecera*, of the county
in which lies Pustunich. The county president, government, registry,
police, court, and priest are all in Ticul. It has a large marketplace, many
stores, bakeries, hardware specialty shops, shoemakers, and beer par-
lors. There are four medical doctors and a small hospital. There are two
movie theaters, a telegraph to Merida, an ice cream parlor, an ice factory,
and several small houses of prostitution.

Most Pustunicheños visit Ticul at least several times weekly for
purchases or pleasure. Bus fare is thirty centavos each way. Two

Pustunich shopkeepers also make several trips daily in their pickup trucks, carrying passengers for the same fare. The distance can be biked in ten minutes or walked in twenty.

Pustunich is a semi-tropical town. Summers are hot. Even Pustunicheños complain of the heat. "How can one hold out on a day like this?" is a frequent lament in May or June when the temperature soars to 110° Farenheit. On such days the line at the Ticul ice house forms at four in the morning, and the price of a cold Coca Cola with cracked ice will jump by five centavo increments each hour of the stifling afternoon.

The rainy season begins as early as April or (calamity) as late as July. The longer the delay, the hotter the days. Typically, a rainy season day sees one short downpour in late afternoon. Should rain fall in the morning, afternoons are impossibly humid and vapor rises from the ground in visible waves. The dry period begins in September or October. Rains become fewer and less frequent, and bush paths turn to powder. Temperatures gradually fall until December. Some midwinter evenings may be very chilly, and early rising villagers go about with head and torso wrapped in cloths or blankets.

The people are of medium to short height, dark complexioned, and handsome. Some of the women are striking. Features run from pure European to pure Maya. A majority of villagers bear Maya surnames, such as Ek, K'u, Canul, and Mis. With few exceptions, the people speak Maya in the home and street. Maya is the medium of discussion at town meetings. Though most older men, many older women, and all youngsters can speak fair to fluent Spanish, it is spoken only with visitors and outside officials and in the classroom. Except a half-dozen individuals, all adults dress in the mestizo fashion—sandals and dungarees for men at work; sandals, white pants, and shirt for after work dress. Women all wear the *huipil*, a white ankle-length "mu'u mu'u" bordered at neck and hem with machine- or hand-sewn floral designs. It is, in fact, dress which marks Pustunicheños as mestizo, in contrast to those who wear shoes and dresses and engage in other than farming the bushland.

There are 1,007 individuals in Pustunich, represented by 203 nuclear family units living in a total of 153 separate households. The town is laid out in the familiar grid pattern of Hispanic-American towns. Roughly at the center is the large, flat plaza.

The paved highway passes through the town, east to west, a block north of the plaza. Before being paved some ten years ago, the road passed directly through the plaza. Of the four stores in town, only one (the newest) now lies on the highway.

Though housing a small population, Pustunich is not small in area, being roughly three-quarters of a mile long east to west (first house to last house) and half a mile in breadth. There is room in the village. Houses are widely spaced in individual *solares* (lots). Usually, unless parents and children or brothers live next to each other and share a single kitchen, adjacent solares will be separated by a low, piled stone hedge. Similar hedges line and define all streets and are whitewashed each year before the August fiesta. An average solar might be ten to twenty meters broad and twenty to forty deep. Each block is rimmed completely with stone hedges and houses, and there are no public shortcuts available from one street to the next.

All parts of the town, except the streets and central plaza itself, are privately owned. Few solares are owned by nonvillagers. Excepting several vacant plots, all solares contain two basic structures—the living house and a separate kitchen shack. Roughly thirty of the houses are completely of *mamposteria* (masonry). Eight of the ten dwellings fronting the plaza are of masonry. The remaining twenty or so masonry homes lie scattered throughout the village with little visible pattern. A majority of houses, however, are of stick (wattle and daub) or masonry siding, but roofed with palm thatch over a peaked pole frame. The basic house, of whatever material, is a single room. Where two rooms are desired, a second, though nearly always palm-thatched, house is built alongside, or a thatched lean-to is added to the existing structure. Though masonry houses are preferred, their cost (up to $10,000 pesos as compared with $1,500-$2,000 for thatch-types)* is prohibitive for all but a few well-to-do. All-masonry homes are presently being constructed at the rate of two to three per year. Several poorer families are constructing masonry houses themselves and adding to them bit by bit as finances allow. Masonry homes are generally a meter or two wider and longer than thatch. All houses have two doors when possible. Locks are almost never utilized. Largely because of the scarcity of empty land within the town, let alone within the plaza, there is no rich neighborhood. Both wealthy and poor (often first cousins) live side by side, mud wall next to smooth stucco, scattered where inheritance, purchase, or in-law goodwill has allotted them a space.

---

*Unless otherwise specified, ($) will refer to pesos, at a value of 12.5 to the dollar.

Only the poorest of the village live in mud-sided houses. Most kitchen shacks, however, regardless of the owner's wealth, are of mud and sticks, to allow the escape of smoke. The kitchen is usually cluttered with a hearth (three or four stones), low benches, gourds, pots, pans, dishes, *metate* (concave stone slab for grinding spices, not corn; Pustunich has had a motorized cornmill for over thirty years), kittens, and chickens. Near the kitchen stands the *batea*, a dug-out wooden or molded cement trough for clothes washing. It may be covered with a crude thatch lean-to for protection against the sun. There may be a pigpen or chicken coop in the solar, or if neither, certainly a few chickens or ducks, one or two turkeys, and, if the owner has "had some luck," maybe a pig or two. Most solares contain one or more raised, dug-out, tree-trunk troughs where chives, herbs, or flowers are grown out of reach of animals. Some yards may contain a corn crib. Only a few village solares sport outhouses, however. Several years ago the Community Development Foundation of Mexico talked some villagers into latrine construction in return for U.S. surplus food. Response was not enthusiastic, as the high bushes against the back stone hedge of the solar are as efficient and less likely to harbor scorpions.

All solares have some variety of trees. Few are primarily for shade. Common are sweet and sour orange, lime, avocado, mango, ramon (for horse fodder—either for one's own animals or to be sold to others), and the round gourd called *jicara*. The jicara, when dried and sawn in two, provides the everyday and extra bowls a family needs for meals in house or field.

Most solares contain at least a few *juano* palms. Pustunich is one of only four or five towns in Yucatan which fall within the natural zone of juano. It provides fine wide fronds for waterproof thatching and can be sold at a good price by the bundle. The stems, moreover, when dried and split, provide straws which every woman and child braids into long strands for sale to the hatmakers of Pustunich, Ticul, and Campeche. In the hardest of times, two, three, or more pesos a day—sufficient for a bare subsistence—can be obtained through sale of the *tejidos* or braided strands. Every solar also contains a cave, from which lime has been dug for contruction. It serves as a cool, damp storage place for split juano. On the hottest days, tejido weaving in the dim caves offers Pustunich women the best escape from the high sun.

Most solares also have wells. The water table in Pustunich is twenty-four meters deep. Starting in 1962, the town has had a central, motorized water system provided by the government. As pipes extend but a block on either side of the plaza, only thirty-five families are presently members of the "potable water association," and the three peso monthly fee also limits membership. Three members, all of them well-to-do, have water pipes tapped directly into their solares. The rest obtain water from four corner hydrants which are now shut off at 6 P.M. following complaints that nonmembers were surreptitiously using them after dark.

The economic focus of Pustunich is milpa—slash-and-burn corn farming. Of the 203 nuclear family heads, less than a dozen make no milpa at present. *All* men have made milpa at one time or another, regardless of present wealth or occupation. There is sufficient land for all, though good fallowed plots closer to the village are at a premium. Some villagers must walk ten kilometers to their milpas. Corn is the staple, grown in the bush on small plots (generally two to five acres). The manner of farming has changed little over millennia. The village ejido lands are used on a first-come, first-served basis. They are leveled by machete and burned before the first spring rains. Grains are sowed by hand in holes made by pointed sticks. The crop is weeded several times during the summer, doubled and allowed to dry, and harvested from fall through winter. The corn (in the form of tortillas), along with beans, squash, peppers, tomatoes, and other vegetables grown in the milpa and home gardens is supplemented with small quantities of purchased meat, home-butchered pork, and the infrequent venison obtained in individual or communal hunts.

Most of what villagers don't grow can be purchased at four local general stores and a butcher's shop. There are also two barbers, three shaman-curers, a tailor, a radio repairman, and a movie theater. There is no bakery or marketplace, and most villagers visit Ticul for any major or semi-major purchases. Market going is also an excuse to walk around the bigger town.

The village school boasts five teachers and about 250 students. Most men, many women, and nearly all of the children are literate. Several newspapers reach Pustunich daily. A number of families own short-wave radios and half the village's thatch roofs bristle with antennae. On most Friday evenings there is a movie. During a typical month, two Tarzan epics, a 1930s U.S. gangster film, an Italian spoof (with subtitles) on Cleopatra, and several Mexican singing cowboy films were shown. As the town has no electricity, power must be rented from the town's wealthiest store owner who rents out several portable generators for fiestas or ball games. He owns the movie theater—which is actually the storage lot behind his shop.

Ball games and major festivals are held in the plaza, which is the town's pride. It is one of the cleanest squares and the most rock-free in Yucatan. Marking its southern boundary is the church. Within memory there has been no resident priest. The church is nonetheless well known, as it houses the patroness of Pustunich, a wooden image famous in much of Yucatan. The annual fiestas in her honor are more crowded and profitable than those of other towns of similar size. She is tended by the *sacristan* (sexton), who is old and lives behind the church in a rickety thatch hut. He, like the one-armed policeman, never married and lives on town charity. Both are *medio inutil* (semi-useless) because they are bachelors and make no milpa like other men.

Across the plaza from the church is the town *comisaria* or office, in which the policeman sleeps. It is his duty to run errands, bike to Ticul for the mail, and mark the hour by ringing the bell over the comisaria. He glances at the old clock over the desk. It marks 11:20 and chimes four times. By this, the policeman knows it is approximately 2:00 A.M. He stumbles out of his hammock (as often as not, he decides not to), trips over the old telephone box, and goes outside to toll twice. The time is actually 2:20.

4

The Histories and Orientation to Change

History and Change

There are two kinds of history. One is the "actual" or scientifically determinable past,[1] the sum of all events preceding the present instant. Such historical events shape the present and attitudes toward it. The second history includes those events remembered, reinterpreted, invented, or assumed to have occurred. This too serves as a referent and mechanism for judging and validating present acts. "History written from the inside view," said Redfield, "is the temporal dimension of world view."[2]

At various times in the past, one or the other of these two histories has been given preference in explaining contemporary world views and attitudes toward change. Not infrequently, too, historical phenomena have been largely ignored in explaining present social structural phenomena. In spite of his lip service to "inside" history, one of the more glaring examples of this latter is Redfield in his Yucatan work.

As we noted earlier, Redfield attributed a high level of homogeneity to Yucatan's historical, economic, and social past. Today, of course, we are aware that events which entered into the creation of modern Yucatan were far from evenly distributed in time or space. The conquest was easier for some native groups (the Xiu, for example) than others (such as the Cocom or Itzaes). Some villages experienced more threatening, others less threatening, contact with colonial Europeans. The northern zone suffered far more disruption from commercial henequen than did the central and southern portion of Yucatan. The Caste War dislocated some communities, while others experienced minimal violence or fac-tionalism.

Each micro-area of the state, if not each community, thus exhibits a variant historical configuration. Each community, moreover, interprets this history idiosyncratically, inventing some elements, misinterpreting or forgetting others. The combination of actual and remembered events is the base upon which local self-image and orientation toward continuity or change are built. All outside influences, regardless of urban or other provenience, must confront this orientation and undergo evaluation with reference to it.

Politics and Leadership

One of the earliest references to Pustunich occurs in the *Chilam Balam of Chumayel*. Both the village and nearby Xocnaceh are mentioned in legend as waypoints on the twelfth-century migration from the south.[3] Today, Xocnaceh is a ruined sugar plantation with crumbling buildings and no one can recall when it might have been a settlement in its own right. As early as 1557, however, Pustunich is recorded as a distinct town with a church of its own.[4]

Prior to the conquest, Pustunich was almost certainly a small tributary of the ruling Xiu family. The Xiu were apparently latecomers to Yucatan and established themselves in Uxmal, some twelve kilometers to the southwest of Pustunich. Subsequently, they managed to gain con-siderable influence in the territory to the north, governed by the Cocom family out of the temple center of Mayapan. When Mayapan was destroyed in the mid-fifteenth century, the Xiu subsequently moved to the Mani area, five short kilometers northeast of Pustunich. Village contact with the ruling bureaucracy likely increased considerably at this time. In 1536, approximately eight years after Montejo's disastrous first sortie into Yucatan, the Xiu leadership, on a pilgrimage to Chichen Itza, was betrayed and decimated by the Cocom.[5] When Montejo's son arrived in Yucatan to finish the work of his father, the Xiu voluntarily united with him, ostensibly to revenge themselves further upon the Cocom.[6] It is also possible that an oracle who resided in Mani around

1500 encouraged cooperation with the Spanish. This famous priest, named Chilam Balam, is said to have predicted, prior to the conquest, that fair-skinned, bearded strangers would come to convert the people and that they should be met with cooperation.[7] Regardless of the cause, the Xiu and their tributary villages such as Pustunich suffered little during the actual conquest.

Both because of its location at the southern fringe of the populous flatlands and because of Xiu cooperation with the colonial regime, Mani was made a separate province and the administrative center of southern Yucatan. Once again, Pustunich was near a major bureaucratic head-quarters.

Shortly after the conquest, Montejo the younger made a *repartimiento* of the Mani province, portioning out lands and inhabitants in a number of *encomiendas* (territories granted to colonists by the King entitling them to receive tribute from the native inhabitants). Rather than the limited grants made in Mexico, the encomiendas of Yucatan were made in perpetuity.[8] Ticul, two miles west of Pustunich, was created an encomienda in 1549, with 3,555 inhabitants listed as residing in 790 locations.[9] Pustunich, however, though only several kilometers from Ticul, fell to a separate encomendero, Francisco Arzeo, who also received tribute from the towns of Chaltum and Xanaba.[10] Insofar as Arzeo's three towns are scattered around the peninsula, it is unlikely that he resided in any of them. Unfortunately, Arzeo was one of nine who failed to respond to the Crown's amazing socioeconomic questionnaire of 1577 which was sent to thirty-three Yucatec encomenderos. We thus know nothing of the town's earliest colonial appearance. It was, however, a thriving, distinct community even at that early date. In 1588 Pustunich, as an autonomous political entity, executed a land treaty with Ticul over water holes.[11] This autonomy, however, was incomplete.

Prior to the conquest, individual towns of the area were governed by local, permanent chieftains (*batabs*) appointed by the Xiu ruler of Mani. Often, the batab was a son or close relative of the ruler. Advising the batab was a town council. Following the conquest, a new governmental form was imposed upon Yucatec towns, consisting of a governor chosen by the townsmen (yet confirmed by the Spanish authority), two *alcaldes*, a justice, and three or more counselors (*regidores*). In many villages, however, this elected hierarchy was actually subservient to a *cacique*—usually charismatic, often an old batab or son of the preconquest batab, and permanent in his position. Pustunich oldsters still refer to leaders of their parents' generation as batabs. In the Mani area, caciques almost always appeared from the ranks of remaining Xiu.[12] Because of their obvious usefulness as local leaders and opinionmakers, Spaniards relied heavily upon caciques, often granting them special privileges. Thus, where they existed, caciques were the major, though unofficial, local power figures. In the treaty of 1588, the "principal man" of Pustunich is listed as Alonso Xiu. Following his name are those of the official alcaldes who are listed as such.[13] In other words, the new political machinery itself was "run" by a cacique, a member of the old royal family, at that.

Because of its proximity to the larger and more important centers of Ticul and Mani and because of the presence of a Xiu cacique, Pustunich had little opportunity to govern many of its affairs, less opportunity even than more isolated towns governed by elected alcaldes and councils.

The encomienda system ended and the political center of the immediate area passed from Mani to Ticul. Though always a separate town, Pustunich's political life was controlled by Ticul through several centuries. Prior to 1939, the town leader (called *cabo*) was appointed directly from Ticul. He and his council held but moderate authority, limited to the adjudication of minor torts. Older Pustunicheños tell of the 1939 visit to the village by Mexican President ("General") Lazaro Cardenas who spent an hour in the pueblo "with his mariachis." He stressed the *campesino*'s right to elect his own *comisario* (mayor) and put the best men in office. With this incentive, the school teacher helped organize a "league of workers" upon which to base future "election" of village officials. However, indirect pressure soon limited candidates to those "friendly" to the *presidente* of Ticul. Often only one candidate was nominated. The present school head has persistently stressed the necessity for autonomous elections with at least two candidates. Indeed, two candidates have sometimes been nominated. (In 1961 both sent turkeys surreptitiously to the Ticul president a week prior to the vote.) Pustunich, it must be stressed, controls no important natural resources, nor does it provide significant taxes to the Ticul treasury. Its political subservience to Ticul has been one of simple tradition. For years, the proceeds of the lucrative annual fiesta in honor of the Virgin Assumption has been confiscated by the country president, and only a small gratuity was given to the mayor of Pustunich. "The town isn't ready to handle its own affairs" was the excuse reportedly given. No one cared or dared to oppose this.

Disinterest in, and distrust of, politics is traditional in Pustunich. Within memory there have been no "political" deaths. While many towns suffered bloodshed during the Yucatec Socialist-Liberal dispute of the 1920s, Pustunich endured a few fistfights and one man reportedly left town in fear of his life. Only a minority of Pustunich actively seek office and its perquisites—the clandestine "deals" with the president of Ticul, the modicum of judicial power over one's neighbors. One mayor who held office continually from 1924 to 1935 is referred to as "a cacique" (political boss). The town still recalls (unemotionally, jestingly) the time Comisario Uinic ordered a line-burning *fagina* (communal labor) "for school improvements." One night, it is said, he sold the entire pile for a tidy personal profit. The last mayor was in his second term. The first time, it is maintained, he was thrown out of office for robbing a poor old villager's house of cash and goods. Yet no loud protest went up when he was reelected after some ten years out of office. There is no rush among Pustunicheños to stand for election.

Though always a distinct community, under batabs, caciques, cabos, and Ticul, Pustunich has had little opportunity to control its important affairs. Always a small, yet centrally located, cog within larger political networks, the village long ago abandoned its direction to others. Others have done its official thinking. Villagers do not view outside political intervention as unusual or disruptive, nor do they view local governmental representatives as leaders and innovators. They have historically lacked a precedent for self-determination and change-oriented action.

Ritual and Religious Hierarchy

As part of the Xiu empire, Pustunich owed both political and religious allegiance to Uxmal. The closest complex of large ruins is that of Xcorralche, ten kilometers to the south and roughly contemporary with Uxmal. Smaller temple ruins can be seen in Dzan, Mani, and the outskirts of Ticul. Pustunich, however, has no such remains, nor does anyone know of any in the immediate vicinity. As vassal of Mayapan, Uxmal, and Mani, Pustunich undoubtedly had to supply labor and, occasionally, sacrifices to the priesthood in the capitals. Since the village is only a three-hours walk from Uxmal and twenty minutes from Mani, it is unlikely that any major ceremonials were carried out within it. The simple milpa ritual, however, was most likely performed autonomously even during the Xiu epoch. In 1548, Yucatan's first Catholic priests settled in the new Xiu capital of Mani. After initial hostility on the part of certain noble factions in Mani, the province settled down to ostensibly voluntary practice of Christianity. By 1557 a monastery had appeared in Mani and a church in Pustunich itself.[14]

The new priesthood outlawed pagan ritual, though as Wolf demonstrates, predominantly the more overt, permanently organized, and public spectacles were immediately displaced.[15] Field and house ritual, being covert, continued to thrive or went underground. After the centralized Maya priesthood was disbanded, local curers and practitioners took over the religious leadership. For the small peasant communities, this was not overly difficult. Polytheistic Maya belief syncretized easily with the multiplicity of Catholic saints. Monopoly of esoteric knowledge and literacy merely passed from one set of priests to another.

Regardless of the presence of a church, however, the conversion of Pustunich was still incomplete. As early as 1558, Bishop Landa found that many newly Christianized natives in Yucatan were "perverted by the native priests and reverted to idolatry."[16] In 1561 or 1562, a certain priest of Sacaba sent several principals to "the town of Quicucche and to the town of Pustuniche, and in these two towns they purchased two small boys which had just begun to walk, and who were bought from Juan Puc, principle Indian and powerful person of the said town of Pustuniche."[17] The sacrifice took place one league from the present hacienda of Tabi, twelve kilometers south of Pustunich.

Appalled by such incidents, which were beginning to multiply, Landa initiated an inquisition in the Mani territory in early May 1562. It was discovered that village leaders (caciques appointed by trusting encomenderos) as well as poor farmers were involved. Landa states in his defense that his friars killed or maimed no one intentionally, and that many natives "hung themselves in the bush and uninhabited sites and hidden places in order not to give [up] the idols nor abandon their evil ways as two or three did [hang themselves] in the province of Sotuta and as many more in that of Mani in the Pueblo of Tekax and Pustuniche."[18] Though such a spectacular phenomenon as sacrifice was soon suppressed, the basic field ritual of Pustunich survived, a remnant of the early tenacity of the town. Centuries later, Catholic Pustunich put as much effort into preserving its saints during the Anti-Cleric era. The image of the Virgin was secreted in a cave and even today the mildew streaks across her face are pointed out with pride as the story is told.

The religious autonomy of Pustunich is of considerable antiquity and continuity. Fray Lopez Cogolludo, writing in the mid-seventeenth century, reports that Pustunich's patroness even then was the Virgin Assumption. Hence, it may be concluded that she has been the only patron saint since the conversion of the village began in the 1540s. Furthermore, the image was important enough to warrant a relationship of reciprocal "visits" (*visitas*) between the faithful of Pustunich and devotees of Ticul's patron, St. Anthony of Padua.[19]

The present church was completed by the Franciscans in 1779. It is typical of many small-town Mexican churches: single-naved, with an ancient stone baptismal font to the right of the main entrance. Midway to the altar are two side entrances across from one another. Just beside the church stands a small ruined building which villagers think was once a monastery. Within memory of the oldest inhabitant no priest ever resided in Pustunich, however. Ticul is the religious center of the *municipio*, with at least one and sometimes two priests. Unlike the general practice in Guatemala, villages of the municipio pay homage to their particular *santos* only and do not regard the cabecera's saints as important to their welfare.

Today both Catholic and pagan ritual exist side by side. Neither has threatened the other for centuries. Both are under almost complete direction of the village. Seldom does a priest visit Pustunich, and then only at the request of someone with the required fee. Because of the expense of priest-directed masses, Pustunich has done without many of the formal trappings of orthodox Catholicism. The most progressive priests are viewed with suspicion, and tales of "Slavery Epoch" abuses are common.

There has been little change in either Catholic or pagan ritual since the post-conquest conversion. The village has held on tenaciously to both, viewing each as generally distinct, albeit complementary in certain functions and somewhat syncratistic in form. St. Michael the Archangel directs the ancient balams of the four directions. On the other hand, offerings to the dead on All Souls Day are those of the milpa and its deities. Should the cha chaac ritual in late spring fail to produce rain, San Antonio's day on June 10 serves as a backstop.

The Economic Past

Pustunich is fortuitously located. It lies snuggling the Puuc Hill range on the fringe of an area which is rocky, generally inaccessible, and impractical to farm on a large mechanized scale. Here, in and beyond the Puuc, the village makes its milpas. As sugar, and later henequen, plantations ate up the flat, arable land to the north, Pustunich suffered no land pressure. Towns surrounded by large haciendas soon found their croplands dissipated and their residents forced wholesale into peonage. Furthermore, as traditional Maya ritual and the making of milpa are mutually dependent, disappearance of one almost inevitably meant destruction of the other. The displaced Indian seemed unable to transfer a ritual attachment focused on milpa over to the paid production of yet another crop—henequen or sugar. Today, few towns in the henequen zone hold the annual cha chaac ceremony unless a good proportion of the men make some milpa on the side. Even so, many towns must import a *h-men* (Maya priest) from other areas. In some instances Maya ritual is a recent phenomenon in henequen-zone communities, for government redistribution of former plantation lands has permitted newly formed cooperative henequen villages to allocate some plots for home-use corn planting.

Some Pustunicheños were certainly caught in debt-servitude to local plantations, due largely to extra cash needs. However, village milpa lands remained untouched in the vast and fairly inaccessible region south of the Puuc. Plantation work for Pustunicheños thus generally meant extra cash rather than actual subsistence. Frequently, one day a week would be given in exchange for cash or debt cancellation. Such service was given on Mondays and nonresident workers became known as *luneros*. For those who worked part-time on plantations, milpa time-requirements were not severely challenged. Until late in the nineteenth century, sugar was the major cash crop of Puuc region plantations. Unlike henequen, the sugar labor-requirement calendar does not compete directly with corn production. It should be stressed that many Pustunicheños, having a solid, autonomous milpa base, simply chose to work part-time for plantations, particularly during periods of peak labor needs. Thus wage labor was established early and existed side by side with the traditional milpa.

Shortly before the Revolution and the breakup of the haciendas, Pustunich had a population of 283 (General Census of the Mexican Republic 1905). By 1940, the population had less than doubled to only 541,[20] indicating natural growth rather than wholesale immigration from haciendas. Since 1943 immigration has been practically negligible and the population has more than doubled. In the census of 1900 the nearby hacienda of Tabi was listed as a rural *finca* of 851 population—513 males and 338 females. All other towns in the vicinity had larger numbers of females than males. This suggests that possibly one-third of Tabi's work force represented males commuting for varying periods from their native villages of Pustunich, Sta. Elena, Ticul, Dzan, and others. Today's Pustunich population of 1,007 is largely a result of internal growth rather than migration from other towns. Slightly over 88 percent of all Pustunich males are village-born. Approximately 75 percent of the women are locals.

The "Epoch of Slavery," as Pustunicheños refer to it, was ended by such state-level heroes as the martyred Felipe Carillo Puerto, who, to hear the villagers tell of it, "personally came to this area and hanged hacienda owners." Such statements help explain Pustunich's antipathy toward local power figures and genuine respect for state-level politicians.

When, following the revolution of 1919, ejidos were established for peasant use, Pustunich merely received formal authority over rather marginally located farm lands which it had been using exclusively for centuries. Now, however, ejidal status carried the added advantage of legal status, giving Pustunicheños the hitherto unavailable clout to collect damages from cattle ranchers whose beasts trampled milpa lands.

Pustunich is well located from another point of view: it is in the center of the state's only juano palm region. Juano is an excellent roof thatching and early became the raw material for a local hatmaking industry. Significant extra income is obtained through selling crude and plaited juano palm. Every village woman and child earns daily juano money. Thus Pustunich has had an income insurance lacking in many other communities. Lastly, the vast bush south of Pustunich is fairly rich in small game. Even today a man can turn to hunting in an emergency. All families have owned shotguns for generations.

Continuity and security are thus major themes of Pustunich economic history. Milpa, wage labor, and small-scale (palm industry) entrepreneurship have long coexisted in harmony and are thus "traditional." Never having been seriously threatened, all are now taken for granted. Also taken for granted are the functionally related elements of social class (mestizo dress), pagan ritual (milpa offerings and communal rain purchase), and possession of "modern" goods via cash.

Outside Contact

As part of the colonial Mani province, three miles from Mani and two from Ticul, Pustunich became an early way station for trade, missionaries, and diplomatic intercourse with Merida. The Ticul-Pustunich land treaty of 1588 indicates an early introduction to Spanish bureaucratic mechanisms. The Puuc, as a natural barrier to southward travel and colonization, became the frontier zone of Yucatan. Important settlements such as Ticul, Oxkutzkab, Tekax, and Peto flourished, linked along with Pustunich by a single road, all lying in the shadow of the hills like knots on a string. The zone was more fluid than other areas, its Spaniards "mixing more easily with the indios."[21] In the Valladolid district (near Chan Kom), natives far outnumbered the Spanish creoles. Yet in 1881 the Ticul district contained roughly equal numbers of Indians and whites.[22] At the same time, traditional activities appear to have continued. During the early nineteenth century, the zone raised two-thirds of Yucatan's corn crop, indicating not only a heavy and continuing reliance upon milpa, but long familiarity with broader cash-based market requirements.[23]

Good roads have linked the village to other towns and to the capital for centuries. The railroad from Merida to Peto runs through the village outskirts. It has offered an inexpensive four-hour means of contact with (and transportation of goods to) the capital for over eighty years. General literacy has been part of Pustunich life since at least 1893, when the first school opened. Movies have been shown by the town's wealthiest storekeeper since the 1930s. Traveling circuses, curers, hucksters, credit salesmen, and con-men have made Pustunich a regular stop for unknown decades. For over fifty years motorized corn mills have freed village women from the time-consuming task of hand grinding. In the early 1930s, a telephone line linked Pustunich with Ticul and several other nearby towns. It was abandoned, however, insofar as there was nothing much to talk about. The phone hangs today in the *comisaria*, a mute reminder that the village had once sampled an element of modernity and had found it wanting.

As a town on a main road, only several miles from important administrative centers, and as a village supplying workers to haciendas, Pustunich had centuries of opportunity to view the Spaniard and the latest of "Western culture." Pustunich witnessed innovations as they appeared among the Spaniards of Mani, the ladinos of Ticul and hacienda—

innovations in logical sequence, with subsequent understanding of their development and relationship to one another. Even so, modernism did not burst upon the village with the opening of a road, nor did it trickle to it with an itinerant backwoods merchant. For centuries in a mainstream of social and political movement, Pustunich has been able to pick and choose what it would, or more realistically, *could*, of "modern" ways.

The Inside View: Myths and Miracles

How does Pustunich view its past? Some villagers say that the town was first settled by the Huites, who subsequently fled during the wars between the Xiu and other royal groups. No one is sure who the Huites were, though possibly they were Indians. Others claim that the first inhabitants were the Ppuses, who preceded even the Indians. In fact, the Xiu are the "legitimate" descendants of the Ppuses. The Ppuses occupied all of Yucatan. They were dwarfs. It is said that at Xocnaceh plantation several miles down the road sixteen stone coffins were discovered which could only have held midgets. The Ppuses (*not* the Franciscans) built the Pustunich church in only two days, as rock was softer then (thus the outside Catholic hierarchy is effectively dissociated from its own works). Later the Franciscans came and rebuilt it. It is said that when the Spanish arrived, they considered making Pustunich the capital of Yucatan, but decided upon Merida because it was closer to the coast.

Spaniards, several old villagers maintain, first came to Pustunich around 1800. After mining iron (there are no known iron deposits in Yucatan), forging weapons, and taking Pustunich women to wife (thus the many present Spanish surnames), they left, promising to return one day and make a grand city of the village. One of these Spaniards stayed to become *encomendero* (land-grantee with tribute rights) of Pustunich, and it was he, it is said, who built the first masonry houses in the village square. This story is in turn contradicted by two rival oldsters, each of whom claims that his own great-grandfather, and no "outsider" Spaniard, built the first masonry houses in Pustunich. Interestingly, both of these old men bear Spanish surnames, though not of the alleged encomendero.

It is certain that village life was disrupted during the Caste War of the past century when less acculturated, more isolated Maya groups rose in rebellion against the Yucatec colonial masters and hispanicized town Maya. Many communities, particularly in the north central portion of the state, were emptied and their populations driven into the bush. Being neither bush Maya nor Spanish nor landless plantation workers, Pustunich was ostensibly "neutral" and an unlikely target for specific attack by either side. Major battles, however, were fought in Ticul and, indeed, the city was under siege during most of the month of May 1848, before falling to Maya attackers.[24] It is doubtful whether Pustunicheños could have remained wholly neutral yet safe during such a period; they may have taken to the bush or joined the native forces or, more likely, simply provided shelter and food for the Maya who were fighting less than a mile away.

Pustunich's own history of this era is sketchy yet important. The war was between the "Indians and the Castillians." The town itself was threatened by the Indians, some of whom even occupied the northern periphery. However, three famous Pustunich witches came to the rescue and sent magical plagues of bats, bees, and *balancabs* (large stinging insects) to drive the Indians off. The people of Pustunich at that time were neither Indians nor Castillians, but *mayeros*. "Mayero," like the Spanish terms molin*ero* (miller), carpint*ero* (carpenter), etc., indicates professional status or expertise—in this case, expertise in the Maya life-style. Villagers refer to the Maya of those days as "legitimate Maya." The Pustunich version of the Caste War thus turns inward, denying disruption, stressing continuity and magical events. It further attributes to Pustunich cultural descendancy from a specific, orthodox ("mayero") life-style (rather than ethnic or racial group) from which it has somehow diverged.

The plantation era, or "Epoch of Slavery," is recalled but hazily, and destinies of rich and poor merge in an aura of past subjugation to secular and religious authority. "I was a slave in the old days," recalls an eighty-year-old man, who neglects to add that he and his father also made milpa. "Yes, we were all slaves," sighs the town's richest man, whose family was long wealthy and never involved in anything but full-time milpa and entrepreneurial activity. Thus grows a tale of homogeneity, uniting rich and poor alike in a past of partial domination by others.

An ancient relates that during the Epoch of Slavery

all the priests made slaves of the people. All the people—even the young—were told when they were to marry, because they didn't [simply] fall in love with their wives. This was permitted because they [the priests] were the authorities. The boy met his wife in front of the authorities; he met her for the first time. The priests who directed marriages said to them: ''There once was the Holy Inquisition, which says to the parents that a woman who marries must wait eighteen days before the mass can be performed.'' So [they took the bride off and] at the passage of eighteen days the bride was delivered to the groom and the priests said: ''she is now crossed with Spanish blood,'' for they had lain with her, ''and all your children will be Spanish.'' All are mixed, all. The bishops were first to get the girl during these eighteen days, and then she was passed on to the lower ranking priests. ''Afterwards we will deliver her to you,'' [said the priests]. ''You will go and say nothing because you are a slave.'' This was said to all boys who would marry. Such were the times. I had not been born yet. My grandfather told me about this. Probably took place before the revolution for independence.

In 1910, when the last of the rebel Maya in Chan Santa Cruz were finally defeated, several Pustunicheños who are still alive were present. Typically, they were not even given the responsibility of bearing arms; instead they were porters and saw no action. This occurred about the time the revolution began. No one recalls any difficulties in the village during the revolution years of 1910-1920. During the rise to importance of the Yucatec Socialists, in the 1920s, oldsters recall some mild factionalism, and one man was reportedly forced to ''flee for his life.'' No deaths, injuries, or physical clashes are remembered.

History and Orientation to Change

The two histories of Pustunich complement one another. They paint a picture of a community with a clear identity, whose ways and families merge in a distant past. At the same time there is a clear tradition of political subjugation. Leaders came from outside, not inside, and neither a tradition nor precedent for innovation exists. The great age, the continuity of economic and ritual institutions, the assumed lack of serious threat to village life, have all combined to produce a self-view of Pustunich as relatively timeless and slow to change. Many present phenomena have the authority of tradition whose roots are lost in time, legend, misinterpretation, falsification, claim, and counterclaim. There is little possibility of anyone's stating with unimpeachable conviction what "things were once like." Even Pustunicheños hasten to qualify most tales of the past with the phrase "it is said that. . . ," or "so they say." "I think so, but who knows?" they answer, when pressed about whether a certain event really occurred.

Chan Kom, it must be recalled, was an isolated community *less than fifty years old* when Redfield arrived in 1930. It was originally and subsequently settled by individuals discontented with or routed from their previous communities. In terms of world view and self-image, Chan Kom lacked a specific tradition and a personality of its own, as compared with Pustunich, whose traditions and families were solidified through at least four hundred years of nonisolated existence. Any middle-aged resident of Chan Kom could say, with authority and experience, that "things were once different." For Pustunicheños of any age, things were always pretty much the same. Yet Chan Kom is still viewed by many as the archetype of Yucatec peasant communities, and its experience with change representative of the problems to be faced by others. It is thus relevant to note that whereas 5 percent of the Chan Kom population dressed in the ladino manner in 1950, less than 3 percent of Pustunicheños were so garbed fourteen years later.[25]

As one of the earliest towns to fall to Spanish rule in Yucatan, and as a town so near administrative centers, Pustunich had early contact with and overt adoption of required European and Catholic socioreligious forms. Hence, the town made an earlier readjustment and had a longer subsequent period of untraumatic "simmering." During this period, Pustunich experienced more or less continuous and relatively unthreatening contact with the European settler. Pustunich views outside forces as paternalistic, self-serving, and generally avaricious, but not as ultimately dangerous. The village thus exhibits no cultural paranoia. It is not consciously protecting its life-style from encroachment by nonintelligible forces bent upon its destruction. In fact, it hardly admits to influence from outside sources. Its marvelous hunchbacked ancestors built the church overnight. Its witches saved the day during the Caste War, preventing possible destruction of the village. The Epoch of Slavery, though an imposition upon village autonomy, was a period less of disruption than of stabilization in a configuration of dependency. And dependency is hardly new to Pustunich.

Although it considers itself to possess a quite specific life-style,

Pustunich does admit to having deviated from some now forgotten standard of cultural orthodoxy established by its "mayero" ancestors. In short, while there is some precedent for change, the precedent is unclear (no one knows how the legitimate Maya lived) and the innovators unspecified. The various "histories" contribute to a self-view which is neither conducive to novel behavior nor necessarily threatening to it. This is not a "nonstatement." It describes a specific situation where innovation is possible, yet where abrupt change is unanticipated and traditional role-encumbents, both within and from outside the village, are not looked to for initiation of change.

Thus we can comprehend how, some twenty-five years ago, a Pustunich boy was able to initiate a vigorous committee system of village communal labor which paralleled the preexisting political organization. This young man was Pustunich's first nonmilpero—a school teacher and son of a highly conservative family. He had created an unprecedented role for himself and organized activity for unprecedented goals (we will examine this more closely in Chapter 9). At the same time, we can understand the minimal use of and respect for priests in the village. Tales of past abuse by the religious hierarchy, and of earlier Ppus (as opposed to Franciscan) architectural ingenuity, serve to reinforce old attitudes toward the Church and its priests as superfluous or self-seeking. This in turn prevents Pustunich from maintaining regular contact with young and eager new clerics whose nutrition-oriented sermons, whose cooperative produce-marketing projects, credit unions, and the like might serve as stimuli for significant economic change.

Pustunich has a pragmatic view of outside role-encumbents and physical trappings. Where such trappings could be utilized, they were. In its baseball team, basketball court, radios, bicycles, plastic hair curlers, general literacy, weekly cinema, and defunct telephone, Pustunich feels itself to be, if not terribly modern, at least one of the less "hickish" villages in the area. In its ubiquitous milpa, mestizo dress, pagan ritual, *curanderismo* (folk medicine), and Maya language, Pustunich feels itself to be linked with a fairly stable, nonthreatening past.

These views, and their effect upon orientation toward change, are the products of history. Pustunich's "verifiable" history is unique, or at most shared by a handful of villages in the same micro-area of Yucatan. Its myths and personal recollections are certainly shared by no others. Thus, the village's experiences cannot be generalized directly to other communities confronting the present. Nonetheless, we profit by the example. Reinforced is the obvious—and for that reason easily ignored—principle that specific historical events play a major role in the development of any community's world view and, ultimately, orientation toward stability and change. Further, we must remember that quantity and frequency of "outside" contact are but two among a host of variables that affect orientation to change. Pustunich's experience demonstrates that centuries of outside contact, if not directly threatening to the economic or social system, may create a stable *modus vivendi*, enabling the community to confront the world with pragmatism and self-confidence. This, after all, is what Foster meant when he described the peasant community as a perennial part-society. This, too, is what Wolf meant when he suggested that peasants, at whatever point in their history, are contemporaneous.

NOTES

1. B. Malinowski, "The Dynamics of Culture Change." In Phyllis M. Kaberry, ed., *An Inquiry Into Race Relations in Africa* (New Haven: Yale University Press, 1945), p. 29.

2. Robert Redfield, *The Little Community* (Chicago: University of Chicago Press, 1958), p. 111.

3. Ralph L. Roys, *The Book of Chilam Balam of Chumayel* (Washington: Carnegie Institute of Washington, Publication No. 438, 1933), p. 72.

4. Ralph L. Roys, *The Political Geography of the Yucatan Maya* (Washington: Carnegie Institute of Washington, Publication No. 613, 1957).

5. Ibid., pp. 61-63 and 69-70.

6. Frans Blom, *The Conquest of Yucatan* (Cambridge: Riverside Press, 1936).

7. *Relaciones de Yucatan* (Madrid: Real Academia de la Historia, Vol. #11, 1898), pp. 44-45.

8. Cf. Lesley Byrd Simpson, *The Encomienda in New Spain* (Berkeley: The University of California Press, 1950).

9. Ralph L. Roys, *The Political Geography of the Yucatan Maya* (Washington: Carnegie Institute of Washington, Publication No. 613, 1957), p. 70.

10. *Relaciones de Yucatan* (Madrid: Real Academia de la Historia, 1898), p. VII.

11. Ralph L. Roys, *The Indian Background to Colonial Yucatan* (Washington: Carnegie Institute of Washington, Publication No. 548, 1943), p. 190.

12. Ibid., p. 140.

13. Ibid., p. 190.

14. Ralph L. Roys, *The Political Geography of the Yucatan Maya* (Washington: Carnegie Institute of Washington, Publication No. 613, 1957).

15. Eric R. Wolf, *Sons of the Shaking Earth* (Chicago: University of Chicago Press, 1962), pp. 69-70.

16. Alfred M. Tozzer, ed., *Landa's Relacion de las cosas de Yucatan—A Translation* (Cambridge: Papers of the Peabody Museum of American Archaeology and Ethnology, 1941), p. 76.

17. France Scholes and Eleanor B. Adams, "Don Diego Quijada—Alcalde Mayor de Yucatan 1561-1565." In *Documentos sacados de los Archivos de España*, 2 vols. (Mexico City: Biblioteca Historica Mexicana de obras ineditas Nos. 14, 15, 1938), p. 101.

18. Ibid., p. 294.

19. Fr. Diego Lopez Cogolludo, *Historia de Yucatan* (Mexico City: Editorial Academia Literaria, 1957), p. 236. The first edition appeared in 1688.

20. General Census of the Mexican Republic, 1905. General Census of the United States of Mexico, 1943.

21. Nelson Reed, *The Caste War of Yucatan* (Stanford: Stanford University Press, 1964), pp. 18-19.

22. Howard F. Cline, *The United States and Mexico* (Cambridge: Harvard University Press, 1963), p. 136.

23. Nelson Reed, *The Caste War of Yucatan* (Stanford: Stanford University Press, 1964), p. 18.

24. Ibid., pp. 91-92.

25. Robert Redfield, *A Village that Chose Progress: Chan Kom Revisited* (Chicago: University of Chicago Press, 1950), p. 40.

5

Economic Life

The Milpa and Its Meaning

Perhaps the best single definition of Pustunich is milpa. No villager recalls a time or has heard of an epoch when Pustunich did not make milpa. Milpa is the focus of a majority of male and much female conversation. The pagan ritual is structured around it. Village dress reflects its importance. It consumes the largest single share of a man's time. Milpa defines a man.

Pustunicheños have been farming the same territory as far back as the oldest inhabitants can recall. There are 126,000 *mecates* in the village ejido, 2,500 of which pertain to the village site itself. At any given time 8,000 to 10,000 mecates are in production, with perhaps 80,000 more lying fallow. This still leaves a residue of over 30,000 mecates of which only a portion is unusable or considered too far out to be desirable except in cases of emergency. There is more than sufficient land.

Pustunicheños know the land is not the best. Rocks as large as six feet in diameter lie an inch or two beneath the surface. Rainfall is good, but not ideal. From centuries of farming and hunting villagers know every trail, deer path, thicket, rock outcropping, ancient well, ancient temple-site, dip, and hillock of their ejido, and each—including features which disappeared long ago, yet whose location is still known—has its name. This name is given to the ejidal comisario in early spring when one registers his milpa. It is more precise than a map coordinate.

Corn is the major milpa crop and three types are grown. U.S.-

developed hybrid is used by only a few men who wish to appear modern. Though it produces more than native varieties by total crop weight, it weighs less and few Pustunicheños can overcome a reluctance to sell more (by volume) for the same price. The many who do not grow hybrid corn claim it does not taste as good as the native.

The two native varieties are *xnuuknal* and *xmehenal*. The xnuuknal has been the traditional major crop. It produces more and its grains are larger than the xmehenal. A disadvantage is that the crop takes four or five months to mature and must be planted later as it requires more rain from the very start. When rain is good, when sufficient corn is left from the previous year to last at least a month or two into the summer, xnuuknal will be planted in May to mature in September or October. If the supply of corn has run out earlier than expected, perhaps due to a baptismal or wedding fiesta, or to the expense of an unexpected illness, the hardier and faster maturing xmehenal will be planted in early April to mature in July or August. In practice, most men will regularly sow a few mecates of xmehenal so as to have at least a temporary crop by middle or late summer. Xmehenal is thus an "insurance" crop, planted as much to obtain an early income as to weather a particularly dry year. As a very general rule, the xmehenal growers in a good rain year will more likely be those who experienced some social or physical crisis during the previous winter which necessitated a heavy expenditure. At present, a good proportion of Pustunich men plant only xmehenal, due to the lingering spectre of a devastating drought that occurred six years ago. More are returning to xnuuknal, however, as the memory fades and good rains continue to fall.

The swidden (slash-and-burn) technique practiced by Pustunicheños uses up the land after a second planting. Thus, after the second crop, new land must be cut. Most men try to cut anew each year, and at any given time have both first- and second-year land in production. New milpa is *milpa rosa.* Second-year is *milpa caña,* which produces slightly less.

The cutting occurs from January to March and must be timed correctly. A mistake, "bad" weather, or postponement could severely affect the year's production. The cut bush is allowed to dry in preparation for burning. To cut too soon might mean subsequent growth of new, less combustible shoots. To cut too late is to court disaster should early rains wet the field and prevent burning. Most milpas are burned in March, and the horizon is obscured by whitish-grey mist for days on end throughout the central and southwestern portion of Yucatan. Before burning, the milpa spirits are offered *saca*, consisting of corn boiled without lime, set in the milpa on a makeshife wooden altar.

The time spent waiting for the first substantial rains is the least predictable of Pustunich's year. All hope that it will be at least several weeks, yet less than a month. Few today believe in the predictive efficacy of the January *cabanuelas*,* though most try to remember the weather then to see, "perhaps," if there might be a correlation (in retrospect).

With no milpa work to do, communal hunts are frequent. Houses are repaired or started, and some wage labor may be undertaken in the village or in Ticul. The men try to stay busy.

Should April turn into May without sufficient rain, worry sits in the face of each villager. Conversation seldom strays far from the matter. Those who were remiss in performing the preceding year's *uahicol* (harvest ritual) now call in the h-men to make amends. Should June arrive without rain, disaster looms. By this time the village has generally performed the *cha chaac* (rain-purchase) ceremony. Cha chaac usually always precedes June 13, the day of San Antonio. It is said that rain *must* fall on or before the 13th, so cha chaac is held prior to the 13th, which then becomes an "ace in the hole." Though novenas in honor of family birthdays (where the celebrant bears the saint's name) are not universal in Pustunich, more novenas are celebrated for San Antonio's people (and thus, rain) than for any other except the national patroness, Our Lady of Guadalupe.

Once cha chaac is past, no further community ceremonials are held. If still no rain falls, individuals begin to offer their own *premisias*. Roast chicken, tortillas, and fresh *pozole* are prepared for offering in the milpa. Candles are lit at home, and the priest in Ticul begins to offer masses for rain. Some Pustunicheños who can no longer bear the tension plant anyway, hoping rain will come to germinate the grain before birds and animals steal too much.

Seldom do the rains come later than early June, however. After the first

*The first twelve days of January represent the coming twelve months. Each day's weather ("it is said") predicts the corresponding month's weather. Again, from the 13th to the 24th (this time from December backward). Each half day from the 25th to 30th again counts as January onward, and the twenty-four hours of the 31st represent the twelve months (and their weather) back-to-back. For a more complete description, see Rubel.[1]

sustained downpour hardly a male can be seen in Pustunich. Planting is not done in regular rows, as the soil is too rocky. Shallow holes are made by fire-hardened or iron-tipped digging sticks four or five feet long. Several grains are dropped in each, and the hole is covered by scraping with the point of the stick. The method is inefficient. When asked why they don't simply push soil over the hole with a foot, villagers respond, "Well, it's the custom to use the stick; who knows why we don't do it another way?" It is not unusual for a man to stab four times at the earth with his stick before it sinks in, unhindered by shallow rocks. No attempt is made to clear rocks beforehand, except for the few which are used to mark off the corners of each mecate.

Following the planting, three or four jicaras of saca are placed in the milpa for the balams. An additional offering is made when the corn sprouts. There is no standard number of jicaras to be placed in the milpa, as these are individual rites and subject to family usage. Most milperos spend from fifteen to twenty days weeding during the growth period. When other crops are planted as well, still more weeding is necessary. From July to September the crop matures and ripe ears are bent over to prevent moisture and birds from destroying them. This is the season for corn-on-the-cob and the sending of pots of sweet, rich *atole* (corn gruel) to friends and relatives. At this time thirty to forty green ears are used to prepare the first atole of the year. From three to nine (individually determined) bowls of fresh atole are placed on the home altar along with nine green ears and two candles. These are for "the Eternal Father" in "thanks for the harvest." After several hours the new atole is shared among those present, and small porcelain pots of it are sent out for distribution to children, parents, in-laws, and friends.

Some ripe ears are sold, and within a two- or three-week period it is once again impossible to obtain fresh sweet-corn in Yucatan. The now-dried *elotes* (ears) remain in the field, to be brought home in small amounts as needed—on a man's back or horse's rump, or in larger batches on rented or borrowed horse carts.

From this time until the following June Pustunicheños will perform the uahicol* as thanks to the milpa balams for a harvest. These are individual ceremonies, though several milperos may, and usually do, cooperate in financing the dinner and paying the h-men.

*Uahicol is a local corruption of the more correct expression *uhanlicol*— "meal of the milpa."

Corn is the staple food, eaten mostly as tortillas. The grains are soaked in lime water overnight and ground at one of the two motor mills in town.

Few families use silverware regularly, except for soups. Tortillas serve as sandwich material, filler, scoop, scraper, pusher, and spoon. Ground without first soaking the grains, the dough is lightly seasoned with pepper and carried to the milpa as pozole—the meal of the field. Pustunicheños, from infant to adult, consume an average minimum of half a kilo of corn daily. A family of seven consumes from 1,400 to 1,700 kilos annually, or, in local measure, from thirty-five to forty-two *cargas* (a measure of roughly forty-four kilos) per year. In a good harvest year the men produce one and a half cargas per mecate. An average family in Pustunich thus requires a minimum of twenty-five mecates of milpa to supply its corn needs.

As usually happens, few families manage to last the year without buying corn. Debts are generally incurred during the early summer and must be paid off after the harvest by selling corn. During the fat months from October to February, corn is sold at or slightly under eighty cents per kilo. Usually, by May or June it must be bought back, often from the *same* Ticul or Pustunich buyers, for $1 per kilo.

A number of other crops are grown in the milpa; the major part of them, particularly tobacco, are for cash sale. Rarely, however, will tomatoes, papaya, stringbeans, melons, or peppers be planted instead of corn. Most milperos manage to earn from $400 to $1,000 annually from subsidiary milpa crops.

Milpa is time-consuming. Though most villagers plant both new (*rosa*) and second-year (*caña*) plots, caña nonetheless requires slashing, and the rosa is virgin second-growth. The following is an estimate of time spent at the milpa, based upon a single individual who is a partner in a milpa group, whose share is twenty-five mecates of rosa, and who plants other crops in addition to corn:

A total of 102 days may be spent each year at the milpa. As milpa involves simple technology and little heavy work, two men produce little more than twice that of one and must each spend roughly 100 days in the field.

Pustunicheños get good value for their milpa time. An average of twenty-five mecates produces roughly forty cargas of corn. A third to one-half the cargas are sold during the year at prices ranging from $35 to $40, totaling $530. The remainder is consumed over the year (estimating a remainder of roughly twenty-seven cargas) and represents an average

Table 1
MILPA TIME DISTRIBUTION

Work	Number of Days	Month
Enclosing milpa with brush to prevent entry of cattle	8	March
Tumba (cutting the brush)	25	March-April
Burning	1-2	April, May, June
Planting	3	May or June
Weeding--six times (depends on amount of other crops and how well one wants to weed)	40	June to August
Doubling the ears	2	August-September
Harvest (one man can harvest two mecates of corn per day. Figure 12 days for the corn and 10 days for other produce grown	22	September to April or May

value of $40 per carga (the price rises as the year wears on), totaling $1,080. Tomatoes, beans, and other produce may have an average value of $750. The grand total is roughly $2,400. Counting produce both consumed and sold, the average milpero thus earns over $20 daily at milpa work, almost double the earnings that can be obtained at most kinds of local wage labor and at least equal to construction and government public works wages.

Milpa, too, is a form of capital investment. Though ejidal lands cannot be legally sold, any "improvements" to virgin bush have cash value. Any permanent or salable addition to the milpa, including the crop standing on it, can be "sold." A mature crop is naturally worth more than a freshly sown milpa. Moreover, many individuals, having made milpa in a single general bush region over a number of years, have built permanent huts and in several cases have established beehives and dug wells. All such additions and improvements to virgin bush, including crops, are referred to as constituting the *position* of the land. Thus, while ejidal lands are not legally transferable, villagers get around this by selling their "positions."

The more improved the "position," the more a piece of ejidal land approaches a private property categorization by villagers. Thus, certain areas of the ejido have been "staked-out" for a number of years by families who dominate portions of land which include both planted and fallowing land. As the wealthiest in town are *not* full-time milperos, such "stake-outs" would only be of interest to full-time milperos and thus do not represent a monopoly of major wealth-sources by the rich. In addition, there is plenty of land.

At first glance one might ask why Pustunicheños are satisfied with a $20 average milpa day and don't simply increase their milpas regardless of the extra labor required. Nothing would suit the villagers more. Time, however, is a limiting factor. Most milpa hours must be spent within a three-month period—from shortly before the rains until two to three months afterward. To surround, cut, and burn twenty-five mecates, a man visits the milpa daily with but few absences during a four- to six-week period. He could not manage to complete a larger undertaking before the rains came. Only by hiring workers could extra land be prepared at maximum economic advantage. However, paid workers would then be required once more during the crucial weeding period when weeds must be trimmed within a limited time. Laborers cost less than $20 daily, but one must have ready cash at a time when most families have expended their corn supply and are laying out extra monies for corn in addition to regular daily expenditures.

Wages, Cash Crops, and Entrepreneurship

The 2,000 or so pesos which the milpero earns from his milpa will not normally see him through the year. The average Pustunich family spends from $3,000 to $5,000 yearly, *apart* from the value of milpa corn consumed. A poor family composed of husband, wife, and four children spends roughly $10 daily over a year for fuel, cooking oil, clothing, and other necessities. A medium poor family spends from $14 to $16 daily. A fairly well-to-do family (with, say, four children, one of whom is mature) spends from $18 to $23. These expenditures vary from year to year as illness occurs, clothes wear out, and daughters become eligible for the traditional and elaborate "coming out" party on their fifteenth birthdays.

With the exception of the few wealthy, all Pustunicheño males over nine or ten years old take on outside labor.

Wage labor is normally available for those who want it. Some milpa help is always needed by area milperos. All men have hired one or more of their neighbors at one time or another and all (again, excepting the few wealthy) have worked on the milpas of others. Bush-cutting work is available during early spring, planting during the few weeks following first rains, and weeding during most of the summer.

Wages range from $10 to $18 daily, depending upon the work and industry of the worker. Most milpa labor is by the piece rather than by day or hour. The harder one works, the more one makes.

Pungent wildflower honey is a major export of Yucatan, and collecting work is available during most of the wet season. Much honey work is obtained through two villagers who serve for part of the year as foremen for large-scale honey producers throughout the state. Foremen choose gangs, and Pustunicheños working on such operations can earn up to $18 daily. Village men who are not relatives of the two foremen or friendly with them—or those who do not care for long absences from the village— can work sporadically for small local producers at reduced wages. Honey is collected each fortnight over a three- or four-month period.

During August, considerable work is available on the three nearby henequen plantations. Weeding is paid for by the mecate and a fast worker can earn up to $20 daily. It is not uncommon to see three generations weeding henequen—an eleven-year-old boy, thirty-year-old father, and sixty-year-old grandfather. Additional henequen work is available during cutting times throughout the year and for transplantation of young shoots. Less than a dozen Pustunicheños work more or less continually on the plantations, however. One villager is a foreman. All workers also make normal amounts of milpa.

Within the town itself no regular work is available. If someone is making a lime kiln, he may hire several workers to chop and stack wood at $10 daily. Should someone need his house re-roofed with juano, he might hire one or two friends to help him at roughly similar wages. At times, the *curanderos* (folk curers) must replenish their herb stock, and a brother-in-law or close friend may be hired to roam the *monte* (bush) looking for plants, at $8 to $15, depending upon distance traveled. Several village hatmakers hire sporadic sewing-machine labor as the demand for hats increases.

Ticul, as a town of 15,000 inhabitants with many private businesses as well as civic projects, offers a number of opportunities for wage labor. Recently, for example, both the county and state governments began projects to extend water and electrical lines in Ticul. A number of young Pustunicheños obtained unskilled jobs. Those working for the state electrical project earned $18 daily, which is the Mexican minimum wage. Such municipal or state jobs rarely last longer than two or three months for Pustunicheños, as Ticul officials are expected to "spread the fat" to a number of communities.

Several young men, in their late teens or twenties, have worked and resided for several months in Merida or outside the state. Jobs in Merida generally involve unskilled construction. News of openings reaches the village by word of mouth and young men may journey to the capital to try their luck. Some arrive too late. Others contract as *brazeros* to cut cane in the Campeche area. They are paid $6 the ton and earn little, perhaps $12 daily. Should lack of rain bring on a poor crop-year, as many as thirty adult males may bus the fifty kilometers to Santa Rosa and spend a week or two cutting cane at $8 to $16 daily. Similarly, in August up to seventy young men might depart for a one- or two-month stay in the henequen zone, weeding for up to $18 daily as they wait for their corn crop at home to ripen or dry. Three men have worked in the United States as brazeros, and two others have applied. Upon their return, the three men spent their earnings on improvements to their houses, purchase of luxury items, or capital investment in the form of an additional sewing machine for hatmaking. The three brazeros provoke interest in travel and short-term high earnings, rather than migration per se. None stayed longer than the minimal contract time allowed.

Labor which requires residence outside the village will be undertaken only if the home situation appears bleak; such labor is the exception rather than the rule among mature married men. By and large, Pustunicheños prefer to work near home.

Since before the sugar plantation was founded at Xochaceh over a century ago, Pustunicheños have been working for others. As "wage slaves" or day laborers on sugar and, later, henequen plantations, villagers have sporadically received salaries while partially or wholly maintaining the milpa economy. Two miles from one large town, five miles from another, and on the fringes of commerical agriculture, Pustunich has seldom faced a scarcity of supplemental income. Working for cash has long served as supplement to or insurance for milpa production. Today's labor opportunities are merely greater than those of the past, and the pay is better.

A variety of available entrepreneurial opportunities add further to the overall income potential. The most lucrative are cattle and honey. Honey is the second most important export of Yucatan, next to henequen. Merida buyers pay from $500 to $1,000 per barrel (300 kilos), depending upon demand. Most is shipped to the United States. Because of the financial outlay required for hives and body-protective clothing, only a handful of Pustunicheños produce honey. More would be produced if it weren't for the belief that bees are bad for the citrus trees in town ("they make the blossoms fall"). Thus, all hives are several kilometers into the bush where it is difficult to transport water and sugar for the bees during the dry season. As a result, a number of villagers have lost considerable investments in honey in the past. Honey represents one of the few instances wherein local belief has effectively blocked potentially useful innovation.

Slightly more villagers own cattle. Initial investment is less, and cattle roam untended (though belled to prevent hunting accidents) in the bush where they forage for themselves. Few of the less than two dozen cattle owners possess more than three or four head.

A growing economic opportunity lies with citrus trees. The federal government has established irrigated lands on the outskirts of many villages in the vicinity. Pustunich boasts two such irrigated *recursos hidraulicos*. Villagers have been allowed to use the land, with the stipulation that they must cooperate in water payments and keep the land under constant cultivation of cash crops. Though distributed on a first-come first-served basis, initial investment requirements have essentially limited use of recursos to the already better off. Perhaps eighteen men maintain such plots. Common crops include tomatoes, lettuce, cabbage, and papaya, in addition to lime, oranges, and tangerines. Corn is also grown by some, but illegally since the government requires that recursos be utilized for cash crops only.

Oranges represent a gamble by the federal government. Southern Yucatan is excellent for Valencia oranges. Present prices for them, of course, remain quite high. While a number of Yucatec entrepreneurs see the potential of being first in the orange boom, the five years required for a mature first crop is still too "potential" for corn-farming villagers. Furthermore, peasants distrust the government to such a degree that few have faith in the continuity of irrigation plants or policies. Pustunicheños still talk of the government irrigation-fee collector who the year before "ran off with our payments and stole the repair kit for the pump motor to boot." The full truth of this accusation is unimportant. Villagers have little faith in promises or in a future free of treachery. Memories of recent droughts reinforce a lack of trust in nature. If nature is to be "beaten," villagers must place five or more years of trust in government policies. This they will not do, regardless of the fact that if present prices remain more or less constant, a mere ten citrus trees at maturity will produce as much annual income *as an entire milpa.* Most villagers presently maintain several orange trees in their solares and are more than satisfied with the regular extra income they provide. Irrigation is by bucket, free and guaranteed.

All men, to varying degrees, engage in entrepreneurial activities. These include sale of lime-rich soil, which is found in every solar, juano leaves, chickens, pigs, ducks, eggs, cardinals, armadillo, and game. For the more ambitious, lime making provides a good source of income. Lime is rarely made more than once a year by any villager and few attempt it unless they themselves have a need—house construction, for example. It is meticulous work, necessitating the hiring of at least two laborers to cut, split, and stack wood and limestone. A hearty meal of *mondongo* (tripe stew) must also be provided the workers.

There are few specialties in town. Three men are hat manufacturers when not busy with milpa and can earn about $20 daily at their treadle sewing machines. They are in the lower middle income range and also work for daily wages whenever the demand for hats falls. The hats are sold to Ticul wholesalers. The hatmakers feel no loyalty to village women who weave hat-strands of juano and instead buy from Ticul and Chetumal jobbers at a savings of from ten to forty centavos per half hat-strand. The most successful hatmaker hires from two to four workers on occasion. All three manufacturers utilize their sons, daughters, and wives at the machines.

In addition to the hatmakers, three village men are barbers on demand, charging $1 per haircut. One village woman acts as midwife. There is one male tailor. One villager occasionally makes hunting lamps, on order, out of flashlight materials. There are four storekeepers, a radio mechanic, two motorized corn mills, one buy-sell husband-wife merchant team, and several female huipil buyers who contract for Merida jobbers with village women, supplying cloth and thread.

Of the specialists, only the single h-men (Maya priest) and the two curanderos have skills which no others are expert enough to perform. The curanderos are sufficiently young and self-oriented to feel no need to take on apprentices. Their skill and fame are such as to prevent any other villager from entertaining thoughts of becoming a curer, even if he could find a practitioner to teach him the trade.

Aside from the curers and h-men, no economic specialty is considered the sole possession of any individual or group. In the past, other stores have come and gone, and other hatmakers have tried their hands. Anyone with a sharp scissors and high chair can take up barbering. All Pustunicheños have made lime, sold juano, owned pigs, ducks, chickens, and perhaps even a cow at one time or another.

Pustunich boasts no economic specialty, which sets it apart from other villages in the area. Curanderos, swine raisers, juano weavers, orange growers, hat makers, milperos, and shop keepers are found in every other town in the vicinity.

Pustunich, however, does lack a number of specialists found in larger towns. The village has no marketplace, no bar, no shoe repairman, no bakery (though one existed for several years over a decade ago), no clothiers, restaurants, ice or ice cream, carpenters, masons, or blacksmiths. Ticul successfully monopolizes these services and provides a bustling, exciting milieu in which to obtain them. The monopoly has grown even more complete since electricity was introduced in Ticul over a decade ago.

Division of Labor

Few activities in Pustunich are viewed as inviolably masculine or feminine. Rather, distinctions are the result of traditional role divisions and de facto differences of interests. Thus, while men make milpa, women may help husbands at any aspect of it. This is admittedly rare, but possible. While only men repair houses, there is no reason why a woman may not do this kind of work. Similarly, though females do the family cooking and tortilla making, it is not uncommon for men to take these tasks over for a wife who is ill, providing there are no capable daughters available. Men will take corn to the mill if necessary, though this is a female activity, closely connected with gossip and relaxation. Men regularly take corn meal to the milpa, however, and prepare their own tortillas. Dishes of venison and other hunt-animals are quite often prepared by the husband, who is regarded as a better cook where such dishes are concerned (the equivalent of backyard barbecuing in the United States).

Women may be as entrepreneurially active as men and are wholly responsible for selling the woven juano hat-strands prepared by other family members. The family pocketbook is essentially communal, though normally dominated by the male through whose hands more family income arrives. Females are expected to purchase food, clothing, and any necessary minor household items. These items often constitute the largest portion of the family budget. For major expenses, both husband and wife will have a voice, though the male's decision is the more potent. Few Pustunich men fail to consult wives over major purchases; in a number of households, the female may dominate all expenditure decisions.

As will be discussed later, the weaving of juano braids for sale to hatmakers is strictly a female activity. Women generally weave these tejidos in company with others. No mature male will engage in this activity without incurring harsh informal sanction. Similarly, hunting is a strictly male activity and in certain respects the counterpart of the female's tejido weaving. Both are economic activities which provide an excuse for pleasant, relaxed interaction with no stigma of laziness so long as other, more immediate work is not ignored.

For the communal hunt, as many as sixty males may gather at 5:00 A.M. and spend the day wandering through the bush of the village ejido. In terms of food, ammunition, and bus fare (if the hunt is to be a longer one in a different area), the operation is generally a loss. But it is always enjoyable.

Women are forcibly excluded from only two activities: lime-burning and the major public Maya rituals. (For the latter, women are essential to preparation of offerings.) A woman's presence may "prejudice" the burning of lime pyres, causing uneven combustion, etc. As a preventative measure or *contra*, a piece of feminine attire is usually placed on top of a burning lime pile, in case a woman should inadvertently pass nearby.

Milpa Groups

Few make milpa alone in Pustunich. It is lonely in the monte, and though village men are minimally wary of the supernatural, it is nice to have a companion around for conversation. Though the heavy work of clearing and fencing fields is somewhat more easily done by two, villagers are aware that many accidents can occur in the bush and that several varieties of poisonous snake or scorpion make their home there. At one time or another most milperos have been carried into the village ill or with a wound, break, or bite.

Most milpa groups average three or four partners. At any given time, a majority of men make milpa with fathers, sons, and brothers exclusively. Following, in their order of frequency, are the most common types of milpa partnerships:

> father/sons or stepfather/stepsons
> grandfather/father/sons (patrilineal)
> brother/brother (and one or more of their sons)
> friends (and sons)
> father-in-law/sons-in-law

Other less numerous combinations, such as brothers-in-law and their sons, cousin/cousin, or uncle/nephew, may be formed. The three-generation patrilineal combination is less frequent than the simple father/sons arrangement, not out of a preference for limiting partnerships to two generations, but because of the death rate of older men.

Only fathers and sons make milpa as a wholly communal venture, working all parts of the field as though the whole belonged to all. Whenever two or more nonlineal partners (for example, brothers, cousins, friends, in-laws) make milpa, slashing and burning are generally the only cooperative activities undertaken. Each partner (representing a distinct nuclear family—and this generally holds for two married brothers as well) plants, weeds, and harvests his own portion. Portions are actually marked off with stone piles. Ideally, each is on his own after the burning. Should one partner's half fail, the other is not obliged to share. Actually, the point is moot, as little can occur to one-half a milpa that does not occur to the other. Should cattle enter, all parts of the field generally suffer. In such an event, however, indemnity for crop damage is sought from the cattle owner. *If* the milpa partners can manage to collect, all will share. Should drought occur, all milpas die.

Milpa alliances change throughout life and few men can say they have never made milpa with other than a father, son, or brother. While working on fifteen mecates of caña with one's father, a Pustunicheño may clear and plant ten of rosa with his brother- or father-in-law. Nonetheless, some nuclear family members are included in the vast majority of alliances. Less than 15 percent of present partnerships include no nuclear family, and the bulk of these are entered into by individuals between the ages of thirty and forty-five. These years are socially the most active, in which the individual is most heavily engaged in the full range of social relationships available to villagers—that is, with affines, (own and children's), friends, compadres, and extended family. Immature sons and the elderly make milpa almost exclusively with father and sons, as their presence often becomes more of a burden than an asset.

As it is difficult to find two Pustunicheños not related through blood or marriage (through self, children, or siblings), nonnuclear family partnerships are chosen on the basis of existing friendships rather than specific kin or nonkin ties. There is no overriding pattern visible in the choice of nonnuclear family milpa partners. Animosities one year can, and have, driven even siblings to separate milpas and partnerships the next. Beyond family solidarity, the partnerships of the summer reflect the alliances and friendships that existed during the premilpa months of January, February, and March.

Milpa alliances such as these are not uncommon in Meso America. Rubel (in personal correspondence) describes them in S. Cristobal, Chiapas, where they are formalized by the title *grupitos*. These, however, consist of individual contiguous, though distinguishable, plots cut and burned communally by members of the grupito. They are planted and harvested by the individual members or owners. Most commonly "grupito" membership consists of brothers and their children.

Wealth Differentials

Milpa, by far the most important activity in Pustunich, provides a major portion of food and income, either directly or through wages. It consumes the largest single share of a man's time and is thus seldom unobtrusive in the daily life of the family. Conversation centers upon it, on the price of corn, on the weather, on the relative merits of this bush area or that. Most injuries occur while making milpa. Insofar as milpa throws individuals together for a season of cooperation and close association, it announces and demonstrates to all the present alliances and the solidarity of the family. Milpa is the focus of the pagan ritual round and as such is inseparable from it. It demands commitment and the cooperation of a majority in the annual spring cha chaac. Milpa is the training-ground of sons. At birth a boy's umbilicus is taken to the monte and thrown away, so he will not be afraid of the bush.

Milpa verifies Pustunich's own self-characterization as a campesino village and, equally important, as a Maya village. It affects the class structure of Pustunich, in that mestizo garb (denims, sandals) is regarded as expendable and is identified closely with the life of the monte. Villagers feel strongly that a *catrin* (the Yucatec term for *ladino*) could not make milpa without ripping his "nice" clothing. Thus, only a mestizo can logically make milpa. Regardless of the presence of a few catrins, Pustunich views itself as a mestizo town.

Milpa is virtually the sine qua non of male identity. Only three have made no milpa—the "policeman" and two retarded youths. They are referred to as *medio inutil* (half useless) because they make no milpa. Several other young men at present make no milpa; as the sons of one of the town's wealthiest men, however, it is felt that they need not farm. Hence, there is a latent double standard: if a man is rich, he need not make milpa; if a man is not rich, he is not a full male unless he does, at least once in his life.

Even the wealthy grow citrus trees and make small to substantial quantities of milpa from time to time. As such, they can and do participate regularly in the major communal Maya rituals—if only as donor of a chicken or cash for purchase of ritual ingredients. Milpa and Maya ritual are inseparable and constitute two of the major features of Pustunich life. To be cut off from both is to stand outside of the tradition and world-view of the vast majority.

As one cannot normally become rich by making milpa, and as most men, regardless of wealth, make some milpa, milpa itself is not a strong indicator of social or economic status. The quantity of milpa varies from year to year for any individual, the most important variable being the number of sons between the ages of eight and thirty. The more mature, unmarried sons a man has, the more milpa he makes without having to share with other nuclear family heads.

Wealth differentials are most readily seen in the rewards of nonmilpa activities: in head of cattle, orange acreage, bees, stores or businesses, wages earned, etc., and in certain aspects of the style of living which reflect them.

Aside from such obvious (and scarce) items as masonry houses, automobiles (there are only three), and the single television set, the possessions of the better-off do not differ significantly from those of the poorer. A few poor families own bicycles, sewing machines, and battery-powered short-wave radios. The better-off merely possess more of them. The mestiza huipils and *ternos* (dressy, more complicated huipils) of the wealthier are better made and have costlier thread, but do not differ in form. They put more meat and vegetables in their soups and bean-potage, and they buy more candy for their children. The dishes prepared, however, are similar throughout the village, and tortillas are the staple. Though all four stores stock canned tuna and small sausages, few families will purchase them more than once or twice yearly. Regardless of wealth, all villagers cook in a stick-sided thatch hut which is behind the house (and from which smoke escapes easily).

The wealthy dress no differently from all other villagers. All are mestizos. All speak Maya in the home. Clemente Perez (store, theater, and television set owner) has great difficulty with Spanish, using it only with merchants and suppliers from Merida or Ticul. The wealthy differ visibly in the better quality and greater number of their possessions, and in the fact that their major sources of income are other than milpa or wage-labor.

There is some argument as to who is the wealthiest man in Pustunich. Clemente Perez and Manolo Cepeda vie for the title. Perez owns the largest store. In a corner of the main plaza his shop and warehouse straddle what was once the main road. The store was his father's and grandfather's before him. It has the largest stock of the four shops in town. Perez has a corn mill run by gasoline motor. Though another individual also owns a corn mill, Perez by far has the largest volume of business. At night, his store is the only building in town lighted electrically, the current being produced by a gasoline generator in the warehouse across the street. He rents out two other generators, along with strings of bulbs, a record player, and records for parties and novenas. His main generator is connected by permanent cable with the church, for which he provides neon light at a fixed fee whenever the church is needed at night. Perez owns a car and a truck which he rents with driver, for hauling. He makes daily runs into Ticul, charging passengers thirty centavos each way.

For over thirty years Perez has provided moving pictures for Pustunich in the open-air storage and parking lot behind his store. His sons built a professional projection booth at its rear, under a permanent corrugated iron awning. Movies are shown at least two weekends per month. Adult admission varies between seventy-five cents and $1.50 depending upon the film; the more recent, the more its cost of rental from the Merida distributor. For the past four years, Perez has owned a television set, for which he also charges admission when special programs are to be shown.

When President Kennedy died, half a hundred villagers paid thirty cents apiece to view the funeral.

Perez also owns citrus land just south of the village. He is a moneylender, charging 10 percent per month. Lacking a liquor license, he surreptitiously sells shots of brandy to village men. Through kickbacks to the major beer distributor in Ticul, he monopolizes all sales of beer for Pustunich festivals. The distributor will sell to no one but him, and at least ten times a year he makes handsome profits—not only as local beer distributor, but also for hauling the bottles to and from the village in his truck.

Perez maintains a family of eight, which includes his wife, two married sons and their wives, and two unmarried daughters. His oldest son, a radio mechanic, operates a repair shop behind the store. He learned the trade through a United States correspondence school. His income is added to the family fund. Perez' daytime household also includes several young nieces and cousins who do domestic work and babysit. They are, however, employees, working for low wages and receiving good food at the family table.

Clem Perez' store, as do all stores in Mexico, has a name: "La Fortuna." Perez himself is referred to as "Fortuna." To the villagers, the nickname fits like a glove.

Manolo Cepeda inherited his henequen acreage from his father, as did his two brothers. The brothers, however, squandered their inheritance on unsure business ventures and lost much. Today they are among the middle well-off. Cepeda's property hems in the east of town and bends to enclose a portion of the south side of Pustunich. He also owns cattle and pigs; a car and truck for hauling henequen to the cortification plants; a good number of masonry buildings on his plantation and two large masonry houses in the main square next to the cuartel.

His wife and daughters contract with village women for the making of huipils which they sell to Merida jobbers. Because his wealth is limited to one major area, and because he lives on the periphery of town and visits the plaza less frequently than most men, Cepeda's wealth is less visible than Perez'. It is altogether likely that he earns as much or more than Perez from the sale of henequen. His yearly income may be in excess of $125,000 pesos ($10,000 U.S. dollars), as deduced from his present holdings and the present price of henequen.

The third wealthiest man in Pustunich is Torcuato Belem, one of the best known curanderos in southern Yucatan. It is not unusual to see a Mercedes Benz from Merida parked in front of his waiting room. The waiting room is new, with a parquet tile floor. Actual consultation is performed in the attached dark, dirt-floored thatch hut which creates the "proper" atmosphere.

Torcuato makes a very substantial living from his cures and diagnoses. He has reputedly charged $400 dollars on occasion for curing nervous disorders of Merida *ricos*. Torcuato also owns henequen land on the southern border of Pustunich, which produces income at least equal to his income from curing. His henequen land is smaller than Cepeda's. His healing business is discreet, and no one knows for sure what he earns from it. As he charges his fellow villagers less than outsiders (he knows what the traffic will bear), villagers assume he earns less than Perez or Cepeda. Actually, Torcuato may be the wealthiest of the three, as a close estimate of his henequen income alone for last year is not too far under 10,000 dollars.

Torcuato lives in a four-room complex in a large solar two blocks from the plaza. He owns a car. His oldest son recently completed a correspondence course in commercial art and cartooning. Torcuato is the only polygynist in town: he lives with two wives and is reputed to have another in Ticul and still another in Merida, both of whom he maintains. He is also a lavish entertainer and will stand round after round of drinks at the slightest excuse.

Though in no way approaching the wealth of the other three, Justo Belem's potential is perhaps greater. Justo is the brother of Torcuato and is himself a well-known curandero. Torcuato, it is said, has been "slipping" in the past few years, and Justo is fast becoming his equal in fame and clientele. Justo, too, has a masoned, tile-floored consulting room in front of his thatched dwelling quarters. He, too, has cured the children of Merida matrons who park Mercedes Benzes in the dusty street. He is an astute businessman, and more often than Torcuato he provides work for the other three poorer Belem brothers. Justo owns the newest and best located store in Pustunich, on the paved highway. Unlike the three other shops, his is spotless and tile-floored, with goods neatly stacked on shelves and well organized without clutter. His neatness, organization, and desire for perfection are reflected in his orange grove, located in the southernmost village recurso. He was one of the first in the entire area to recognize the potential of oranges, and his entire allotment is under citrus cultivation. The trees are in exactly placed rows, forming a straight line when viewed from any angle. "Look," he exclaims to any visitor, "try to find a weed—even one." He sprays regularly and his trees, though just reaching maturity, are already bearing twice as much as any others in the vicinity. Recently, Justo was appointed president of the Yucatec Orange Grower's Association, more in recognition of his showplace grove than for administrative functions which are limited to sporadic meetings with Merida agronomists.

Justo recognizes the potential of lush Quintana Roo. He plants from three hundred to six hundred mecates of milpa in Quintana Roo yearly. He and his poorest brother, Juan, rotate visits to the area on a twenty-day-on, twenty-day-off basis during the growing season. There are six hired men at the milpa during much of the year, and at peak cutting, weeding, and harvest periods as many as twenty laborers from Pustunich and other nearby towns will be hired. Justo chose the location on the basis of productive potential rather than ease of accessibility. The milpa can be reached by truck during a few months' period in the dry season. For the rest of the year, he and his crew must walk for ten hours through dense bush after leaving the bus on the main road to the British Honduras. Justo also owns private milpa lands to the north of town and is involved in at least several other enterprises to which he alludes but does not describe.

Clem Perez, Manolo Cepeda, and the two Belem brothers are never addressed as other than "Don." They are treated with considerable respect, and their counsel is heeded when it is asked. They are among the first seated at any dinner, the first served at a party.

With the exception of Torcuato, none spends much time in conversation groups. Perez' storefront is a major congregating place, but he rarely appears from behind his counter. Rarely does he leave his store-theater-house complex. Cepeda seldom walks the five blocks into the plaza unless drunk and looking for jovial conversation. Of the four, Torcuato is the most garrulous. He is inebriated most days and staggering drunk most weekends. His daily expenses are ten times that of the average family's. He is reputed to be heavily in debt, owing $5,000 pesos to his brother Justo and over $10,000 pesos to Manolo Cepeda. Having put up his henequen land as collateral for Cepeda's loan, he recently defaulted on part and lost over half his henequen acreage. To most villagers, however, owing 20,000 pesos is as exotic as owning it, and Torcuato has not lost prestige. His expenses are enormous. He himself claims to spend over

100 pesos daily. He estimates that he has over 1,000 compadres. Likewise, the other ricos have stood as godfathers more than any other villagers.

Of the four, only Perez has served as comisario. Justo Belem recently ran and lost. Since the time he held office, Perez has done nothing for the town without receiving his profit or vigorously attempting to. Each year at Carnival, however, he condescends to play "King Ugly," in circus barker's costume and false whiskers. The crowd has grown to love this exhibition, as it is so distant from their expectations of him (and the wealthy in general) as social participant and jolly comrade. Nonetheless, Perez makes a profit from rental of the loudspeaker through which he announces the Carnival events. He charges 15 pesos for rental of the auto battery and public-address hardware used each Sunday to announce the village baseball team's games. His cost is roughly 3 pesos for a battery charge. Recently, the progressive schoolteacher obtained beer for annual fiesta sale directly from the bottler in Merida instead of through Perez and his distributor. The bottler gave a substantial discount, advertised the fiesta over Yucatec radio, and provided free tables, chairs, and beer glasses. Perez could have provided none of these benefits—only beer. He immediately retaliated by raising his generator and public-address prices for town affairs.

Following the same fiesta, many hundreds of empty beer bottles were missing, representing a good loss in deposits. They had been secretly garnered by another storekeeper for surreptitious return and a quick personal profit.

Though a part of Pustunich, the wealthy and most of the merely well-off neither lead nor aid it more than do any others. In fact, the contrary is more true. They are socially conservative. The donations of the wealthy for public works, though higher than any other villager's (it is expected of them), in no way approach the fair share commensurate with their incomes. They innovate principally in their costly purchases which, more often than not, are turned to making a profit off the village. Indeed, such things as movies and TV programs would never have reached Pustunich had there been no profit for the rich Perez. In dress, the wealthy are among the more conservative of Pustunich. In terms of profession, two of the wealthy (the curanderos) represent perhaps the ultimate economic and prestige achievements of "nonmodern" role configurations.

On a hypothetical ten-point scale from 1 (poverty) to 10 (very wealthy), the four ricos occupy level 10, with the remainder of Pustunich distributed between 2 and 4, most falling in levels 2 and 3. No one approaches the wealth of the four ricos.

When asked to rate all village families by economic level, seven informants (two each from levels 2, 3, 4, and one from 10) unanimously agreed on the ratings of only eleven people. Three of these were placed in category 10, two in 4, and seven in the lowest category, 2. Of the four ricos, only Torcuato Belem received second category votes, and these were given by informants of the two highest categories (which included his brother Justo). The better-off, who are quite ready to include themselves in the same category as a traditionally wealthy individual, can more easily recognize his slipping finances. To the two lowest categories, however, Torcuato is immensely wealthy. To a man, the poorest informants placed him in the highest economic level.

That informants failed to agree on all but eleven individuals is indicative of the fluidity of economic status in Pustunich and the absence of broad economic class distinctions. Ten individuals were categorized in class 4, only two unanimously. These latter included one of the four shopkeepers (the mayor) and a full-time honey foreman who often shows up in town driving a company Jeep.

Past wealth is of relatively little importance except for its lingering tendency to elicit deference. The teacher's father, once one of the wealthiest men of Pustunich, now lives off his sons. The seven informants accordingly rated him as category 2 (lowest), though he is highly respected and an ex-mayor. Inheritance is generally behind anyone in second or highest level economic status. Whereas Perez and Cepeda represent long well-to-do families, the Belems are descended from a line of curanderos (both male and female) who, though comfortable, in no way approached the entrepreneurial status of the two present curing brothers.

There is considerable disagreement over categorization of the sons of the wealthy. Two opinions predominate: "Sons are as wealthy as their fathers because the fathers are wealthy," or, "They are not so wealthy because it is their fathers, not they, who are the established, wealthy ones." The latter is said more often in reference to Cepeda's boys. Unlike the two Perez sons, they work the land (henequen), dress mestizo more often than do the Perez boys, and one lives apart from his father in the town's center. Perez' sons both dress catrin, live and work within the paternal store-cinema compound, and are rated as wealthy as their father.

Economic differentiation, though broadly apparent at any given time, is an unstable typological mechanism on the whole. Even the wealthy may fall. Old man Gomez, once one of the wealthiest in Pustunich, today lives with a young married son who buys his clothing for him. Cepeda's brother received a roughly equal inheritance from the father and squandered it on gambling. Today he is the town's butcher, living in a smoke-stained thatch house. Avila the mayor was once a cantina owner. Hercila once owned a store and went broke. Alejos and a Gomez were lucky enough to find work as well-paid honey gang foremen. Mex saved and established the town's second corn mill. Ek studied at home and now is a well-paid secretary in Oxkutzkab. Pustunicheños do not stereotype whole families because, excepting Clem Perez, *every* family in town has a son, brother, or father who is predominantly a milpero of lowest or second lowest economic category. Even Perez has poor cousins.

Aside from the wealthiest men, neither major occupation, sideline, specialization, nor economic condition serves to distinguish a recognizable group or clique who must be treated or viewed in a special fashion. (The two curanderos are exceptions, but they are among the wealthiest.) While there are indeed obvious differences of wealth and possession among individuals, these differences are not evident in day-to-day interaction. Though the food, beverage, and entertainment provided at parties and novenas reflect the economic condition of the host, guest lists reflect blood, affinal, and friendship relationships rather than economic position. Conversing groups of men in the plaza reflect no purposeful economic segregation.

It is at marriage, however, that economic considerations may play an important role.

Excerpt from field notes, March 1964:

Eulogio Guzman (twenty-seven), who got married about a month and a half ago with much splendor and a $4,000 price-tag was divorced today. His wife (twenty-nine years old) just left his house and returned to her parents. I had expected a solid union, as both are quite old for a first marriage. Her stated reasons were that the Guzmans (including Eulogio, the father, mother, Eulogio's brother, and his wife and children) were too cheap. She said she didn't like eating beans every day, and when the elder Guzman brought the usual Sunday meat ration of one kilo home, she became exasperated, shouting that "one kilo is enough for my dog for one week, but not for eight or nine people."

Manolo Guzman (Eulogio's brother and five or six years his senior) says that an economic difference between families can be troublesome. Eulogio's bride, for example, was used to better food. He says that when a woman is brought up on a basis of plenty and then marries a poor man, dissatisfaction can result. For example, he says look at Clem Perez' daughter who is being courted by Jaime Guzman (Manolo's cousin's son) who comes from a poor family. "She's used to eating meat three times a day. How can she hold out married to him?"

I asked Alonso Gomez [the teacher] about the matter and he claimed it wasn't only the food. There was also the lack of room and privacy in the small house with so many people. Another point, he added, might be the fact of her once being Justo Belem's mistress, and the inevitable jealousy.

Though this divorce was as much the result of personal incompatibility between two late-marrying and long-independent individuals, the stated reasons indicate the view of Pustunich on matters of economic inequality. It is not by accident that Clem Perez' three daughters—all older than seventeen—are as yet unmarried. Nor are the four daughters of two other storekeepers of mid-range economic comfort married. Young village men describe themselves as "afraid" to approach them and believe that they could never get used to less than plenty. This view of marital economic inequality, however, is ideal rather than overwhelmingly behavior-orienting. There are many "unequal" matings. Yearly individual income fluctuations and the ubiquitous food customs make it impossible to type any number of families as permanently unsuitable for supplying marriage partners. Furthermore, in all families, the woman's work is virtually identical. She rises early, prepares tortillas, soaks the corn, takes the corn to mill, mends clothes, washes clothing and dishes, feeds the solar animals, shells beans, and weaves tejidos. This is as true

for Clemente Perez' wife as it is for the wife of the poorest individual,
though Mrs. Perez may vary her day by tending to the store while a hired
girl washes the clothes and makes tortillas.

Pragmatics, Potential, and Continuity

In its continuing preoccupation with milpa, Pustunich maintains a
persisting link with the traditional past. This link is multifold in that the
influence of milpa goes far deeper than the comparatively good income
and subsistence which it actually provides.

Milpa is a major factor in male identity. Since milpa is the focus of the
male-organized pagan ritual, each reinforces the other and further contributes to the definition of other male activity spheres. The pagan ritual
ideally demands the cooperation of all farming village males at least once
a year in a ceremony which all know to be Maya and specifically
campesino. It further necessitates a h-men whose presence strengthens
the village image as Maya and campesino. As milpa work is strongly
identified with clothing, and thus social class, a preoccupation of adults
with milpa strengthens the mestizo identity of the town. (See Chapter 6.)
Equally important is the fact that milpa reinforces and demonstrates
family and affinal solidarity and friendship alliances through semi-
cooperative or fully cooperative work groupings.

Because these concomitants of making milpa are so all-pervasive, to
make or have made any milpa at all is to experience, at least minimally,
the phenomena noted above. All males in Pustunich, including the
wealthy and their sons, have made some milpa, or at least worked a
limited recurso plot. All are thus typed as campesinos by outsiders and
Pustunich consciously embraces the stereotype to a man. "We're all
poor—campesinos," says wealthy Clem Perez in halting Spanish.

The attitude prevails, even though villagers spend more of their total
work hours away from the milpa than on it. However, milpa does
consume the largest single share. Exceptions are the four very wealthy,
the two honey foremen, the teacher, a secretary, several *medio inutiles*,
and perhaps Gerardo Alvarado who, with his wife, spends most of his
time in trade and merchant activities. Ek (the secretary), the foremen, and
Justo Betem (a curandero) *do* make some milpa annually, however.
Thus, of over three hundred male residents, only seven do not make
milpa at present. To live in Pustunich is to make milpa, especially if one

is not wealthy. To escape milpa, one must escape the town itself, as have perhaps a dozen young men in the past ten years.

Though milpa is a major economic focus, wage labor must not be underestimated. It is familiar, quite traditional, and easy to obtain. Sufficient opportunities are available to minimize the necessity for binding one's self to a single job or for lengthy migration to another zone for work. Most wage labor is within Pustunich or commuting distance. Some young men have worked in Merida. Only a minority actively seek city employment, however, and it is from this group that the infrequent emigrant arises. The majority, even when working for a number of weeks on plantations in Campeche or near Merida, work only with other campesinos. Here, the peninsular cultural homogeneity serves to minimize the exchange of radically new ideas. Though more conservative in many respects than full-time henequen workers, it must be remembered that Pustunicheños live on a main paved road, own many dozens of radios, see movies regularly, receive several newspapers daily, and interact with travelers, merchants, and Ticuleños on a day-to-day basis. Pustunicheños learn little, if anything, new from their fellow Yucatec workers, and return to town with a heavier pocketbook, secure in their knowledge that twenty-five or thirty mecates of good corn immunizes them against general layoffs or a depressed labor market.

The century-old availability of wage labor, coupled with milpa and the day-to-day entrepreneurial activities of tejidos, huipil sewing, milpa and garden produce, sale of fruit from solar or recurso trees, juano, fowl and game, provide a varied and highly secure economic foundation. The economic pie is virtually unlimited in size. A "limited good" value orientation is absent. The success of each activity makes the abandonment of any one neither advantageous nor desirable for the majority of Pustunicheños. The addition of new cash avenues is also quite possible, provided, of course, that they do not compete with related existing time requirements or value systems. Thus, the rather present-oriented peasant finds it difficult to invest in oranges which promise no return for five years. The difficulty is simply one of lack of investment funds, however, in that a number of villagers are attempting, albeit cautiously, to raise citrus trees in the government-irrigated projects. It is interesting that villagers automatically began pagan ritual rounds for maintenance of the irrigated citrus groves, thus endowing orange growing with "legitimate" agricultural status. Similarly, the attempt by the ethnographer to introduce a small-scale hunting-lamp factory in the village succeeded and attracted considerable general interest. (See Press.[2]) It later petered out from lack of experience at ordering, salesmanship, and the like, rather than any intrinsic distrust of unprecedented cash sources.

Thus, the village economic configuration is simultaneously a force for stability and change. It is successful, open, and not defensive. It offers physical security, sex-role differentiation, and leisure-time validation. It also strongly influences maintenance of peasant (campesino) identity and of class (dress) and pagan ritual behavior.

NOTES

1. Arthur J. Rubel, "Prognosticative Calendar Systems." *American Anthropologist* 67 (1965): 107-110.

2. See Irwin Press, "Innovation in Spite of: A Lamp Factory for Maya Peasants." *Human Organization* 25 (1967): 284-294.

6

Class and Identity

On Being Maya: Names, Mates, and Mobility

Pustunicheños stand united in referring to themselves as Maya, mestizo, and campesino. To them, these categorizations are evident from their home and street language, dress, economy, style of life, and appearance of their pueblo.

A majority of marriages are endogamous. A typical comment is one young man's when questioned about desirable marriage partners. "It's better to marry a local girl. If you get a girl from a big place like Ticul, she's used to walking in the plaza and lots of excitement. Here the life is boring. A girl from outside would soon get bored in a small village like this." Ticuleños have obliged in the past by referring to Pustunich as a "forgotten village," the stereotypic rustic, hick town. The president of Ticul tells how for years Pustunich has been used by people of the region as a classic example of naivete, much as Peoria, Illinois, has been characterized by midwesterners in the United States.

Though agreeing that Ticul folks are used to more excitement, Pustunicheños know the larger town too well and have too many kinsmen or friends there to stand in awe of it. All of the Ticul tradespeople and storeowners speak Maya. Pustunicheños have sold sufficient produce in the single Ticul market to know that the city-dressed, educated elite of Ticul eat very familiar foods.

Still, Ticul is different. City people, doctors and lawyers, for example, *do* live there. Its two movie theaters, electricity, cantinas, shops, and services make it a metropolis compared with the dusty village. While not feeling greatly alienated from Ticul, or nervous and overly out of place on her streets, Pustunicheños nonetheless feel themselves to be different. Most Pustunicheños have been to Merida at least several times and always feel ill at ease, conspicuous in their "mestizoness," wary of clerks, awkward in their usually adequate Spanish, and hesitant to use Maya. As a result, visits to Merida, for specific purchases, governmental business, or pleasure, seldom result in exploration of new ground. The restaurants, stalls, shops visited the last time and the time before are again patronized.

Most Pustunicheños will readily admit to being Maya, but not "real" Maya. The "legitimate Maya" lived long ago, during and before the Caste War.

Though Maya, Pustunich is not agreed upon its categorization as "Indian." Some suggest that all in the village are Indians (*indios*). Others claim that no one in town is an indio. The indios are probably bad people, probably not Catholic. These "Indians" are equated with those who supposedly did damage to the village during the Caste War. If many Pustunicheños were asked to describe an Indian, the description would be that of a Sioux or Apache, seen in cowboy films shown regularly in the "Cine Perez." "They say there are Indians south of here, in the forest," comments one villager, "but we've never seen any." In actuality, typical Yucatec "Indian" dress, visible mainly in Quintana Roo, today involves the wearing of white shorts, white shirt, and an apron (for males) in front. The present catrin schoolteacher's father, in fact, wears this garb on occasion, yet is described as being mestizo, not indio.

Other categories in which villagers lump others include the following: gringos, who come from any country other than Mexico, unless the specific country of origin is known (one can be both a gringo and a German); Mexicans from Mexico proper; Yucatecans; Turks, generally associated with Merida shopowners and most any merchant who comes through town; Chinamen, with Chinese characteristics; Negroes, who are anyone very dark with or without Negroid facial characteristics and generally assumed to come from Belize. Toward none of these does Pustunich exhibit overt distrust or inhospitality. Only local and lower ranking state and federal government officials are treated as suspect.

Pustunicheños vary in physical appearance. A majority combine degrees of Maya and European characteristics, ranging from phenotypically Maya to apparent European. A few villagers reflect the migration to

Yucatan of Negroes from the nearby British Honduras and of oriental merchants who followed the *chicle* boom in the early twentieth century. It is reported by villagers that Hacienda Tabi, eight kilometers south, once employed numbers of Chinese. Old Pustunich men still chuckle over the "huge battle" among a group of "chinos" some years ago during the annual fiesta of Ticul. "There they were—a mountain of Chinamen, all fighting."

Most Pustunicheños are olive complexioned. Some range to dark (called *moreno*), though more "swarthy" than Negroid. The villagers are of medium to medium-short height. Few are over five feet eight or nine inches tall; few males are under five feet four inches. The single six-footer in town is accorded special status as "official" policeman (bouncer) at public events. Beards are most often sparse. Only one very old man lets his beard grow, and less than half a dozen men sport mustaches.

There is little correlation between physical features and surname or family. Though the most Maya in appearance are generally also Maya-named, strongly Maya features can be seen among the Spanish. One of the darkest complexioned (*morena*) girls, a storekeeper's daughter, comes from one of the oldest and largest Spanish families. The wealthy Clemente Perez combines oriental and Maya features, not European. Village boys say that it is better to marry a girl lighter than they. Morenas, some state, aren't the most desirable girls, yet Pustunich has mostly morenas. Though a lighter complexion is regarded as ideal in a potential spouse, the ideal, when realized, is more frequently fortuitous than planned. More important in choosing mates is family, general appearance ("looks"), and idiosyncratic personal attraction.

There is also little correlation between language and other characteristics of identity. Maya was the first language learned by all present villagers. With few exceptions, Maya is spoken by all Pustunicheños among family, friends, in the street, shops, and at town meetings. Though Spanish is, and has been, the language of the school, Maya is spoken by the children from the moment classes are dismissed each afternoon. All shopowners in Ticul speak Maya. Few of the traveling merchants or of the sixteen bus drivers who stop momentarily in Pustunich each day cannot carry on a minimal conversation in Maya. Local, state, and national political candidates from Yucatan often deliver two speeches in the Ticul square—one in Spanish, and a shorter, "homier" version in fluent to broken Maya. With the exception of the schoolteacher or ejidal comisario, no Pustunicheño would have a frequent need to approach a governmental office in Merida where Maya might not be understood. In the mass market of Merida, however, Maya is the *lingua franca*. For the necessities of daily or occasional interaction, purchase of a TV set, or travel on a train or state highway bus, no Pustunicheño need speak Spanish.

Most adults and all children nonetheless speak fair to fluent Spanish. Only the oldest women and one or two old men are Maya monolinguals. There has been a school in Pustunich for over sixty years, and Spanish has been the required language of classes. Movies, radio, travelers, and travel have made Spanish a useful, though not essential, skill. In its almost universal ability to speak the national language, Pustunich feels itself to be modern. It is Maya, however, which gives voice to the important thoughts and interactions of the village. Those few families which are actively attempting to teach Spanish to their young children as a first language are also those which attempt to dress them catrin (ladino). As catrin and milpa are incompatible, the emphasis upon Spanish indicates consistency in their attempts to commit children to a different mode of life. At present, the *only* adult who is more fluent in Spanish than Maya is the catrin, educated schoolteacher.

A more complex category of identity lies with the distinction between *dzul* and *mazehual*. As in Chan Kom, the terms are basically referents to patronymics,[1] with additional overtones of life-style. A Maya surname is mazehual; a Spanish, dzul. As also noted in Chan Kom, an individual whose father had a Maya surname and whose mother was Spanish is a *kaz dzul* or semi-dzul.

Dzul and mazehual are also cultural referents. Anyone with a light complexion, if not a known campesino (typically, a gringo or catrin of Merida), is a dzul. That this does not refer to color alone is evidenced by the separate Maya word used by Pustunicheños for albinos or blonds—*chel*. Mazehual is also used as a general referent to the poor, Maya-speaking peasant, regardless of surname. "Frijol k'abax," says one mazehual, "is the meal of the mazehuals. Black boiled beans with salt and *silantro*, mixed with broken tortillas to make a *sopa*—the meals of the mazehuals—the poor. The very mazehual eat *chai* [a low-growing plant]. They eat the leaves. Cattle eat it, but so do people. Boil it with salt, ground calabash seed, some lemon juice, and *chile habenero* and you have a big, cheap meal with tortillas. Actually, though, *everyone* eats these things; everyone. We say they're for mazehuals because the old timers ate it. It's a local dish. If you live here, you know it." In this recitation, the typical mazehual dish is for the poor, and everyone in the village eats it. Everyone is thus viewed as mazehual in at least this respect.

Again, if pressed, Pustunicheños *may* state that the *dzulob* (plural of dzul) are *buena gente*, good people. However, there is no complimentary description for the mazehuals, though they are not *mala gente*. All will agree that a person with a Spanish surname can be a bad person. It depends on the individual.

While Pustunicheños are quite aware that a Spanish surname has had and does have an advantage over Maya (after all, both the wealthy Perez and Cepeda families are Spanish, and certainly most outside officials are dzulob), surname means little in terms of individual everyday prestige. Wealth, comportment, and sociability label a person as buena gente more surely than surname. Though 44 percent of the village is composed of dzulob (by patronymic), dzul is a term most often used to refer to outsiders of different appearance. In daily interaction, in conversation groups, in partnerships for sponsoring a fiesta mass, in the roll of contributors to cha chaac, in the roster of past village officials, *no* patronymic discrimination is visible.

By both father's and mother's surname, composition of the village is as follows (patronymic precedes matronymic):

Maya-Maya	*Maya-Spanish*	*Spanish-Maya*	*Spanish-Spanish*
43 percent	13 percent	13 percent	31 percent

Thus, 56 percent of villagers bear Maya patronymics and 69 percent bear at least one Maya surname, with little differences between distribution of male and female surnames.

Though dzul and mazehual have little meaning in terms of daily interaction, surname distinction does appear to play a subtle role in choice of marriage partners. The following table of marriages (by patronymics of the partners) is instructive:

Overall, 56 percent of native-born village women bear Maya patronymics. Thus, on the basis of random mating, 56 percent of all men, whether Spanish or Maya, should marry Maya-surnamed women, and 44 percent, Spanish women. Overall actual marriage patterns show that 64 percent of Spanish men marry Spanish women while 66 percent of Maya

Table 2
MARRIAGE DISTRIBUTION BY PATRONYMICS

Marriages		% of Men in Various Age Categories Marrying Either Maya or Spanish Women			
Husband	Wife	51 and Over	36-50	26-35	Under 25
Spanish	-Spanish	53%	67%	58%	79%
	-Maya	47%	33%	42%	21%
Maya	-Maya	75%	67%	62%	53%
	-Spanish	25%	33%	38%	47%

marry Maya. Again, overall, Spanish men exhibit a 20 percent preference for Spanish women, while Maya men exhibit a 10 percent preference for Maya women.

The above table is meant to be indicative of trend rather than an absolute measure, as the sample (which includes every village marriage) is nonetheless small and the age categories are arbitrarily chosen. The under twenty-five group, for example, contains only half as many marriages as the two middle groups. In general, a fairly clear trend toward increasingly preferred marriage with Spanish spouses can be seen, on the part of both Spanish and Maya males.

Though Pustunich is strongly endogamous, women have been imported throughout the present three generations. There is no difference in frequency of exogamous matings between Spanish- and Maya-surnamed men. Roughly 20 percent of each group marries exogamously. Of exogamous matings, however, three-fourths of the wives imported by the Spanish and one-half of those imported by Maya men are Spanish surnamed. Reflecting the lower number of Spanish surnames thirty to fifty years ago, 83 percent of the Spanish wives of men fifty-one and older are imports.

The high proportion of Spanish wives among exogamous matings reflects more, however. To marry exogamously is to contradict the self-stereotype of Pustunich as a dull little place from which any outside woman will eventually flee. Exogamous marriage denies the attractiveness of the town, and of its women, whom the majority marry. It further denies the utility of strengthening ties with village families. It is thus not surprising that a majority of exogamous matings are with Spanish women, for to marry outside in the first place is to demonstrate some degree of dissatisfaction with the status quo, be it of the local, mundane female crop, or of one's own surname. No uniform or easily expressed reasons for the trend toward Spanish matings can be obtained from Pustunicheños themselves, as close to a third of younger and older Spanish adults have themselves "intermarried." In addition, a majority of Maya boys *do* marry Maya girls. It is also impossible to find any Pustunich family which does not include both Maya and Spanish agnates and/or affines.

The dzul-buena gente configuration is more a matter of lip service to an older, outside-originating discriminatory device than a reflection of a well-internalized phenomenon affecting views of personality and character within the village.

The encomenderos, *hacendados*, wealthy Merida merchants, local and state politicians, and even most of the wealthy families in Pustunich have been Spanish-surnamed. Though the mazehual Pustunicheños have had little lack of pride in their Maya surnames, the Spanish have traditionally been associated with prestige. During the past century, furthermore, a Spanish surname facilitated expeditious treatment while a man was away from the village on governmental or general city business. The increasing preference for Spanish wives is thus not a simple indication of changing values. A Spanish surname has been more advantageous for centuries. The preference for Spanish wives is most clearly understood as part of a far longer trend which began as soon as Spanish migrants to the village began allowing their sons and daughters to marry into the local Maya population. This trend is gradual, perhaps 10 percent over a generation, and varies considerably as the ratio of sons to daughters in the minority Spanish population has varied from generation to generation.

While the advantage of a Spanish surname has long been clear to the village, it must not be forgotten that surname is only the *least* visible among a number of other characteristics traditionally conferring class status upon Yucatecans and affecting the type of interaction between the pacesetters of Merida and others. Far more visible and immediately identifying are language facility, facial features, and dress, followed by provenience (*campo* or city) and work. Traditionally, there has existed no possibility at all that an educated, Spanish, Merida civil servant would allow his daughter to marry a son of the mestizo, campesino, Maya-speaking Clem Perez, even if the Spanish Perez' income were ten times that of the Meridano. By criteria of racial characteristics, Maya language, and dress (not to mention economic base and "campesinismo"), until quite recently, Pustunich was overwhelmingly homogeneous. Indeed, over 95 percent of the village is still virtually identical in language, dress, financial worth, and economic base. Thus, in Pustunich, Spanish surname in a spouse, and to a lesser degree lighter skin, is desirable, though not essential to major intravillage identity or prestige. Gross behavioral and social significance of the preference for Spanish mates is tempered by the degree of intermarriage both past and present. Though rich Manolo Cepeda himself is married to a Spanish woman, all his sons have married Maya women. Two of his three brothers are married to Maya women, and they all married while still in the flush of a fine inheritance. The rich Belems had a Maya mother. One of Torcuato Belem's two wives (his first) is Maya. The rico Clemente Perez is himself married to a Maya woman, Sarah Tum Pech. Sarah is the daughter of Pablo Tum Gonzales and Elena Pech. However, she has adopted the name of her paternal grandmother, Gonzales. Clem Perez' children are thus called Perez Gonzales rather than the more correct Perez Tum.

Though there are similar cases of surname transposition, the vast majority of Maya-surnamed individuals with Spanish matronymics retain the Maya. Such a name option, where it is exercised, is usually in cases where a Maya-Spanish woman weds a Spanish male, or where a Maya-Spanish woman, unmarried and with illegitimate children, chooses to provide the offspring with a Spanish surname. As such children generally carry the mother's surname even when the father is known, there is no rigidly correct form, and the option may be taken. There have been no cases of outright hispanization of Maya names as is described by Goldkind for Chan Kom.[2] In fact, Pustunicheños, *including* the Belems, think that Belem is a Maya surname, though it is actually of pure Spanish origin.

Dress and Life-Style: A Different Kind of Mobility

Regardless of family or surname, all adult Pustunicheños—excepting the schoolteacher, five women, and eighteen unmarried young males and females—are full-time mestizo dressers. A typical male wears ready-made denim shirt and trousers, thonged sandals, and medium-brimmed straw hat. Work dress usually includes these "blues," though "whites" may be worn if the wife does not mind the extra washing involved. White clothing is also slightly less expensive. Work (milpa) sandals are most often contour-cut pieces of auto tire, with thongs of deerskin which fit between the great and second toes and bind the ankles. Only small children go barefoot. Mestizo dress-up wear may involve the more conservative white pants and shirt or blue gabardine slacks and sport shirt, but *always* sandals. Dress sandals have tire outer and deerskin inner soles, with a broad strap binding all of the toes in front. A hat is considered standard dress-up wear for a male. Most male garb is store-bought. Few women today bother to cut and sew pants and shirts.

A typical female wears the huipuil: a white cotton shift, square cut with hand, machine-sewn, or ready-made floral bordering at neck and hem. Though inexpensive huipils with printed bordering can be purchased, all women make the bulk of their own wardrobes. Many own treadle sewing machines. Those who do not may rent a machine in Ticul, use a neighbor's, borrow one from a relative in town, or use the communal machine in the town square's Centro de Salud. Everyday huipils may have either machine bordering or sewn-on printed strips. Women have a number of these, and they are washed frequently. Few women don soiled huipils at the day's start. For more formal occasions, all women own hand-embroidered huipils of better cloth with thread of faster colors. This is worn with a white slip showing from beneath. Bras are exotic new items, slowly being accepted in Pustunich. Several younger girls and matrons wear them at present. The female dress-up ensemble centers around the *terno*: a two-piece tiered gown, of white cotton, with machine- or hand-bordering at four points. It is ideally worn with gold chains (if available) around the neck and, invariably, modern flat- or high-heeled shoes. Everyday wear for women may involve either sandals or, more frequently, flat modern shoes. Sandals are definitely not worn with ternos, even though the terno is traditional mestiza garb. The terno is like a formal gown in the United States. Almost every woman has owned one at some time. As they change little in style, most mothers pass them on to daughters, who wear them at the annual jarana dance during fiesta week—an opportunity to show off in one's best before the shy, admiring single males.

The opposite of mestizo is *catrin* (*ladino* in other parts of Mexico). For males, to be catrin is to wear shoes regularly. It is also assumed that men who wear shoes will not wear white (mestizo) clothing. To be a catrin woman, one wears a fitted, store-bought dress rather than huipil. As with men, it is also assumed that the woman wearing a dress will not wear sandals. A catrin from Pustunich is indistinguishable from a catrin of similar economic means in Merida or any other Yucatec town.

To Pustunich, mestizo and catrin go far beyond immediate dress. A number of villagers have worn shoes, suits, and a tie on at least one occasion, either their own or another's wedding. Though dressed catrin, they were not regarded as being catrin at the moment. When the mother of a legitimate catrin girl shows a photo of her daughter in mestiza garb at a festival, she laughingly and fondly says, "Look at the pretty 'mestiza,' " and the quote marks around the word "mestiza" are absolutely implicit in the statement.

More than form of dress, mestizo and catrin reflect commitment to a way of life and specific values. The mestizo is a campesino, a milpero, a laborer, and perhaps a small shopkeeper. If none of these, he at least lives among them. He speaks Maya as a first language. The catrin does little or no manual labor. He definitely does not, nor can he, farm. "How can a catrin make milpa?" asks a villager. "He'll ruin his good clothes." "How can a catrina live with a campesino?" asks a woman. "The work is hard, and she often has to go out to the milpa, or collecting leña (cordwood), and a huipil is cheap to fix or buy. But a dress? No, sir!" That Pustunicheños equate mestizo and catrin with life-style rather than with physical or innate qualities is indicated by the statement that mestizos are darker than catrins—but only "because mestizos are farmers or workers and thus burned by the sun."

As a value common to all Yucatecans, "catrinness," like Spanish surname, is granted higher prestige. Less a mechanism for active discrimination, "European garb is the symbol nowadays not so much of the status of a privileged class as of opportunity in a freer and more individuated society."[3] Still, discrimination exists, as much in the minds of the mestizos as among the catrins who traditionally occupied a higher status. Yucatan, however, has not proved immune to *indigenismo*—condescending paternalism and admission of the Indian to "kinship." Indeed, Yucatan, through over a century of hostility toward mainland Mexico, and with a healthy respect for the Maya who almost succeeded in driving the Spaniard out during the Caste War, has more of an ambivalent attitude toward its indios than most other Mexican states. The elite of Yucatan identify with the Maya campesinos both as "our Indians" or "our people" and as the opposite pole of that scale which makes the elite a worldly, "cultured" group capable of confronting one another and outsiders with confident erudition.

Rather than force servants to learn Spanish, most of the older elite of Merida learned Maya. For an elite person to speak some Maya is to indicate that one has servants or was raised with them and, not incidentally, that one is a native Yucatecan, not a *huach*. Meridanos readily admit (not without paternal pride) that many Maya words form part of their daily vocabulary.[4] In Pustunich, as elsewhere in Yucatan, the first dance of the annual fiesta, the *vaqueria*, is for participants in mestizo dress only. The greater the number of known catrins attending in mestizo garb, the more successful it is regarded. When Ticul holds a vaqueria, the price of admission is steep, and it is tacitly understood that the dance is mainly for legitimate catrins. This tradition is an old one in the vicinity and was noted in Ticul by Stevens in 1840.[5] This switch of costume is indicative of an identification with the indigenous population not similarly exhibited in Guatemala or Southern Mexico. Though the mestizo voter in PRI-dominated Yucatan is easily swayed and unnecessary to woo, few serious candidates for political office of *any* level do not own a mestizo dress-up outfit (the *chamarra*) with gold studs, and their wives usually own an expensively embroidered terno and impressive gold chains.

The identity between Yucatec mestizos and catrins is further overtly sustained through the dress worn during official state-pueblo ceremonies. Outside of Merida, the governor and his retinue are never received without a bevy of pretty mestizas among the welcoming party. This holds for Valladolid and Ticul as it does for Pustunich. It symbolizes representation of all the peoples. In Pustunich, for example, on the two occasions of visits by the governor of Yucatan, the welcoming committee consisted of town officers (in mestizo garb, as they are full-time mestizos) and a party of pretty girls in huipils bearing bouquets. Only one of the girls was a legitimate mestiza. The girls all belong to the school auxiliary, those with high school educations (all catrin) being thought to be more "qualified" to greet outside officials. In addition, it shows that Pustunich is an erudite, educated town. No mestizo in the community thought this act incorrect.

With exception of the schoolteacher, all adult Pustunich males are mestizos. The wealthy Perezes, Cepedas, and Belems are mestizos. Indeed, Clem Perez wears only "whites," an even more conservative form of dress than blue dungarees. All the wealthy have mestiza spouses, excepting Torcuato Belem, whose junior wife was brought from another town.

The schoolteacher's usual dress consists of tee-shirt, white short-sleeved shirt, gabardine slacks, shoes, and sox. He wears sandals only while resting in his house or during relaxed moments in the village streets. He makes no milpa, though he does help his father and younger brother if pressed and available. He is viewed as modern, highly literate, and knowledgeable. He can administer injections and tend minor wounds.

Several other adult males dress catrin for their work, which is outside the village. All, however, make small to considerable quantities of milpa as well. Two are foremen of honey-gathering gangs (one of these is the teacher's brother) contracted by large honey producers throughout the state. A third (the ejidal comisario) is a secretary in an Oxkutzkab office. He boards the bus at seven each morning in gabardine slacks, white shirt, shoes and sox, and a short zipper jacket. When he returns in the late afternoon, he most often slips on sandals and an older pair of pants. Less as ejidal comisario (a post he has held for two years) than someone who can obviously hold his own verbally and in manners with outsiders, he shares the stage with the teacher on special occasions more often than does the town's own mayor. He, however, never left Pustunich. He commutes fifteen minutes to work. When able, he helps his father with milpa labor. As he owns shoes, it is regarded as only natural that he wear them on his infrequent trips to Merida. He does not flaunt them in front of the village. Though most villagers view him as almost being a legitimate catrin, he himself says: ''I don't dress like an Indian because we must adapt to the times. I do dress catrin sometimes, but I don't think I'm catrin. Mestizo, remember, means 'mixed.' We're between Indian and Spanish. We dress, really, for the moment—for one thing catrin, for another, mestizo.''

Of the six catrin women, five came from larger towns; only one, the teacher's spinster sister, is a native of Pustunich. The five are: the wife of the teacher himself; the younger wife of Torcuato Belem, who assists him at all major cures; the wife of Avila, the mayor and storekeeper; the wife of storekeeper Orozco; and the wife of a respected village milpero. All of the catrin women are themselves of Spanish surname and married to Spanish, though mestizo, men (excepting the teacher, who is catrin, and Belem, who is regarded as Maya-surnamed).

There are about twenty catrin youngsters in Pustunich, each of whom has been attired in catrin clothing since birth. Their status was determined solely by their parents, they themselves having no voice in the matter. The five catrin mothers in town have dressed most of their children as catrin. The wider implications of dress are most visible in the exceptions. Orozco the storekeeper has two daughters in their early twenties and a fourteen-year-old son. The younger and prettier daughter is catrin. She aids her mother in light housework, weaves tejidos, and spends many hours tending the small store. The older, less comely sister is more of a household drudge, a mestiza, who does heavier, dirtier work. The son is mestizo—his father's right hand, helping him in heavy, dirty work and aiding in sporadic milpa production. Avila, the mayor, has six children. The oldest son and daughter, catrins, have left the village; one is a garage mechanic in Merida and the other is a practical nurses' aide in Mexico City. Three remaining daughters are catrin. The younger remaining son's dress-position is ambiguous. He helps the father in the store and wears sandals unless forced to dress in shoes by his mother. Torcuato Belem has several children. The only catrin is a son who manages the father's business affairs and aids him in the henequen business. He also works sporadically for low-budget Merida and Mexico magazines as a corresponding commercial artist.

Though Clem Perez and his wife are both mestizos, all of their children are catrin. All are high school graduates. The family has no need of making milpa. Pepe, the oldest son, is a radio mechanic, having taken a correspondence course from a Texas school. He very often wears sandals. His wife, however, is a village mestiza. Their children are catrin and bear Anglo names such as William. Israel, Clem's younger son, is married to a catrina from Merida, cousin to the single noncommercial villager with a catrin wife (also from Merida).

The teacher himself has four children, all catrin. The remaining catrin children are all of wholly mestizo parents. As is the case with the Orozcos, some children of these same families are mestizo. In such cases, boys are more usually "maintained" as mestizo, as the father is a milpero and needs their help in the fields. As catrin children are effectively cut off from the more arduous work of home or milpa, a majority of catrin-dressed youngsters are girls.

Though mobility between the two statuses is not closed, no adult Pustunicheños have been known to change their dress. Unlike Chiapas or Guatemala, one's past and ancestry are *not* taken into account in ascribing such status. "Passing," however, is not easy. Including the schoolteacher, all catrins were either dressed catrin since childhood or married into the village as catrins. An individual mestizo cannot become catrin by mere change of dress. He would be labeled a "catrin forzado" (forced catrin). He would be "putting on airs" and would be chided. Bonfil Batalla notes that in Sudzal, should a young man leave the village and decide to return "de vestido," he exposes himself ". . . to being the object of insults and jokes on the part of his acquaintances."[6] Should a person simultaneously abandon milpa, Maya language, and mestizo dress, however, passage would be easier. Complete acceptance is most readily achieved by prolonged absence from the village—perhaps ten or more years, as in the teacher's case. Should the individual return as a catrin, he would be accepted as such, providing his general life-style also appeared to fit the village concept of catrin. The fact that his family in Pustunich was still mestizo, the fact of his local birth and initial mestizo status would not prevent his becoming a full catrin in the eyes of his former neighbors. The catrin schoolteacher's father, for example, is one of the most conservative mestizo dressers.

One occasion on which nonmestizo outfits are worn wholesale is carnival. It must be stressed, however, that there is no such thing as a "mestizo costume." Pustunicheños, like Mexico City's elite, are well aware that "costume" implies dress which represents something the individual is not. No costume is mestizo yet "different." Pustunicheños thus attend Carnival as clowns, circus barkers, or Mexican Charros. All costumes are rented in Ticul.

Though no one will deride an individual for being catrin if the decision was made at birth by his or her parents, mestizo parents incur gossip by dressing their children in this manner. The gossip is less an expression of indignation than a pragmatic recognition of the estrangement from the way of the parents which a catrin child represents.

That the catrin status of its youngsters *is* accepted by Pustunich is indicated by the fact that villagers do not show indignation but rather a sense of ambivalence. Catrin children and young adults interact as do any other youngsters. Play and friendship groups or *diads* do not reflect a clique or incipient class. Yet this is understandable. All in the village are close acquaintances, and almost everyone's parents dress alike.

It is with regard to marriage, however, that the degree of commitment to the status of the young catrins becomes evident. With only one exception, no catrin girl has yet married, and at least seven are over sixteen years of age, four being in their middle twenties. In Pustunich, an unmarried girl of twenty is rare, and by mid-twenty she is already a *soltera*, to the despair of her parents.

The one catrina who did marry was from a poorer, though highly respected mestizo milpero family. Her mother is a religious singer, being hired to lead prayers and songs at private novenas or general church occasions. The girl is but fifteen. She had only a year or two of grammar school before dropping out because, as she admits, her "head was hard." She is illiterate and speaks poor Spanish. Both she and her ten-year-old catrina sister are the apples of their parents' eye. The mother trained them to sing and dance to Mexican Charro music. They possess little Mexican cowboy costumes, painstakingly sewn by their mother, who is very nearsighted. The older once performed at all village functions and has now turned this role over to her little sister. The girls, however, are catrin in dress only. Used to the life of the mestizo household and frequent trips to the milpa and bush, they are mestiza in act and view. The fifteen-year-old married the son of a well-to-do and equally respected mestizo family. He is mestizo. Both sets of parents worried about their ages. He was seventeen, she barely fifteen, and the whole village was amused by their whirlwind courtship. The marriage took place in Pustunich. As is the case where at least one spouse is catrin, the bride wore a gown and the groom appeared in shoes, suit, and tie. The bridesmaids, several of them mestiza, also appeared in catrin dress, purchased for them by the groom's family. Suits for the groom and groomsmen were rented in Ticul. Both sets of parents, however, appeared in mestizo dress; to do otherwise would have courted ridicule. The ceremony's physical trappings were for the children.

The bride's father also has a ten-year-old son. He is mestizo and already takes a good share of milpa work. The parents claim to speak Maya with the son and Spanish with their two catrin girls. They do, when they remember or don't lose their tempers. Most often, in the midst of a heated conversation or to give cryptic orders, Maya is used with all three children.

Some of the groom's friends believe that the young catrina will change back to mestiza in time. After all, she is now living the life of a mestiza.

Villagers guess that the remaining catrin girls in town will have to marry Ticul boys or else choose a Pustunicheño and probably become mestiza. "You can't live the life of a mestiza as a catrin," say the townspeople. All catrinas own huipils anyway, and wear them frequently for dirty house or yard work. Married to a mestizo, a girl would wear the huipil far more often than she did at home, where her parents tried to vary her work to fit her dress.

Orozco, the storekeeper, despairs of his pretty catrina Rosa marrying. "Who knows if she'll ever marry?" he laments. "I sure hope so, but she dresses nice, and is used to good food, jewelry and other things. And so the boys are afraid of her . . . they feel they couldn't afford her." Village boys compensate for their wariness of marrying a catrina by accusing Orozco of purposely keeping Rosa single. She does too much good work in the house and the store, they claim, and Orozco doesn't want to lose a good worker. Orozco does want a catrin for his catrina and discourages Rosa from seeing village boys.

Clem Perez' three eligible daughters face an even harder road. Not only are they catrina, but they are immensely wealthy in the eyes of Pustunicheños. Only one has a suitor at present—one of the few catrin village boys. He is three or four years her junior, and much gossip has flown. Village boys admit that they are "afraid" of the Perez girls when it comes to thinking of them as potential spouses.

It must be remembered that the young catrins of Pustunich are a result not of their own desire for different status, but the desire of their parents. Of the two dozen young catrins, seventeen are the children of individuals who earn the greater part of their living away from the milpa. Perez, Avila, and Orozco (three of the four storekeepers) account for twelve of the young catrins. The teacher's three children make fifteen. Torcuato Belem has a catrin son. The teacher's brother, a honey foreman, has another catrin child. Though all have made some milpa in the past, all today make it infrequently. To these men, a catrin child does not represent a threat to eventual economic security. A catrin can tend store without incongruity. To the nonstorekeepers (the foremen, teacher, and curandero), their children will become professionals some day. The remaining seven catrin children belong to milpa families. Only three are boys. All four of the girls are completing high or normal school. One of the boys is already teaching, and another is completing high school.

These catrins represent less the projection of deviant parental desires for social mobility, than (1) the economic ability of the parents to realize an *old ideal* which is familiar to all villagers; and (2) the rather recent availability of an outlet for the newly created catrins. This is to say that the presence and availability today of high schools, normal schools, teaching and new white collar employment opportunities are as much an innovation as creation of catrins by mestizo peasants. There is hardly a Pustunich mother or father who would *not* wish to be well-off—able to part with the services of and boast of a catrin child or two in higher schools or prestigious jobs. For a milpero, however, a catrin child is a hardship. Some parents prefer to "better" their children more cheaply, by speaking Spanish with them in the home. This creates no problem of identity or economic security.

Identity: Inside and Outside

Pustunich is aware of a number of categories that identify kinds of individuals and establish them as different from others. The strongest categories are those which tend to lump the greatest numbers of people. Even the rich and Spanish-surnamed in the town readily agree that Pustunich can be absolutely characterized as Maya ("ethnically"), milpero, poor, campesino, mestizo, Maya-speaking, and mazehual. Simply being from the village implies all. So interconnected are these characteristics, in fact, that to be different in one or two does not deny the rest and, thus, the overall identity of the individual as "one of us." As no individual is without some (often considerable) family in the town, he cannot escape identification with others. Hardly a family exists which does not contain both Spanish and Maya surnames among agnates, affines, or direct ancestors. The wealthy Perez makes no milpa and is indeed dzul; yet his wife is mezehual. He and his wife are mestizo and neither speaks much Spanish. Yet their children are catrin and speak fluent Spanish. Perez' catrin son Pepe married a mestiza. His children are dressed catrin. Aside from the mestizo, milpero (etc.) majority, no sufficient number of characteristics is concentrated in any single individual or group as to definitively establish them as different from the rest.

Several of the Perezes are fairly poor, and many Maya are better off than Spanish neighbors. Individual characteristics, rather than family or groups, serve to differentiate one from the majority. That man is "Don Torcuato," not "a Belem." This one is "Don San the cat" (the best tree-climber in town) rather than "a Mis." Proportional numbers of dzul and mazehual men have held major office in the town during the past forty years. For leadership on any occasion, universalistic criteria or charisma most often direct the choice. Ek Canche, the mazehual ejidal comisario, is a regular speaker whenever distinguished outside visitors come to Pustunich. Ek is glib and makes a "good presentation." To lead a traditional communal hunt, on the other hand, dzul Antonio Orozco Castañeda is most often chosen, as his command of bush lore and byways is better than anyone's. His cousin Panfilo Orozco is the poorest man in town and has been fined or jailed on several occasions for petty theft. Another cousin is one of the four shopkeepers.

Certainly some of the identity categories are associated with outsiders, the city, and city ways. Yet in its ricos, nonmilperos, dzulob, teachers, Spanish language, and catrins, Pustunich simply shares in the broader identification mechanisms of Yucatan and Mexico. The town is thus not on the *verge* of confronting change. It has *long* confronted it and is continuing to do so. The preference for Spanish wives is an old phenomenon (roughly a constant 10 percent over each generation). Dress change is not merely the adoption of new values; these values were already present. The *opportunity* rather than the value per se is the more recent phenomenon. The present configuration reflects a blend of conservatism and modernity rather than disorganization. No adult has changed his dress. Commitment to the standing mestizo identity of Pustunich is overwhelming. Young children, however, may be successfully dressed catrin, as their major adult role configurations are not as yet established.

More important than the mechanisms of dress change are the highly pragmatic and flexible views which the change in dress expresses. The creation of catrin children is not a general blind attempt at identity modification. Theoretically, anyone in the village could dress his child in this manner. Few actually do so. That far more girls than boys are catrin indicates the clear understanding which Pustunicheños have of the implications of dress change. That far more catrins are children of minimally milpero families further indicates the very practical considerations which guide the change. A child catrin is a child lost to milpa and, in the eyes of villagers, traditional housework.

For this very reason, the creation of catrin children is no immediate threat to the community. Teaching and shopkeeping could only accommodate a half-dozen or so non-mestizos. Catrins, therefore, *must* emigrate or revert to mestizo dress. Thus, while on the one hand parents may obtain satisfaction (including vicarious mobility) from raising their children's position vis-à-vis national class standards, the forced departure of catrins means that few, if any, non-mestizos will remain into adulthood and thereby disrupt the community. It is more than likely that having an absentee catrin child will gradually become a new symbol of village status. The result will not threaten village continuity. It will simply throw another ingredient into the simmering pot.

NOTES

1. Robert Redfield and Alfonso Villa Rojas, *Chan Kom: a Maya Village* (Chicago: University of Chicago Press, 1962), pp. 101-102.

2. Victor Goldkind, "Class Conflict and Cacique in Chan Kom." *Southwestern Journal of Anthropology* 22 (1966): 326.

3. Robert Redfield, *Race and Class in Yucatan* (Washington: Carnegie Institute of Washington Publication No. 401, 1938), p. 513.

4. See Alfredo Barrera Vasquez, "El Idioma Español en Yucatan." *Enciclopedia Yucatanse* (Mexico City: Gobierno de Yucatan, Vol. 6, 1946): 341-375.

5. John L. Stevens, *Incidents of Travel in Yucatan* (Norman: University of Oklahoma Press, 1962). Edited and with an introduction by Victor W. Von Hagen.

6. Guillermo Bonfil Batalla, *Diagnostico sobre el hambre en Sudzal, Yucatan* (Mexico City: Instituto Nacional de Antropologia e Historia, 1962).

7

Becoming a Pustunicheño

Early Preparation

Most Pustunicheños are born at home. A Pustunich or Ticul midwife attends, aided by the expectant mother's sisters, mother, and perhaps a few close friends. Birth is in a hammock. The umbilicus of a baby girl is buried under the kitchen hearth so she will be a good wife; that of a boy is carried out into the bush so that he will not fear the monte. There is no specific rule for naming. Frequently, the name of the day's saint is used. Sometimes, the child's father's or mother's name is chosen. There is a beginning trend for American and other foreign names such as William, Wilbert, Roger, and Leydi (from the English "Lady").

For nine days following birth, child and mother must not leave the lying-in house, so as to avoid evil winds. At this time, both are highly susceptible. During the next three months, the child is carried outside only when completely covered by the mother's *rebozo* (shawl). Vulnerability to the evil eye lasts into the second year. One need not be malicious to harm a new child. It will fall ill should a drunk look upon it, or a pregnant woman pass its mother without speaking to her. In this latter case, diarrhea will result unless the pregnant offender urinates upon the child.

From about the third month onward, the child is gradually introduced to the village as its mother neglects to pull the rebozo tight. It is introduced to modern medicine early, when taken to Ticul for vaccination. Many visitors come to see it. The child sleeps with the mother for the first several months "because it's easier to feed." During the day, the baby rests and sleeps in a hammock within the house. The string-mesh sides of the hammock rise to prevent the child from falling out, yet allow a full view of all household activity. The child is cuddled, kissed, and played with by father, mother, and siblings. It is allowed to creep about on the floor with the chickens, and, near the end of the first year, out into the solar within viewing range.

Children are breast-fed, on the average, until one-and-a-half or two years old. Some adults feel that it is wrong to breastfeed a child longer—not for health reasons but because it "looks bad." During the first four months the child receives no solid foods. It is given the breast on demand, though supplementary liquid corn gruels may be offered from birth. Solids begin with softened soda crackers or oatmeal. As the proportion of other foods increases, the breast increasingly takes on a role as pacifier or diverter. Weaning is not abrupt, but may occur during an eight-day period. Should gentler methods fail, the breast may be smeared with a bitter substance. The most common weaning device is diversion. Solid foods and late hours keep the baby full or too tired to pursue the breast with much energy. The easy availability of modern canned, sterile powdered milk and various infant formulas (stocked by all four Pustunich stores) makes weaning easy for Pustunich mothers and gives them wider choice in timing it.

Toilet training is permissive and gradual. Very early, when the baby urinates or defecates, it is simply held out at arm's length. An attempt is made to get the child outside first, though floors are usually dirt. Its pants or huipil are then changed. There is no chastisement during the first eighteen months or so. Little concern is given to soiling the hammock, as it is string mesh, dries fast, and is easily washable. As the child learns to walk, it will be taken out to eliminate whenever family members themselves feel the need. As its understanding increases, the child is talked to, admonished to leave the house, or communicate its desire to someone. Once the child indicates that it understands what is desired of it, it will be punished (slapped) for soiling the hammock, house floor, or clothing. Most very small toddlers of both sexes wear only the huipil, without pants, which permits "accidents" with minimal clothes soiling. Parents expect such accidents and try to avert them by learning the child's moods. "There's so much to wash when you have a baby," sighs one mother resignedly.

There is tolerance for the acts of young children in Pustunich. Some believe that even a two- or three-year-old is incapable of control because he's "only little and doesn't know anything. He can't express himself. He can't really talk. So why punish him hard?" "A baby or young child knows nothing," says one very old man. "It's like a bird, eating everything, even chicken droppings." A young father takes this attitude: "Try to reason with a child before punishing it. When you do hit it, use your hand or a piece of rope—but don't hit hard. Try to *teach* them what to do or not to do." While adult men sit talking quietly at the central water pump in the early morning, children play nearby, often running noisily between conversing adults. Unless the whole group of youngsters runs about at the same time, or repeatedly interrupts the men, nothing is done about this. The men continue their conversation above the noise.

This is not to say that childhood is a largely permissive time. The older the child, the more responsible behavior is expected of it and the more frequent or harsh the punishment for failure to perform. Either parent will deliver corporal punishment (hand, rope, or switch). Older siblings may also punish the younger, within limits. Older children themselves will receive punishment for abuse of younger.

As boys and girls become of increasing economic importance to the family, they are punished less for "badness." Ideally, a father has the right to punish a child physically until he or she marries. Actually, punishment of young adults rarely occurs and for a father to strike an eighteen-year-old is cause for gossip. Most youngsters in Pustunich have common responsibilities. During school or work hours, therefore, there are few unoccupied older boys or girls available to tempt others. Girls beyond the age of seven seldom leave the house or converse with other girls unless running errands or busy babysitting or weaving tejidos.

Toward the end of the first year the child leaves the house more frequently, on the hip of an older sibling. Boys and girls may care for infants of either sex, though girls are felt to be more nurturant and less likely to abandon babies momentarily for stick-ball or marbles. When the baby begins to cry, it is usually brought home to be fed, whereupon the sitter may escape to play with friends.

Whether outside with parents or sibling, children of one, two, or even three years are seldom allowed to walk. Infants are constantly carried. Girls and boys of five and six strain heavily to lift and carry a child twenty feet, though the child is capable of toddling the distance unsupported.

This, in fact, permits greater mobility for the very young, as they travel greater distances and with better vantage than would be theirs through self-propulsion.

In the afternoon, when the father has returned from the milpa, bathed, and changed into fresh clothes, he may take the baby for a bicycle ride. Most men who own bicycles also have little wooden seats on the crossbar for the baby to ride on.

At four or five years, the child begins to run about more freely, but seldom far from the house. It may visit nearby relatives and considers any house with an open door as enterable. At this age, boys and girls run errands (however, they are not trusted with more than one or two pesos), play at making tortillas, and begin to learn how to weave long hat-strands out of juano. Children of six and seven exhibit remarkable motor skill and produce salable strands. Until five or six, boys and girls run together; thereafter, mixed groups are less frequent. Girls play in the house or sit around and watch the boys, no different from the older girls and matrons who sit at the peripheries of ball-games. Girls may participate with boys in the mob kite-catching game, but are strictly excluded from peg-and-stick, stick-and-hoop, and marbles. The larger the group a game customarily embraces, the more likelihood for inclusion of both sexes.

All babies are dressed in the female shirt-like huipil for the first year or two. The first formal recognition of sex difference is the *hetzmek*, which occurs at around six months. The hetzmek is a ritual of role-differentiation. The child is placed astride the hip of the godparent of the ceremony—a godfather for a boy, a godmother for a girl. The godparent places articles in the child's hands which it will use (or hopefully acquire) in adult life—a book (for literacy), tortillas, needle, thread, mixing spoon, and other female items, or book, machete, shotgun, money, pen, and other male items.

A more noticeable distinction occurs when the child begins to walk freely. The genitalia of girls are covered either by short underpants, long huipil, or both. Boys are allowed to run about naked or with short shirts only. By three, however, they are fully clothed. A naked or partially exposed child of three or four is a matter for negative comment by elders.

By six or seven, the sex role becomes even more sharply differentiated. As soon as she is able to carry a five- to ten-pound bowl of maize, a girl begins to make the daily trip to the corn mill. Boys rarely do this, and adult men only in case of emergency. When not at school, girls aid their mothers in the kitchen. Through playing at tortilla making and cooking while younger, the girl has progressively participated more in the preparation of the meals. As her dexterity increases, she gradually assumes a major role in meal production and housework. The seven-year-old girl makes tortillas scarcely inferior to her mother's. She may produce from one to three pesos daily through tejido making. By eight or nine she is taking her first tentative steps toward designing and sewing her own huipil. Indeed, by fifteen, most girls are capable of producing huipils on consignment to other Pustunich women or Ticul jobbers.

From the boy's point of view, tejido weaving is a childhood duty. Women will continue with them throughout life. But men do not make tejidos. The only adult male known to weave tejidos was a crippled Ticuleño with no legs. By the time a boy begins to play in segregated groups, he will begin accompanying his father to the milpa. At this time he, too, is producing from one to three pesos daily at tejidos. At first, the boy merely watches men work the milpa. As he goes with greater frequency, he babysits and weaves tejidos less. Gradually, the boy gives increasing aid to the father and his milpa partners until, imperceptibly, he is doing a man's share. At no time can a maturing boy say, "Now I am a man. *At this moment* I have made a milpa."

After age eight or nine, a boy may be able to obtain work as a simple day laborer with one of the henequen plantations nearby. He may also accompany his father to work on the milpas or lands of other Pustunicheños or outsiders.

As with babysitting and the weaving of tejidos, religious participation also begins as a general activity and gradually falls into sex-divisions.

Pustunich parents like to see their children baptized within a year of birth. Within two years, they are confirmed, depending upon the bishop's schedule and the parents' finances and desires. Boys and girls both will be brought to the village church at a very early age to gain grace. The squall of babies is common during any church service. All children are taught to cross themselves and perhaps say the *Ave Maria* or *Padre Nuestro* in preparation for future confession. The various novenas, processions, and the splendid annual fiesta teach the child a basic stock of songs: "Oh, Mary, mother mine . . ."; "Don't cry, Jesus, don't cry. . . ." During the last nine days of May (the "month of Mary"), parents dress their little boys and girls in their best clothing and send them down the church aisle to place a May flower in the big hole-riddled *M* in front of the altar.*

Boys soon notice that few men attend church or take active part in novenas or home observances, though they may aid in preparing or constructing altars. Boys of seven or eight rarely participate in the responsive chanting at novenas. Catholicism, it soon appears, is pre-dominantly an activity for women, little children, and old men (excepting fiesta masses—see Chapter 8). The traditional Maya ceremonies for rain and harvest-thanks are strictly male domains. By four or five, boys attend Maya rituals and are allowed to sit in the front row as observers. Girls and women must remain far away, making the essential corn patties for ritual offerings. Women cannot approach the altar area. As attendants, boys must partake of the ritual offerings, as do all other males present—before the women are brought their shares. Several boys must take an even more active and essential role in the cha chaac ritual by sitting beneath the altar and croaking as frogs to signal the coming of rain.

By nine or ten, boys and girls are busy most of the day at husking, shelling, cleaning, babysitting, and other duties. Boys, however, may run about unattended with others of their age. At night, girls are never allowed out alone. Boys make more frequent trips outside the village, both alone and with fathers.

Organized sports, involving baseball and basketball, are strictly male activities. During Sunday games, only men crowd around the plaza ballfield. Women, however, appreciate the action and on nearly every doorstep around the plaza sits a group, watching and weaving tejidos. Basketball games, being limited to the cement court in front of the mayor's store, are harder to see from a distance; the crowd consists of many women (mostly teenagers), who giggle as their favorites bound past in short shorts and numbered tee-shirts.

Children of both sexes attend school. At present, school enrollment is 234, almost a quarter of the total village population. There are six grades, taught by five teachers, and all classes are coeducational. Recess periods are generally spent in segregated groups, and boys are more frequently absent due to seasonal demands of milpa work. Not all the children finish

---

*Not all children will do this. It depends, of course, on whether the child's parents have decent clothing for it, and more than anything, the present mood of the parents.

the six grades, yet few leave school without knowing how to read and write at least minimally.

Curriculum strictly follows the federal government's teaching guide, with government texts. All five teachers have been trained at federal normal schools. Of the teachers, only one is a native Pustunicheño (whom we referred to as "the teacher" in earlier chapters), and only he resides in the village. The others commute daily from Ticul.

Pustunicheños are in favor of formal education and generally try to keep their children in school for the full six years. Often enough, it is impossible. Village fathers are always ready to aid in any school building project, and the present school houses, school yard, stage, and basketball court are all results of voluntary *fagina*. On "talent night" at the end of a school term, several hundred adults jam into the school yard. Programs rely mostly on the more "vivos" (brash) of the students, and children of all ages perform.

Though the teacher continually exhorts village parents to keep their children in school, he knows that milpa is a necessity. Being a native villager, however, he is familiar with the work round. He knows whether field demands are legitimate and personally contacts parents of overly absent boys. He does not hesitate to bring the matter up in front of others. He expects that up to about age ten, a boy is still too small to be of critical economic importance to the father.

Courtship and Marriage

By the time males and females reach marriageable age, they have acquired full life-skills. Moreover, their activities do not change with marriage. By fifteen, girls are adept at preparing all portions of major meals, at weaving, housekeeping, caring for infants, water hauling, washing, sewing, and bargaining in the Ticul market. They have cared for younger siblings or tended the children of older sisters and brothers. Males of fifteen are already valuable milpa partners and wage earners. They know how to make lime and graft trees. They own or regularly use shotguns in the communal hunt. They can build a house. They now congregate in their own age group alongside mature men in the light of Clem Perez' plaza store after the sun has set. For the most part, they are free to wander or travel to Ticul after dark, and the lateness of their day no longer depends on parents' wishes, but on duties which they themselves feel await them at home, or on the earliness of the next day's work.

Marriage, to Pustunich boys and girls, entails no change in activities—neither new duties (aside from sex) nor abandonment of old activities. Indeed, the major players on both first- and second-string baseball teams are all married. At marriage, only the bride changes domicile, to move a few doors or blocks into her husband's parents' home. Her duties remain the same. The boy after marriage neither makes more nor less milpa than before, nor does he seek more wage labor than before.

Marriage today is based on choice. Male and female have known each other through years of play, schooling, and meeting in the village. Once past thirteen or fourteen, girls exhibit greater cognizance of their appearance. For fiestas or special parties, girls will travel the eight miles by bus to Oxkutzkab for a *mulix* (permanent wave of short, tight curls). Large pink plastic hair curlers are no rarity in Pustunich, and teen-age girls squeal with embarrassment should a boy see them. As girls do not go out alone, nor is it acceptable for them to parade in an obvious fashion, they contrive situations for showing themselves off. Just as tejido weaving—an appearance of busyness—serves as an excuse for women to sit and gossip, so visiting the cemetery to set flowers on the graves is an excuse for parading. In best huipils and chains, bearing bouquets, groups of six to ten walk the half-mile to the cemetery on the outskirts of town. No special holy day is necessary. Any fine Sunday will do, and most often an attempt is made to pass through the center of town. The girls do not stay at the cemetery. They deposit the flowers and immediately parade back. If asked, they admit to "taking a walk." But just taking a walk is insufficient for a woman. Women must keep busy. A reason—in this case flowers for the graves—is always given and expected.

By the time a boy and girl reach marriageable age, they know more or less whom they want. Through gossip and the "grapevine," the word gets to the preferred party. Generally, feelers are extended by the boy rather than the girl. An attractive female receives many, and can choose among them, though one or two will be favored.

Because of these feelers, few approaches are made without some prior hint of acceptance or favor. There is no dating in the North American sense. Informal contacts are limited to street conversations and perhaps a dance or two at a novena or fiesta. If a boy has interest in a girl, he makes a point of meeting her with more than chance frequency. A boy showing such an active interest is said to be "walking behind" the girl. A boy can be seen talking to a girl or dancing with her two or three times with little comment resulting. More than this, and the gossip begins in earnest.

Aside from chance meetings on the street, most overtly flirting contact between the sexes occurs in groups—three or more boys joking with three or more girls. To talk purposely with a girl alone is serious business. Such group or part-of-a-crowd contact *is* dating, and any overture or joke between a boy and girl is cause for speculation.

When the boy begins to be seen at the girl's doorstep, conversing with her in plain view of parents and passersby, they are known as "lovers." Though no formal notice is issued, they are regarded as practically engaged.

It is at this stage that some sexual activity may begin. Pustunich boys guess that half of all couples engage in intercourse before marrying, so that the boys can "see if they're virgins." The young informants are overstating the sexual activity. There is little opportunity to see a girl alone in an isolated spot. Villagers estimate that in very few cases are babies born less than nine months after marriage.

Kissing, handholding, and timid embracing are common on the doorstep, when parents aren't looking. Boys say that most girls will neck today. Some, it is said, will sneak off from errands to meet a boy in a secluded spot. Should the couple be discovered, marriage is mandatory. Again, however, such behavior is rare among couples not at least contemplating marriage and is likely to represent a small minority of couples.

When the couple wishes to formalize their intentions, the boy asks the parents for the girl's hand. Ideally, the boy suggests a period of time for "ripening" the relationship—usually six months to two years. This period constitutes the formal engagement, and from the moment of talking with the girl's parents, the boy and girl are called *novios*. Should the girl's parents frown upon the match, elopement is possible. Generally, the couple will flee to another town, returning after a child is born. Or, the boy may merely bring the girl to his house and spend the night with her. Parents may inform the authorities; two years ago, in fact, a Pustunich boy spent eight days in jail for "stealing" a Ticul girl. Ideally, marriage must follow such an act. Actually, many village unions are common-law, and the very fact of elopement (as opposed to casual sexual relations) represents a manifestation of responsible behavior.

At the end of the "ripening" period, the boy brings his parents to visit the girl's nuclear family, bearing traditional gifts of bread, chocolate, and brandy. A date is set for the wedding, usually within a month or two, and *padrinos* are chosen who will bear expenses of the priest, ring, and wedding chain.

Couples are married both civilly (about a week before the church affair) and religiously. Blood tests are required. Villagers tell of one boy who was "turned down." "He had even bought all the clothes for the girl, and everything was ready. So, they gave the marriage up." Regardless of civil marriage, until the religious ceremony the couple sleep apart in their respective houses. The wedding may take place either in Pustunich or Ticul. Villagers are bitter over the prices charged by the present Ticul priest for the marriage mass—$125 for a Ticul ceremony and $175 for a Pustunich mass. His prices vary considerably, however. In one instance, a brother of the curanderos was complaining about the fee demanded by the priest. This Belem was fifty years old. His first wife, an older woman whom he admits he married for money, had died several months before. His bride-to-be was a lovely twenty-year-old. Because his brothers were rich, claims Belem, the priest demanded $340 for the mass and service ("Just for ten minutes work, mind you"). Belem refused to pay more than $100. They bargained for some time until Belem claims he walked out, crying, "Dammit, I'm already married civilly and don't really need you." The priest yielded and a price of $125 was agreed upon. The priest *will* marry villagers for less—indeed, for nothing. But one must plead poverty. Most pay the asking price.

Today, few unions begin as common-law. Villagers have more money than they did in past generations and can afford the costs of a church wedding. In addition, there is the prestige of an elaborate ceremony. The cost of church weddings has been the factor for common-law unions. Pustunicheños prefer legal marriage. About twenty years ago a mission priest visited the vicinity, holding masses, baptizing, and marrying free of charge. In Pustunich alone, *forty-four* previously common-law couples were married (among them rico Clemente Perez) and many children were groomsmen and maids-of-honor. This was an unusual opportunity, however. The priest performed the marriages *in* town and charged nothing. Today, stable common-law unions are unlikely to be formalized, as couples are not in a rush to spend the money. The reason is not fear of permanent ties. All children are recorded and would be provided for by the father at any rate; and civil divorce is easy to obtain in Ticul.

Today's church weddings are elaborate affairs, involving as many as eight groomsmen and bridesmaids, and often requiring the rental of suits and gowns. The groom's family pays for everything but the actual ceremony and its symbolic paraphernalia. Most weddings today also involve the rental of an automobile to bring the wedding party and invited guests from home to church—be it from Pustunich to Ticul, or from the bride's home to the Pustunich church door; in one instance the distance was less than 200 yards. The festival afterwards is held at the groom's house. There is recorded music (records, machine, speaker, and battery rented from Clem Perez), *aguardiente* and Coca Cola, beer, sandwiches, and either of two formal-occasion hot dishes of turkey in black or white sauce. Total wedding costs to the groom's father may run from $400 to $1,000. While the women gossip and the men gossip and gamble, young unmarried boys and girls stand shyly around the dance floor beneath the blaring loudspeakers until one couple (generally engaged) begins the dancing. Little by little, the floor fills. Still, many girls end up dancing with each other. To ask a girl to dance is a serious act in Pustunich.

The honeymoon is short and rarely interrupts milpa work. It is thought best to provide privacy for the young couple. Often, where both the bride's and groom's families live in one-room houses with outlying kitchens, this period is limited to three or four days during which the couple occupies the kitchen. In other instances, a thatch addition or separate dwelling is constructed next to the groom's parents' house in anticipation of the wedding. Marriage residence is almost always virilo-cal. This is a preference, not prescription, as the availability of better facilities at the bride's parental home may attract a couple. As father and son generally constitute an economic (milpa group) unit, co-residence is a convenience.

There is little privacy. Sexual intercourse in a large family is not a spontaneous act. It must be planned, entailing a move of hammocks for the night or a trip to the monte.

"To have intercourse while kids are in the house is impossible," maintains one thirty-eight-year-old informant. "There are kids who don't sleep, so you have to send them out to a movie or to play, or something. Once a kid is three, he's too old to stay in the house. That's why one needs a separate house when one has kids. Or, take your hammock out into the kitchen, and when you're finished, return to the house. Some kids are real little bastards—they pretend they're asleep, but watch to see how it's done."

Intercourse occurs mainly in the hammock, less frequently on the floor of the house. Should a woman become pregnant, claims one village man, sexual relations may be maintained until the birth of the child. "It's not like a horse—when a horse is pregnant she stops it." Still another villager disagrees. Intercourse during pregnancy is bad for the woman. He, however, speaks with the experience of nine miscarriages, and his wife is noted for pregnancy troubles. Her last child (the third only to survive) was delivered in Merida by Caesarian section. Most appear to cease sexual relations during menstruation. "It's bad—the woman can get sick." After the birth of a child, sexual relations are halted for two to three months—"until the woman is all cleaned out." It is admitted that "a man could run around with another woman during this time, but not all do it." It is believed that no matter how frequent the relations, a woman cannot conceive during the six months following childbirth.

There is no specific pattern to intercourse frequency. "When I was young and living with this girl," comments the thirty-eight-year-old quoted earlier, "I did it *every day* for three years, not missing a single day. Now, every fifteen days or maybe once a month—more often if the woman's interested. When you reach forty you've about had it. At seventy or eighty you're through. You can't."

"There's too much sex today," comments a fifty-year-old man. "In the old days people lived much longer. They didn't marry when they were twelve or fifteen like they do today [this, in reference to the fifteen-year-old catrina]. They're not ripe yet. The blood will tire. In the old days, a young married couple would spend three whole days indoors and get it out of their systems. Afterwards, intercourse only one night out of every thirty or so. Their parents would tell them when and this was strictly followed throughout their lives. Thus the blood remained strong. And they lived longer." He is here referring to the "time before his."

An informant judged to be highly sexually active and of considerable experience claims that fellatio is nonexistent in the pueblo, though "it is said" that some prostitutes in Ticul practice it. Cunnilingus is viewed as something very few women want or permit. A majority of couples would rarely even think of it.

Homosexuality is known, and all agree that there is none in Pustunich, though a soft-featured catrin boy of ten is suspected of future potential. Ticul, however, is known to have four or five. One Ticuleño is called a "queer" (in local dialect *mamflor* or "suckflower") and is reputed not to be able to engage in intercourse with his wife without first commiting sodomy with a male.

Though marriage entails new obligations toward one's in-laws, these are not burdensome. The groom's father-in-law may ask help in any number of projects, though his own sons will normally offer to take the heavier work. The groom, in turn, is expected to respond positively. Son-in-law and father-in-law may make milpa together on occasion, but this depends as much upon the needs of the groom's own father and brothers as upon the amicability of the relationship between son- and father-in-law. Brides now become part of the patrilocal household, working no more nor less than the groom's mature unmarried sisters. Regular gifts of food are brought to the bride's parents, especially at times of surplus (including the groom's hunting kill or share) and the season of sweet, fresh atole.

Relations between the couple and their in-laws are generally good. In their lip-service approval of boy or girl, the two families had already considered factors of friendliness. The usual attitude of the groom's household toward the bride is one of amicability, cooperation, and, initially at least, a fair degree of forced (and sometimes awkward) solicitousness.

With the birth of the first child, both husband and wife are now entitled to be greeted as Don and Doña. Women are more frequently addressed as Doña by village men, unless they and their husbands are close friends. Most village men are on a first-name basis, though younger males will generally address old people as Don and Doña. Women refer to all married village males as "Don so and so," unless very friendly with them.

The ideal of a house of one's own is not easily attainable. Many married couples live their lives out in a semidetached addition to the groom's parents' one-room house. Where the boy's father owns a substantial solar, the couple's home might be at some yards distance. A vacant village solar may cost as much as $2,000 or $3,000; with a well, and possibly a thatch house on it, it may cost as much as $4,000 to $6,000. Few young men could even contemplate such a purchase during the first five years of marriage, nor in most cases could their fathers aid them substantially. As lands adjacent to the paternal solar are usually owned by other families, sons not residing in the solar of their fathers live scattered throughout the town on whatever land was available at the time of their ability to purchase. This has generally prevented the growth of large extended-family clusters, though a few exist. Even where sons do manage to find a solar of their own, the youngest son generally resides with his parents until their death. For this "service," he inherits the house.

Though a separate nuclear family, the new couple generally shares a fireplace with the groom's parents. To a considerable extent both families share a single pocketbook, as most major expenses involve milpa, house, solar, and economic implements rather than clothing and other individual items. While the groom is ostensibly economically independent upon his marriage, the facts of common residence, house maintenance, and milpa partnership effectively ensure that he will remain substantially dependent upon others.

Maturity

Entrance into adult political and social activities generally occurs after marriage. Only for the past nine or ten years have active school organizations existed which demand creative participation on the part of students and which give them a taste of office. At present, there is a "student society," the school government of four student officers, a "school sports committee" (five officers), "order and discipline committee" (three members, all girls, whose major function is to inform on misbehavior), "hygiene and health committee" (two members), and two-member committees of "social action" (chooses talent for the annual school talent night), "punctuality," "school savings" (presents short talks on the virtues of thrift), and "library and handicraft." Most members are twelve or thirteen years old. School-head Gomez states that he formed these committees (many of which admittedly do little work) only to groom the present group of children for future responsibility and "public service to the community."

The only specifically youth-oriented nonschool posts in Pustunich belong to the "Cultural Group of Young Men and Woman" (*Grupo Cultural de Jovenes*), which organizes receptions for distinguished visitors and from time to time presents adult-oriented skits for the school talent night.

Few unmarried men attend town meetings, though if older than sixteen or seventeen they would not be barred. The youngest official in Pustunich is the ejidal comisario, Ek. All other town officials—mayor, secretary, president of the betterment committee, etc.—are men in their forties, with a few over fifty. During his fortieth to fiftieth years, a Pustunicheño is at his social prime. He is physically strong and experienced. The eldest of his children are as yet unmarried or newly married, his sons are maturing and maximally productive, his income from milpa is as large as it will ever be. His household, including daughters-in-law, is swelling. His parents are often still alive, as are his brothers, sisters, and age-mate cousins. He hunts regularly. He is close enough in age to both younger and older villagers to be included in their activities. The mature male of fifty has married and produced children. He has provided for them and has allowed his sons and daughters to attend school. He has taught his sons to make milpa and, through his wife, has raised competent, marriageable daughters. He has attended town meetings, perhaps served in some official capacity, attended cha chaac, and participated in communal hunts. Traditionally, there is little reason for his ever having to say, "I could have done better."

As the village male or female ages, more burden is gradually placed upon the remaining children or daughters-in-law. While entry into active adult life is imperceptible, the aged's departure is almost a mirror image of the early years. There is no specific time or age at which a man is expected to retire. Men of seventy-five still seek and obtain work in the henequen fields and accompany strong sons and grandsons out to the milpa. Slowly, the burden of work and earning passes to the children. While participating in pagan ritual no less than before, Catholic religious participation increases. The old man shows up inside the church with more frequency, though still less often than women. Increasing dependence is viewed as natural by the male or female. First, it is barely perceptible, and, second, it is their due. Old people are owners of their houses and grounds until death. The youngest married son is likely still dependent upon the old couple for shelter. Older people are almost invariably addressed as Don or Doña. They are seated first at the parties of others and are given places of honor at the festivities of their own family.

At the same time, control of the family holdings—cattle, oranges, milpa position, etc.—though nominally in the oldster's hands, is in actuality exercised by the older sons. As the young sons of Pustunicheños are of ambiguous economic status, so too are the old patriarchs. Father and son are not automatically equated. Actual control of property is of greater importance than titular status. Informants consistently rate old men as one or two levels lower in economic position than their wealthiest sons.

Continuity and Orientation to Change

Socialization in Pustunich provides a good example of Benedict's "continuity," wherein little that is learned during the maturation process need be "unlearned."[1] Both the assumption and relinquishing of active adult role behavior are gradual and barely perceptible, unmarked by clear "firsts." As new roles require learning, abrupt role changes imply "spillage" from previous roles and thus constitute a potential cause of anxiety to individual and community.

The life cycle is thus not unlike the history of the community, in that each acts as an "orientor" of perception and evaluation of change. Maturation in Pustunich ensures a smooth and well-internalized longitudinal passage through the social byways. *It serves to minimize the anticipation of change.* Such continuity is not unusual, of course, for peasant communities. The important point is that commitment to adult social, economic, and sex role values occurs early, is taken for granted, and continues unthreatened and consistent. Whether this will remain the case in the future, however, is another matter. The increasing number of catrin children is an indication of new action and the beginnings of new alternatives for village parents. In an interesting TAT study of Pustunich males, David Gutmann has found a significantly higher amount of "generalized guilt" among younger mature men than among older Pustunicheños.[2] Elsewhere, I have suggested that this differential may likely be attributed to the opening of these new alternatives to young parents. They face the choice of whether to deny tradition or deny their children new opportunities for mobility. Either way, the result may likely be conflict and, thus, guilt. The older village males, on the other hand, could reflect an older, low "achievement and anxiety state," common to "all past Pustunicheños who were secure in the limited choices they made and entertained no alternatives to being . . . mestizo and milperos.[3]

It should be stressed that even the new catrin children face little discontinuity through maturation, in that their activity is consistent with their divergent dress style. They do not make milpa or engage in much physical labor. Furthermore, because the school teacher is the only local role model for catrins, many catrins are being funneled through full high and normal school careers. Indeed, as a result, it is likely that the catrins of Pustunich have had far greater education than the catrins of the ''city'' of Ticul. Still other changes are occurring within the political sphere as new expectations of political participation and leadership arise.

NOTES

1. Ruth Benedict, ''Continuities and Discontinuities in Cultural Conditioning.'' *Psychiatry* 1 (1938): 161-167.
2. David Gutmann, ''Mayan Aging—A Comparative TAT Study.'' *Psychiatry* 29 (1966): 246-259.
3. Irwin Press, ''Maya Aging: Cross-Cultural Projective Techniques and the Dilemma of Interpretation.'' *Psychiatry* 30 (1967): 202.

Houses on the periphery of the village square. The school bus arrives from nearby Ticul with four of the five teachers.

Awaiting the mid-morning bus to Ticul for daily shopping. Their men are at the milpa.

Friday night at the movies. Women in their better huipiles, *men bathed and in clean white shirts. Within minutes Tarzan (Johnny Weismuller) will swing across the rear wall of wealthy Clemente Perez' storage yard.*

Drawing water at the central pump, she notes the opposing line-ups for Wednesday's baseball game. The notice reads: Baseball Wednesday 18 of March 1964. Anniversary of the Petroleum Expropriation. Game between students of the school of this locality and students of the school of the barrio Guadalupe of Ticul. A ceremony will occur in view of the students' wearing of their new uniforms for the first time.

Baseball fans on the basketball court watching the game.

Returning from the milpa late in the afternoon. Firewood carried by tump-line and the now-empty water gourd over his shoulder. He will bathe and then his wife will pick the ticks off him.

Family economic scene. Father at hammock, everyone else over the age of four at work on tejidos *or braided hat-strands. The shortwave radio on the table is powered by a car storage battery below. Wires from above descend from antenna wire stretched across the thatched roof.*

Hat maker at work. Today he didn't go to the milpa. His hammock is drawn up to the ceiling out of the way. His wife's daily huipil *wardrobe hangs behind him.*

The mayor's four catrin daughters (one seated in background). Two other catrin children work in Mexico and Merida. His youngest son (left) he maintains as mestizo to help him with store and milpa labor.

The catrina on the right has just married into this mestizo family. Here she sits with her new sister-in-law in a very mestizo kitchen making tortillas for the men who will soon be returning from the milpa. It is doubtful whether she will be able to maintain her catrin identity for long.

A winsome six-month-old in the arms of her very proud mother shortly before the ethnographer's wife became active as godmother in the hetzmek *sex-role ritual.*

Unable to run and play, he must baby-sit with his younger brother. The baby (actually 2 years old) still goes about naked from the waist down.

Less than eight years old, they bring home daily cash through tejido *making. But shortly they will begin going to the milpa with their father, and never again engage in this woman's activity.*

In the schoolroom. The teacher (later mayor) drives home a point. He is the major new role model in the community.

Trying to look nonplussed, his pride at shooting his first deer nonetheless pours through.

Very aware of being looked at, these eligible young women wait outside the mill as their corn is ground. They are overdressed for corn grinding, but not for husband hunting.

Awaiting the start of a meeting called by the teacher. These are the core of "cooperators" who spur each of the teacher's new projects.

Two elders relax on the road to watch the comings and goings of bus travelers. The man on the left is the catrin schoolteacher's conservative old father.

Women, at a good distance from the altar, prepare offerings for the harvest-thanks ritual under the eye of the h-men, *or shaman-priest.*

The h-men *in action, holding aloft a bowl of rich offering soup. Note the cross at right forefront, with offerings of cigarettes, incense, and corn* pibs *nearby.*

After the uahi-col *harvest ritual, all present must taste of the offering soup. Here the* h-men *ladles out bowlsful to the young boys who, by their very attendance, are active participants.*

In front of one of the village curanderos' house sits a taxi that has just deposited a patient from Merida, the capital city.

8

Social Organization

Every Pustunicheño belongs to several groups, membership in each of which is of greater or lesser importance to him in his daily behavioral routine. In some, the criteria for membership seldom surface, or stimulate behavior only sporadically. For example, the Pustunicheño is a Mexican only insofar as he knows and behaves as though he were. His Mexican status serves as a focus of behavior primarily during school days, when lessons must be learned for history classes. As he listens to his home or transistor radio he shows a lively though detached interest in international news. He is apathetic toward state and national politics and seldom votes. When voting, reading national news, or greeting non-Mexicans, his primary identity focus is that of Yucatecan, Pustunicheño, or Maya campesino—not Mexican. He is a Yucateco, not a Mexican. Mexicans live in Mexico.

As a Yucateco, the Pustunicheño knows that peoples of other states are not as good a person as he. Chiapanecos, for example, "use steel" rather than "words" during arguments. He knows that the "legitimate" Maya are from Yucatan. He knows that Mexicans were brought in to destroy the Maya of Quintana Roo. He knows that Yucatan has a governor (he visited the village several times) and that Merida is the state capital. The Pustunicheño's being a Yucateco, however, seldom, if ever, results in more than conversation stirred by radio news items. An exception might be the two brazeros who complained of the small quota of men chosen from Yucatan. When he goes to Merida, the villager does so not as a Yucatecan, but as a tourist, purchaser, or citizen of Pustunich. He knows full well that he can travel anywhere in Yucatan and speak the familiar Maya with people who understand the milpa and Maya ritual. As such, Pustunich rather than Yucatecan membership is the element which grossly influences his behavior with others outside his community. In this, the Pustunicheño is like most other peasants.

Outside Contacts

Pustunich's contacts with the outside are numerous and complex. Wage labor, communal hunts, hourly busses, easy access to larger towns, traveling circuses, visiting salesmen, politicians, all ensure a constant coming and going of villagers and others, and maintenance of a wide variety of personal contacts with outsiders.

All village women maintain relationships with itinerant tejido (hat-strand) buyers. All village males deal with Ticul corn and other produce jobbers and have established credit with them. Since there is no village bakery and little local butchering of meat, villagers are further dependent upon the Ticul market. The fluctuation of outside citrus, meat, corn, wheat, tobacco, and other prices has a considerable effect upon the town. This effect is taken for granted, however, and is not viewed as a specifically "outside" phenomenon or as something mysterious or uncontrollable, ultimately functioning to take advantage of the little community. The town is considerably self-sufficient in corn and produce and can obtain at least minimal quantities of meat locally and through hunts; hence, the effect of outside price fluctuation is not critical. While lower henequen prices spell disaster in the commercial crop zone to the north, the result in Pustunich is lower supplemental income from wage labor. As wages are supplementary rather than focal, local milpa production serves as a buffer against world market fluctuations.

Contacts with "official" outside elements have increased significantly in the past thirty to forty years. Blood tests and civil marriage ceremonies are mandatory. Since Ticul is so close by, villagers have long taken advantage of the courts and notary publics for the legalizing of land transfers. More recently, large numbers of village men have enrolled in the ejidal loan system and are becoming dependent upon the ejidal bank for cash advances on their crops. Whereas government interest charges remain constant and repayment is deferred, corn prices tend to fluctuate by as much as 40 percent over the year. The ejidal bank loans are thus granting Pustunicheños a degree of freedom from the scarcity cycle and giving them more choice in timing sales of stockpiled corn.

A further official contact lies in the first catrin and teacher produced by Pustunich (See Chapter 9). After leaving the village school for an administrative position in the union offices in Merida, Carlos Perez subsequently moved up to the state advisory council for government school teachers. Through his influence, the governor has visited the town on various occasions and has supplied aid for the central pump construction and a small industry. Perez is "our man in Merida" and in him, villagers feel they have a direct link to the political hub. Both his father and father-in-law are among the town's most conservative and respected old men and Perez still maintains a house on the outskirts of Pustunich. His visits to the town always stir excitement. He is a collective rather than individual link to the top officialdom of Yucatan, however. No villager would dream of disturbing Perez for help in strictly personal matters, though on occasion he has interceded for groups of villagers having difficulty extracting milpa damages from nearby wealthy cattle ranchers. In this and in his known acquaintanceship with the governor, Pustunich receives benefit and glory enough.

The baseball team has been the most important recent source of nonofficial outside contact. In the past ten years both first- and second-string teams have visited literally scores of towns, establishing a wide network of casual friendships for the young village players. On a dozen or more Sundays during the year, visiting teams, and all the supporters who can fit into a rented truck, spend the day in Pustunich.

The number of Pustunicheños permanently residing outside the town has been insignificant, though slowly rising, as catrin youth mature and emigrate. Today there are approximately half a dozen. Because of the lack of local opportunities for catrins, none of them lives in the immediate vicinity. Several reside in Merida (one is an auto mechanic, the other is married to a Merida male), one teaches near the British Honduran border, several teach in Campeche, and one is a nurse's aide in Mexico City. Their contact with Pustunich is infrequent and limited to yearly or biannual week-long visits. They are thus less important links with the outside than is the baseball team. Several village men have been to south Texas as brazeros. They spent their time with other Mexicans and traveled little due to lack of English; their contact, then, was mainly with Mexicans from other parts of the country rather than with American social or cultural elements. They brought back little besides a full pocketbook and a jumbled series of impressions of the Mexican countryside as seen from the back of a truck. Pustunich brazeros undertook the work for adventure and extra, rather than critically needed, cash. They were not slow to appreciate the advantage of their positions as contrasted with many others of their countrymen who made the trip desperate for cash. As noted earlier, the two brazeros are small-scale entrepreneurs who make hats in addition to milpa. Both put their wages into additional sewing machines for their shops.

A byproduct of the many types of outside contact—and in itself one of the strongest links beyond the village—is the outside origin of approximately 20 percent of all Pustunich wives. Affinal relationships have been established with most communities in the neighborhood, particularly Ticul. Several wives, in fact, come from Merida. The force of village life-style is such that all brides of local milperos become behaviorally *amestizada* in short order, regardless of whether they affect catrin dress. This transforming force is not lost on villagers. Wife importation thus involves no clear threat to local identity or continuity. Here again, the unique homogeneity of Yucatan ensures that no new bride, regardless of her town of origin or life-style, will be unfamiliar with any element of village life, be it Maya language, milpa procedures, or pagan ritual. Such importation nonetheless brings with it a continuous source of communication with external values and the vigor of the "simmering" process is maintained.

Overall, in its many physical and structural links with the outside, Pustunich is more able to control its destiny than would be the case in distrustful semi-isolation. No element of outside contact overtly threatens the community, and thus new links are readily forged while "old" ones, such as the ten-year-old baseball rivalry with the town of Peto, become tradition. Engaging in an ever widening arena of functionally diverse social relationships with culturally empathetic individuals, the Pustunicheño acquires new roles which do not compete with, and frequently aid him in meeting, traditional role expectations.

Family

As Pustunicheño, the individual is automatically typed by others and himself as campesino, mestizo, Maya, poor, and unworldly. Each villager is tied to all others in living within all or much of this stereotype. Each villager is further tied to most others through kinship, marriage, and fictive kinship and each sees the other frequently at parties (*rosarios*), ball games, public dances, hunts, religious rituals, in the streets, conversant groups, in the field, town stores, council meetings, or fagina.

The town has only one physical focus—the plaza. In it are the baseball diamond, basketball court, church, school, town office, health center, two stores, the major corn mill, and a movie theater. The two remaining stores, the main road, and the bus stop are all within a block of the plaza. Because of the electricity in Perez' store, and the yellow kerosene-lamp glow from the door of the mayor's store, some light is always cast on the terraced water pump and basketball court. After dark, the plaza becomes the only natural meeting ground for those who wish to converse and recognize each other.

Because of its high degree of endogamous marriage, Pustunich is, furthermore, an in-bred town. Few families cannot trace some actual or possible cognatic or affinal relationship to most others and the distinction between cognate, affine, and friend is often unclear. Milpa groups, while usually consisting of fathers, brothers, and sons, are in no way limited to nuclear family members, and most men make milpa with nonagnates at some time in their productive lives. Hunting, fagina, and religious activities are not dominated by any noticeable group; participation varies from occasion to occasion or year to year. Political participation is still tentative and, traditionally, important matters have not been in Pustunich hands, let alone those of a particular subgroup.

For these reasons, no single group membership below the Pustunicheño level clearly and inevitably monopolizes all or most activities, or dominates the type of interaction required under most situations.

The most consistently interactive and cooperating group, as well as the most nominally long-lasting, is the nuclear family. Within the nuclear family, however, are a number of major subrelationships. In rough order of resistance to rupture they are: mother-daughter, mother-son, father-daughter, brother-sister, father-son, brother-brother, husband-wife. Though initially somewhat fragile, the spouse relationship, once it matures, is generally stronger than any remaining kin or nonkin dyads.

Aside from the fact that nearly all marriages result from mutual affection, marriages are often unstable during the first year or two. Though separations are common, so too are reconciliations. Few couples who separate do so permanently. Where there are children, separations are less likely to occur or are utilized by one spouse or the other for "political" strength in "negotiating" some marital difficulty. These difficulties are highly varied and do not represent a pattern beyond the personalities of the partners and the idiosyncratic phenomenon of compatibility, which differs from union to union.

Marital problems most frequently result from strained in-law relationships, adultery, slovenliness, lack of industriousness on the part of either spouse, wealth-related life-style differences, or other, personality-derived incompatibilities. In only a minority of separation cases is the matter taken before the comisario—as much because of the general lack of respect for the office of mayor as for the publicity that would result. A favorite argument of the comisario in resolving these disputes is the high cost of separate maintenance and formal divorce.

Most married couples with children enjoy a union of general equality and harmony. The opinions of each have considerable weight with the other and are almost always solicited before any major action or purchase.

Should a wife be ill, the husband will haul water, take corn to the mill, and prepare meals for the family—chores which are definitely part of the female's role. Men boast that certain dishes, such as venison or armadillo, are best when prepared by men. Women, too, will aid in the milpa if such help is necessary. Both men and women, along with their children, sit and shell beans or husk corn together.

While arguments do occur, seldom are they accompanied by physical blows, which are considered serious marital offenses. During the year of study one couple, who had recently arrived from Campeche, stirred strong village sentiments when the husband publicly struck his wife at an evening dance. They left Pustunich shortly thereafter, partly because of the subsequent gossip and partly because of their boredom in the backward, quiet town.

Pustunicheños pride themselves on being mild, friendly people. Displays of violence, whether within public or private domains, are swiftly condemned and often a matter for the comisario. Where violence occurs, it is most often preceded by alcoholic consumption. On the occasion of his brother's wedding, one young man became drunk and boisterous, disrupting the postnuptial celebration. His father and older brothers felt no hesitation in hauling him before the mayor for a three-hour jail sentence. As there are no cantinas in town (contrasted with three, four, or more in henequen zone towns of similar size), drunkenness is infrequent and generally limited to festival occasions. Pustunicheños, when drunk, tend to be maudlin, embracive, or passive rather than belligerent.

Though more likely to rupture, relations of fathers with sons are closer and more affective than are relations of fathers with daughters. From the boy's eighth year he shares in the most important economic work of his father. He is a co-participant in the male milpa ritual. Leisure activities are with males (hunting, etc.). A boy is tolerated as silent observer and sometime participant in male conversation. Similarly, mother and daughter share in major economic and leisure activities that largely or completely exclude males.

It is precisely because father and son operate within the same role and activity continuum that competition, difference of opinion, and ill will are far more possible than between father and mature or maturing daughter. The mother-son bond is an emotionally charged one. The most vehement curses and verbal attacks involve slander of one's mother. Pustunich shares in that Mexican ideal which equates "Mother" with the Virgin Mary and thus effectively prevents the establishment of an easy camaraderie between mother and son.

Whereas disciplining of young sons is carried out by both parents, mothers generally tend to the behavior of daughters. It is felt that children need a mother more than a father, a feeling reinforced by the fact that a father must spend many hours away from the house. Should a wife die, another mature woman almost inevitably moves into the house—either a married daughter, sister, or mother. Both parents, however, expect and receive courtesy from their children, and well into young adulthood expect prompt compliance from them.

Visits and gifts of prepared food are frequent and informal between married children and parents, though they tend to become somewhat less frequent through the years. In many instances, the bond between parents-in-law and sons- or daughters-in-law parallels the parent-child relationship. In all instances, however, cooperation and good relations with parents-in-law are expected. Face-to-face contact and sharing of extra or special foods are almost daily occurrences, in spite of aversion to uxorilocal residence. "Not even the devil wants a man to live with his father-in-law," maintains one informant who gets along quite well with his wife's parents. "If you live with your wife's folks, and you want to relax in your hammock for a minute, they'll say you're lazy. If some little kid wants something or other you have to get it or you'll be called a bum." "Sure, the wife has to live with her husband's parents, but well, that's life. The man or the woman must direct, and it's the man as a natural thing."

Households

While there are 203 nuclear families and remnants of nuclear families in Pustunich, it is somewhat more difficult to state the number of households. With few exceptions, all Pustunich houses are single room affairs with thatched kitchens either apart or attached. With slightly more exceptions, each nuclear family resides in its own house. Quite often, however, siblings or parents and one or two married sons will share the same solar, though they reside in separate houses. In addition, similar arrangements occur with siblings or parents and married children residing in separate, though adjacent, solares. As a general rule, nuclear families sharing the same solar tend to share, to a greater or lesser degree, a single fireplace and pocketbook, most particularly if one or more of the male family heads is young. If we define a household as consisting of all those individuals who more or less equally share a single fireplace and pocketbook, there are approximately 160 such units in Pustunich.

By this definition, common residence in a solar need not constitute membership in the household of another residing in the same solar. There are at least half a dozen instances of two or more nuclear families (siblings or parents and children) in adjacent solares, with stone hedges as separation, who share in cooking and economic maintenance of both families. Similarly, there are as many instances of brothers who live in the same solar and, though often sharing a common cooking pot and expense of food, maintain all other economic interests apart from one another.

Extended or joint-family households tend to be more cohesive and nonindividuated the younger its constituents. Thus, when a boy marries and begins residence in the solar of his parents, he shares with his father in most economic pursuits. Should the boy find work on his own, the earnings are earmarked for general household expenses, though as a rule, clothing or personal items of either parent or child are more frequently purchased with the earnings of the respective nuclear family head. Food, utensils, sewing machines, radios, tools, fodder, and medicines are purchased in common. As the boy grows older, such sharing decreases.

Frequently this is a result of the subsequent marriage of younger brothers who also move into the solar, and/or the increasing aid given the parents by older siblings who no longer reside within the solar. As parents age, each child (males more than married females) assumes a greater share of the responsibility for them while at the same time becoming more assuredly the head of his own household.

The types of households to be seen in Pustunich, and the frequency of their occurrence, are shown in Table 3.

The large number of nuclear family households does not necessarily indicate a desire for neolocal residence. The average number of children per family is five. Numerous families have that number of sons alone. Few solares in Pustunich are large enough to accommodate more than three nuclear families comfortably (with room for fowl, gardens, and bushes for excretory privacy). Even though money should be available for purchase of a solar, all solares within the village limits are privately owned and in some years none may be up for sale. The sale of a solar is a serious matter, as solar ownership constitutes a major criterion of village identification. Solares will be sold only in extreme emergencies, or where the owner is a bachelor, widow, or widower with few or no male children. Solares, as mentioned earlier, are expensive. Most families cannot afford one without saving for years. Should a married male desire more privacy, he may build a house at one edge of the parental solar. If the solar is large enough, stone hedging may be placed between the portions, though this is more often the case where two brothers (as opposed to father and son) share a single solar.

The typical male resides within his father's solar—and often his house—during the first months or years of marriage. If possible, a separate house will soon be built near the father's. As additional brothers approach marriage age, or as other living opportunities open, the young man may move his residence, either to the solar of a brother who has a piece of land, or perhaps to the solar of his father-in-law, aunt, uncle, grandparent, or other relative who has the room and would appreciate the companionship and/or financial assistance. That the average age of the head of a nuclear family living alone in a solar is forty-four indicates the difficulty of a younger couple's affording their own land. Indeed, of the one hundred and seventeen nuclear family households, in only *twelve* are the male heads under thirty years of age. In addition, the parents of a forty-five- or fifty-year-old man are likely deceased; what was once the solar of an extended family is now divided among two or more brothers

Table 3
HOUSEHOLD TYPES

Composition	Number of Instances
Nuclear family only (male and female with or without children)	98
Nuclear family remnants widow and unmarried children widow and bachelor son (45 years old) widower and unmarried children	15 1 3
Married couple plus single niece	1
Extended family (parents, married son, and his children, plus other unmarried children)	21
Extended family (parents plus two or more married sons)	5
Extended family (parents plus a married son and a married daughter and spouses)	1
Extended family (parents plus a married daughter)	2
Extended family (grandparent, parents, plus married grandson and spouse)	2
Extended family (parents, married son, plus father's unmarried brother)	2
One grandparent and married grandchildren	2
One grandparent and bachelor grandson	1
Single male (49, 58, and 60 years old, respectively)	3
Single female (54 and 63 years old)	2
Aunt and married nephew	1

who often build a stone hedge between their portions, thereby creating visibly, and conceptually, separate solares.

The three instances of uxorilocal residence reflect less a retention of some earlier Maya residence preference than the simple logistics of *lebensraum*, which is most responsible for overall village household patterns. This is not to suggest that most village boys champ at the bit to move away from the father's solar. Village youth find it advantageous to reside with their parents and milpa partners during the first years of marriage. The presence of their families eases the transition period with a new bride and provides immediate economic security during these initial years of childbirth expense and minimal capital accumulation.

In terms of the "developmental cycle" of the household in Pustunich, as new families of procreation come into existence, they usually reside virilocally, creating an extended family household. This period may last for three to six years. As new nuclear families form there is pressure for previously married sons to move. The wealthier the overall household, the sooner this move occurs; the poorer, the longer the membership in the parental household prior to neolocal residence. As older sons move off, the younger marry and take their place in the extended household. The "final" household is generally that of old parent and youngest son or sons. Thus Pustunicheños are members of extended family households at the beginning and end of their married lives, with a relatively long period of conceptually independent residence during active mature years. The simple act of building a stone hedge between houses is sufficient to create two distinct families out of one.

Kinship, Family, and Behavior

Just as the composition of households varies, so too does the pattern of behavior and cooperation.

There are three-generation, extended family households which share in all economic gains, live clustered together in the same solar, cook together, and cooperate in most undertakings. There are brothers who not only live apart, but vilify each other within the limits of village propriety. Sons revere their fathers and sons have murdered their fathers. Villagers tell of the shooting of Jose Maria Puch by his son Ramses. Jose Maria was a noted drunk and eager fist-fighter. He was "a loco who claimed he could beat twenty men. Every day he would get drunk in Ticul and have a fight on the road back.'' One day, about five years ago, he returned home and began to insult his seventeen-year-old son. Ramses took his *xbut bi tzon* (muzzle-loader) and met the old man outside the house. Jose Maria ''put out his hands as if to ward off the blow and pleaded. But Ramses shot and killed him.'' The son went to jail in Ticul and, as the story goes, killed a fellow inmate with a knife. Shortly thereafter, he himself was slain by a group of enraged inmates. He was known as the ''penal tiger.''

A different perspective is provided by the gossip about ''old man Velasco,'' who is universally viewed as a miser. Though his whole cattle range is in his son's name, the son lives on a pittance while the old man lavishes his wealth on two nephews who live with him. He has given one nephew a home in Ticul and is reputed to have also given him periodic gifts of up to 1,000 pesos.

Hermilo Villa lived with his parents in a distant town. The elder Villa died, and Hermilo's mother, being from Pustunich, returned to live in the village. Shortly thereafter, she began to live in common-law with Pastor Uc. Hermilo married a village girl and lived with Pastor and his mother for a year. During that time he made milpa with Pastor. Pastor, however, ''gave nothing'' to Hermilo besides room and board—''not a centavo for spending money.'' Hermilo left the house and moved in with his wife's parents. He has lived with them for over three years and now makes milpa alone.

Brothers, too, may fall out. Gumersindo and Alberto Caeh made milpa together. Several years ago they separated hotly. Alberto accused Gumersindo of stealing a watermelon from his portion, and Gumersindo accused Alberto of taking fifteen or twenty ears of corn from his. Tense petty accusations were merely symptomatic of deeper grievances between the two. The two Belem brothers, both wealthy and renowned curaderos, rarely visit one another and are rivals for the patronage of municipio residents.

Bonds between affines may also be subject to strain. An excerpt from field notes, November 17, reads:

Yesterday, the justice of the peace from Ticul was called into town to see the signing of a statement by Federico Mendez, whose health is rapidly failing. Federico is Santiago Be's brother-in-law, and had lived with San while San was married to Fed's older sister. Federico's sister was much older than Santiago, and it was she who owned the house in which all three lived. Federico would make milpa and contribute to the running of the household. Upon the woman's death three months ago, ownership of the house passed to Federico. According to Federico's subsequent tale, Santiago forced him to sell the house dirt cheap to Santiago's older brother. San subsequently treated old Federico badly, and he finally had to leave and take up residence with another sister. Now he feels himself to be dying, and has called in the JP to witness a statement in which he accuses Santiago of mistreatment, so as to force Santiago to pay for burial when he dies—which he feels to be soon.

In another instance, a Mrs. Canche brought her husband before the mayor and threatened him with separation unless he threw his father out of the house. The old man, she claimed, was constantly browbeating her and complaining about her housekeeping and cooking.

There are yet further instances of hostility between friend and kinsman. Desiderio Cowoh finds his wife rolling in a henequen field with Mario Cetina. He kicks her out of his house and she stays with Mario for several days. They quarrel and she takes Desiderio's three children with her to her parents' house in Ticul. At the moment she and Desiderio are together again. It is said that Des had the right to kill Mario, but as Des also had a sweetheart on the side, he did not feel justified in making too big an issue out of the matter.

An uncle complains of not receiving an invitation to his niece's wedding. A shopkeeper warns others not to loan money to his first cousin, who is a "dead-beat." The teacher informs to the police that a cousin has been selling horsemeat as beef. The fathers of a boy and girl who had lived in common-law for several years and subsequently separated have a fist-fight at six one morning. The girl has gone to Merida for a day of sightseeing. Coincidentally, the boy also happens to be in Merida at the moment and his father greets the girl's with "so she couldn't keep away from him, eh?"

Such instances indicate the types of tensions and schisms that arise—however infrequently—and suggest the pragmatic and nonpedantic way in which social relationships are viewed. This is to say that aggression in Pustunich is not strongly patterned.

To Pustunicheños, animosities may arise from any number of highly idiosyncratic antecedents, few of which are viewed as so standardized as to exist constantly or result inevitably in hostilities. Pustunicheños do see hostilities or difficulties as likely between married persons of unequal

wealth, between rival shopkeepers and rival curanderos (everyone knows
the story of how Venancio Cocom's grandfather was gelded by a rival
h-men). Hostilities are possible, yet somewhat less likely, in marriages
between persons of different religion or dress (the girl knows she will
surely be doing the work of a mestiza). In these instances, however,
villagers agree that "mutual respect" of and "accommodation" to the
other's life-style or views can result in a happy union.

For a hint as to the genesis of the pragmatic basis for interpersonal
relationships, it is interesting to examine the change in kindred as the
individual matures. (See Figure 1).

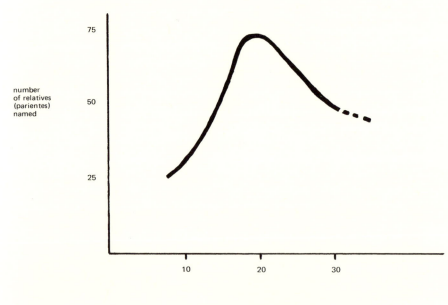

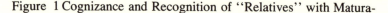

Figure 1 Cognizance and Recognition of "Relatives" with Matura-

When asked to "name all of your relatives,* six male children ranging
from eight to twelve years of age could name only an average of twenty-

*The request was stated in just that manner, leaving ambiguous the question of
whether affines, spouses of agnates, or deceased persons should be included.

four, the highest number being thirty-six. Eight-, nine-, and ten-year-olds begin their listing with age-mates and are unsure as to their relationship with them. Following age-mates, the youngsters name aunts and uncles, mixed with names of *some* of their children—individuals whom the child sees with frequency. The three twelve-year-olds named eighteen, nineteen, and nineteen relatives, respectively. By this time active in milpa and other economic work and having less time to play, the twelve-year-olds begin the list with either parents, siblings, or fathers' brothers, all of whom they must often help or with whom they make milpa. They follow these individuals with names of grandparents, mothers' siblings, and first cousins. Here there is much skipping back and forth, reflecting frequency of social contact.

By thirteen and fourteen, the child has completed school and knows more or less intimately every age-mate, both male and female, in the village. A boy begins to stay out later in the evening, gossiping with others in the plaza. He goes to Ticul with his friends to look lustfully, though bashfully, at the girls and make comments about their bosoms and legs. He may play baseball or basketball, sports in which fifty or sixty other boys are actively engaged. He begins accompanying adult males on communal hunts. Though economically active, young adult males still share in the economic security of their fathers. If younger boys display a lack of exact knowledge of their kindred, young men in their late teens to early thirties reflect a lack of "discrimination" and a propensity to include every possible kinsman. Compared with the children's average of twenty-four, the young adult males name an average of seventy-one (range: 46-90). They tend to include relations such as grandfather's siblings and their children, plus most males and females who have married either maternal or paternal collateral kin.

When the young man marries, his obligations increase and begin to exhibit a focus. He must provide food for a wife and children, plus sufficient cash or produce to cover his share of the extended family's household expenses. In addition, he must send more or less frequent gifts of food to his wife's parents. As he matures further, the focus grows smaller. He generally becomes head of his own household. He becomes a prime candidate for any communal labor and is expected to be "responsible" and independent. He exhibits more caution in economic collaboration. He may have an "enemy" or likely refuses to mix socially with three or four other villagers unless it is unavoidable.

The mature male once more names a restricted number of kinsmen (range: 14-54). The list reflects an increased discrimination in the general lack of young kin, such as nephews and nieces, and of broader collateral kin such as grandparents' siblings and their children. (See Appendix II for a full kinship terminology.)

Descent in Pustunich is bilateral. Individuals formally bear both patronymic and matronymic. While duties, affection, and "feelings" of kinship are extended equally to both parents' families, the patriline is clearly favored as an identificative category. For a woman, marriage does not override her initial affiliation. It is rare that one refers to a married woman by other than her maiden name. Thus one must know the village families and their history to determine maternity and marriage links from the commonly used surnames.

If we may designate all those bearing the same patronymic as constituting a single "great-family," there are forty-five "great-families" in Pustunich. Of these, twenty are represented by two male nuclear family heads each. Of the total 203 nuclear families, sixteen surnames account for fully 165. Sixty-eight of the town's 203 nuclear units contain male or female representatives of but three surnames. Eight more surnames are represented in an additional ninety-five nuclear units.

There is no fixed rule that unites in kinship all those who bear the same surname. If the relationship is known and readily traceable, two individuals will admit kinship without exception. Beyond three generations, however, relationships become unclear. Two individuals who bear the same name and yet are unable to establish clear linkage are free to claim kinship, admit to its possibility, or deny it. Similarly, individuals with different surnames may claim or allude to kinship. Marriage, it must be recalled, is largely village-endogamous. The household is rare that cannot trace some consanguineal or affinal tie to most other households in the village. Which bonds are claimed or emphasized is largely a matter of personal choice and of the need at any given time for identifying another as kinsman. Thus a poor representative of the large Novelo family claims that all Novelos are kinsmen. Carlos Perez, the Merida union official, states that he is not related to rich Clem Perez, even though the surname is identical. "Oh, perhaps we're related, but I don't even think we're cousins." One man says of another, a close friend who lives next door: "We're only neighbors, but we're almost relatives because he married my cousin."

"Family" in Pustunich has no fixed meaning. In its most frequent usage, it has a narrow reference. "La familia" refers to one's wife. In order of next descending frequency, "family" is given the following usages by males or females: the household; the household plus parents and/or grandparents and own siblings; the household plus grandparents (parents if not in the household), siblings, aunts, uncles, and cousins; as above, plus other kin and "political" relatives (see below). While spouse's parents, grandparents, and siblings tend to be referred to simply as "family," further affinal extensions are generally specified as belonging to "her" (the wife's) family or "my husband's" family.

The larger the number of those bearing identical surnames, the less likelihood of "family" ever being used by anyone of that surname to describe and include all others. There exists no occasion upon which more than the families of orientation and/or procreation would be required as participants. All other friends and kinsmen are present as invitees—guests. Villagers in general would rarely, if ever, refer to an entire surname group as "they." Exceptions are the smaller great-families. The fewer the households, the more likely that most or all have been involved in some incident or embrace some history or common pursuit which could lend itself to a stereotyping ("The Cepedas squandered their father's money"). No surname grouping monopolizes wealth, prestige, good or bad reputation, poverty, or modernity. There are poor as well as rich Perezes, admired as well as distrusted Orozcos, progressive as well as conservative Bes. No "great family" has monopolized the *comisariada* or other town offices, and two recent comisarios have been of families with only one or two nuclear representatives.

The existence of the category *pariente politico* (political relative) further exemplifies the minimally ascriptive nature of affiliation. In practice, relationships so designated behaviorally reflect just what the word "political" implies—choice, alliance, and experience. Some define parientes politicos as those who marry cognates. Designation of an individual as politico places him apart from consanguineal kin. Some view as parientes politicos two persons with identical surnames (either mother's or father's) who do not regard themselves as related or who have forgotten the degree of relationship uniting them. In this sense, one does not expect much cooperation resulting from the relationship, though ideally one should receive aid more readily from such a "pariente" than from a mere acquaintance. "At the very least," comments one young informant, "a pariente politico will take your side in a fist-fight." On the other hand, the term may be used to include an outsider within the kinship structure. "If [for example] an aunt dies and her husband re-marries, his new wife is a 'tia politica' "—a political aunt.

Aid and Cooperation

Whereas relations between brothers and other kinsmen are normally close, the degree and type of cooperation exhibited among them must be qualified. Indeed, "qualified independence" best describes the principle that governs relationships between individuals or nuclear family units. This principle derives from an interplay of ideal and actual situations.

Ideally, one should neither solicit nor rely upon the aid of others. Various villagers state that even brothers will not borrow horses and implements from each other but will rather pay for their use, "and the same goes for cousins and other relatives." Again, milpa partners who head their own nuclear families ideally cease cooperation following the burning of the land. The behavioral ideal is reinforced through an explicit "cult of poverty."[1] "Help is not given," says one villager, "because one brother or relative is just as poor as the other." "There's constant want here," says another. "If there's enough to buy shoes, the shoes are bought at the expense of no shirt, and vice versa. If something is bought for the kids, nothing remains for the mothers." "We're all poor here," agrees wealthy Clem Perez. In Pustunich one never says, "I'm going to make a profit" or "I sure hope I make a profit." Rather, one says, "Let's hope I can break even," or, more frequently, "Let's hope I can save myself."

In practice, considerable support is lent to the ideal through the realities of village life. Though far from being as poor as they claim, there does exist a general homogeneity of possession and income among villagers. Brothers, cousins, fathers, sons, and friends seldom differ significantly in source of income or net worth. Only one or two men in Pustunich control facilities or own implements (horse carts, trucks, etc.) not available to others. Such cooperative ventures as milpa partnerships and hunting produce a yield which is more in a 1:1 rather than geometric ratio to total man-hours, thus limiting the absolute advantage of economic cooperation. Even in the communal hunt, he who makes the kill (and seldom do more than 10 percent of huntsmen make a kill on any given outing) receives the major share of it. Furthermore, since little could occur to one portion of a milpa that would not equally damage the other, milpa partners almost inevitably sink or swim together, regardless of how independent they may be in the later milpa stages. Thus seldom, if ever, would any situation arise which would directly challenge the ideal of milpa independence beyond the burning stage.

The Mexican *envidia* (envy) syndrome is but weakly institutionalized in Pustunich. Anyone may actively seek a profit in a host of ventures and many earn considerable portions of their annual cash incomes outside the village or milpa. Excepting, to a degree, the young married male who still resides virilocally, profits belong to the nuclear family head. These profits—aside from gifts to parents and others—are distributed outside the nuclear family only insofar as the family must share household or production expenses with others. One brother or friend rarely gives selfless aid to another's *profitable* undertaking without being "cut in on the deal." Such "deals" include lime making, cardinal catching, tobacco curing, purchase and butchering of beef. It is often the case that in lieu of outright aid, brothers, cousins, or friends are given preference when a hired hand is needed. Thus the younger Belem curandero has permanently hired two of his elder brothers—one to clerk in his store, the other to tend his showplace orange grove south of town. Furthermore, Belem frequently hires the brother-in-law of his store-clerk brother to trek through the bush on herb-quests. This is done as a personal favor to the clerk-brother, who recently married a girl thirty years his junior. By obtaining work for her brother, the clerk satisfies both his bride and the gossips who look unfavorably upon his "cradle-robbing" marriage.

Among lucrative ventures calling for a group of men, lime making is somewhat of an exception. The principals who provide cash for the purchase of stones and payment of labor indeed share equally in the profits. However, it is traditional for lime making to culminate with a large dole of mondongo (tripe stew) as the pyre's flames begin to reach twenty or thirty feet into the night sky. Numbers of men may contribute an hour or less of their time as the work draws to a climax, and still others drop in for the meal without having worked.

Just prior to and during the burning, the profitable (to its sponsors only) lime burning becomes a social event created and capped by the serving of mondongo. Similarly, any nonprofit or profit undertaking, if traditionally capped with a generous dole of food or drink, becomes in part or whole a social event. The lime burning becomes social only toward its climax. House moving, on the other hand, is viewed as a social event from start to finish. From another point of view, any undertaking may serve as a focus for social reunion if it is clearly an undertaking which does not merely save the sponsor a well-established cost. The moving of a frame and thatch house from one site to another is such an undertaking. It has no price. No one would hire labor. The move, which involves several dozen or more men, is always a communal effort, from the removal of side walls to the placing of braces in the new location. It is very difficult work in that once the braces are removed the heavy house must be transported in one nonstop action to the new bracing poles. Always, mondongo or some other rich meal is served at the conclusion.

Roof thatching is an example of noncommunal work. Though easy labor, thatching has an established price. Only brothers, close kin, or close friends will aid one another in repairing roofs without remuneration, though palm-fronds (which in bundles of certain quantity represent a standard peso-value and are often used in lieu of cash) must be supplied by the house-owner.

As all steps in the building of a house have their specific labor-value and involve different specialties such as beam hewing, wall building, jambing, or plastering, houses are not communally built. Cooperation in the building almost never extends beyond fathers, sons, or brothers. Some villagers claim that should a new resident move into Pustunich, communal labor would build his first house. This might be true if the house were of the thatch variety. During the year of observation only one new resident came to Pustunich, and he rented a dwelling. During this same period, four masonry houses were started by village residents, at their own expense. Only one was completed, that of a well-to-do man who contracted with Ticul masons and carpenters at a cost of over 8,000 pesos. The other houses go up bit by bit, as their less well-off owners (sometimes with the help of a father, son, or brother) put in sporadic hours after the day's milpa or cash labor, without the aid of professional artisans if possible. Usually, however, completion of a new dwelling involves an "open-house" at which any villager may stop for a beer or snack. Some such festivities are quite elaborate, often involving the blessings of a priest and full-course dinners for an invited core.

It is usually the case, in times of emergency, that some kinsman or friend can be found to supply medical, nutritional, or financial aid. Should the father of a family be ill or unable to work, or should an individual of a poor household be ill and unable to afford medical care, the matter may be brought up before a town meeting. If an aid effort is undertaken, a committee will be chosen to head an appeal and money will be solicited from townsmen. It must be stressed that such action will not be taken (or if decided upon, will have little positive response) until the village has satisfied itself that all possible avenues of aid have been exhausted. In fact, it is a rare man who could obtain no aid through private means. Assuming for the moment that all potential benefactors of a needy individual are economically equal, aid petitions will first be made to fathers and sons, then sons-in-law, siblings, compadres, collateral kin, and neighbors or close friends. This ordering is not absolute in practice. The extent of an individual's need is the basic factor in choice of a benefactor. Should his need be small, he will approach first those with whom he is close, regardless of their *formal* relationship to him. The greater his need, the smaller the circle of potential benefactors; yet still the ordering of petition follows degree of affect.

Ritual Kinship

It is possible to acquire compadres (ritual co-parents) on five occasions in Pustunich. The classic form is that of baptismal sponsor, and both a godfather and godmother are necessary. Following the ceremony, the child's parents are compadre or comadre to the baptismal sponsors, who in turn are *padrino* and *madrina* (godfather and godmother) to the child. At some time during the child's first year, generally from the sixth month onward, a single ritual sponsor is acquired for the *hetzmek* or sex-role ceremony. A padrino is required for a male child, a madrina for a female. At any time from the third to the tenth year, the child is confirmed in the Catholic Church and a single sponsor of appropriate sex is again required. While most children are baptized and undergo the hetzmek ritual, not all are confirmed. Should a girl's parents have sufficient funds available, they will celebrate her fifteenth birthday (*compleaños*) much the same as a U.S. girl is given a "sweet-sixteen" party. Here, one or two padrinos will be obtained to sponsor the young woman at a church mass. Marriage marks the last occasion upon which a young Pustunicheño obtains a ritual parent (in this case both padrino and madrina) and the last upon which the child's own parents obtain compadres. Of these five occasions, only the hetzmek occurs outside of the church, and only the marriage sponsors are chosen by the sponsored individual.

Baptismal sponsors are by far the most important to both the sponsored and their parents. The godparent-godchild bond is nominally life-long. It binds the child and his ritual parents in an ideally reciprocal relationship. The padrinos are expected to raise the child and make a "good Christian" of him should his own parents die. The padrino is a stern yet understanding pseudoparent to whom one may go for advice and aid. When the padrino or madrina meets the godchild on the street or comes to visit, it is expected that a small gift will be given the child—a sweet, a toy, or perhaps a *toston* (fifty centavos).

Between baptismal compadres there exists an ideal bond of loyalty and reciprocity. A compadre should be a person of respect and confidence. Respect is almost a universal quality desired of a compadre in Latin America. It refers mainly to the compadre's behavior outside the ritual kinship context, although implicit in respect is fulfillment of reciprocal obligation. A compadre with respect does not become drunk or boisterous, make a fool of himself, or acquire a bad reputation. Says one villager, "Better to have one 'docile' compadre who doesn't drink or fool around with women than a bunch who do. How can you respect them?" This same informant has never been asked to stand as padrino. "I think it's because I'm not religiously or civilly married to my wife," he muses. Actually they have been "married" for over fifteen years and have four children. The state of his marriage is less important than the reputation for untrustworthiness which he has acquired.

The pragmatic Pustunicheños refer to confidence in the context of confidence in a compadre's willingness to give aid.

The utility of ritual kinship as both horizontal and vertical security and solidarity mechanisms has been described by Foster, Paul, Mintz and Wolf, Ishino, Press, and others.[2] The operation of this mechanism is not simple, however. Vertically speaking, those who would make socially and/or economically advantageous compadres for less well-off persons receive numerous invitations to stand as spiritual sponsor to the children of poorer, less advantageously placed, or dependent persons. The curandero Torcuato Belem claims to have over 1,000 of all five compadre types. The more compadres an individual has, however, the less able he is to fully accommodate the demands of each. Furthermore, the greater the economic or social distance between compadres, the more reluctant the poorer is to approach the richer. The bulk of compadre reciprocity and interaction thus occurs within the context of horizontal or near-horizontal bonds. Vertical bonds are not expected to yield high returns over the long run. In reality, one can expect nothing more than a "15 percent discount" or aid ''at cost'' from a more advantageously placed compadre—whether it be in time or money. Thus, Humberto Be states that he buys all of his corn from a Ticul merchant at only $37 per carga, though the price to the public is $45. The merchant's younger brother and partner is Humberto's compadre. Gilberto Orozco, one of the town's poorest men, receives for his son every year (on the boy's birthday) used clothing from his wealthy compadre, Dr. Asuncion Peralta of Oxkutzkab. Gilberto receives far more meaningful aid from his own father, who is also padrino of Gilberto's eldest boy.

One's own parents, in Pustunich, are the preferred godparents of one's children. Most Pustunicheños ask parents to sponsor the baptism of their first child. There is no clearcut preference for husband's or wife's parents. One villager, with ten children, has sought only one compadre—his own father-in-law—who has now served ten times. ''This way,'' he explains, ''we can't say anything bad to each other. No fights. No words. Otherwise, it's possible.''

Next to parents, uncles and brothers (plus their wives) are preferred compadres. Approximately half of all villagers go no further than close kinsmen for their children's padrinos and madrinas and have sought no compadres from outside the village. Overall, solidarity rather than instrumental criteria are clearly emphasized.

Roughly 95 percent of the compadres of young men in their twenties are parents, brothers, or close affines. At this point, most young men are still residing virilocally and have little social prestige. With the third or fourth child, and as the thirty- or thirty-five-year-old villager extends his social and economic contacts (and as his concept of ''family'' shrinks), there is a tendency to seek nonrelated individuals as baptismal sponsors.

While the compadre relationship may serve as a social and economic security mechanism, there is no overall manifestation of a tendency to maximize the number of compadres or utilize those bonds to the full potential. In Pustunich, one finds no maximization of sponsor-obtaining occasions as in Moche[3] or complex system of *compadrazgo* as in Pascua.[4] If Pustunicheños expect less from compadres than might be expected from the ''ideal'' Latin American bond, it is primarily because of the frequent identity of kinsman (usually father) with compadre. One interacts with one's father—and expects aid from him—as *father*, not as compadre. The initial compadre bonds of most Pustunicheños are established to honor the ritual sponsor rather than foment reciprocal security ties. It is likely that such a preference reflects an earlier colonial tradition. In isolated X-cacal territory (Quintana Roo), Villa Rojas reports that parents are virtually prescribed as godparents for one's children and that it is thought sinful if different godparents are chosen for subsequent offspring.[5] Common in Pustunich are statements such as: ''Compadres can't really help you, because they're as poor as you are.'' Or, ''Compadres don't help one another. If you need help, go to a friend or relative first, because it's a bad thing if a compadre refused you—a shame for him and for you.'' Both statements reflect a lack of reliance upon compadres as major sources of aid.

Even where compadres were chosen for their relative social and/or economic position, there is no compulsion to maximize the number of such links. A poor spinster with three illegitimate children sought one padrino only for her offspring. ''We asked him three times because he treats us well. If he has a turkey, he give us. Why change?'' A young man of twenty-nine has but one compadre—his father-in-law. When asked if he might solicit others for future children, he replied: ''Well, as long as my father-in-law doesn't deny me, we'll stick with him. Anyway, the more compadres you have, the more opportunity for bad words, lack of respect and the denial of requests.''

Though maximization of compadre links is not a goal of Pustunicheños, there is a tendency for poorer individuals to seek out more padrinos for their children than the more well-to-do. Those at the bottom of the economic range average 0.4 compadres (padrinos) per child, while those near the top average less than 0.2, or one padrino for every five children.

Those who have nonvillage compadres, rather than being poorer individuals anxious to secure favor or aid from wealthier outsiders, are rather generally better-off economically or more politically active than their fellows. Compadres are useful only insofar as they are available when needed. Furthermore, the more frequent the contact between compadres, the more likely is the creation of a strong bond. To a poor, little-traveled villager, outsiders are not convenient in cases of emergency. Those who have more outside compadres tend to engage in various economic undertakings which make outside contacts convenient. Hatmakers and former comisarios are typical of those with relatively more outside compadres than others.

Compadre bonds in Pustunich are neither exploited nor ignored. Those who can utilize them do. Because close kin tend to monopolize compadre groupings of most individuals, compadre identity is subservient to kinship identity. Both because of this and the desire not to embarrass or be embarrassed by refusing a compadre or his refusing you, the ideals of compadrazgo are seldom put to the test. The overall ideal of independence further tempers the relationship, and villagers explicitly refuse to impute great importance to it. Where aid does enter into the bond, it is more often through its vertical than horizontal extension, and the direction of favors is heavily loaded toward the compadre of lower status. Within the village, bonds are almost wholly horizontal and are viewed as such regardless of the wealth of the compadres involved. Storekeeper Belem "favors" his compadres by soliciting them before others for work on his private fields near the village. At the same time he exploits them in return by paying minimum or, on occasion, substandard wages. Overall, if extension and utilization of compadre ties can be viewed as an indicator of socioeconomic *in*security, then Pustunich is a secure community.

Village Interaction

As Pustunich is small and major paths are few, most villagers see most others at least once a week. Village men enjoy animated conversation, and a majority spend at least several minutes daily in casual conversation groups. Though there are four major conversing-spots in or near the plaza, these do not fill up until after the dinner hour. Rarely do groupings larger than six men occur. During a three-month period in which records of conversation groups were taken, most village men were seen numerous times in conversation with others. Though cliques of close friends exist, there is considerable flexibility in the choice of conversation-mates. Taking as an example ten separate observations of a dozen different men, each was seen talking to from fifteen to twenty other men, or an average of two "new faces" each time he conversed. Most conversation groups begin with two or three men and grow as others wander by and join them.

No meaningful discrimination (by name, wealth, or dress) of conversants is to be seen, aside from age-division. Rarely do unmarried boys form part of a grouping which consists of more than three adults. Furthermore, younger men prefer to squat on the ground as they converse. Older men find this position uncomfortable, and thus the group sitting on the ledges of the plaza water house tends to be elderly. The town's wealthiest men seldom find time to join in conversation with others, away from their places of business. Villagers see no reason to converse with kinsmen more often than nonkinsmen, merely on the basis of kinship alone. If two brothers reside at some distance from one another, no special effort will be made to seek one another out for trivial conversation or gossip unless the two happen to have some immediate, mutual concern. Close kin *do* tend, however, to have more specific interests in common at any given time (milpa, parents' or grandparents' welfare or health, sisters' or cousins' situation). Thus they tend to meet with one another relatively more frequently than they meet with others for specific purposes.

While close affines, cousins, and others are expected to be intimate and friendly, residence, history of the relationship in the past, and present state of interaction may greatly modify actual behavior. Outside of the families of orientation and procreation, it must be stressed that friendship and solidarity *may* correspond with kinship.

There are few social occasions in Pustunich which demand a limited number of specified guests. Small family or friendly dinners are exceptions and invitations are casual, with preparations leisurely. For larger events such as wedding parties, compleaños, rosarios, or house warmings, it is understood that while no one will be denied entrance or refreshments, the invitation is not general. Invitations are issued verbally to friends and friendly kinsmen, with the understanding that others may attend. Noninvitees who show up are generally those with whom the host is on good terms at the moment, and always more attend than were personally invited. At a large event, generally sponsored by one of the more well-to-do, perhaps a quarter of village adults will drop in over the course of an evening. Following the nuptials of the younger son of Clem Perez, over 200 children arrived singly or in small groups to receive a sliver of wedding cake.

As parties and rosarios are not infrequent (the Pro-Electrification Committee also sponsors frequent dances, basketball games, etc.), and as weekly movies, radio shows, and trips to Ticul or Oxkutzkab are readily and cheaply available, private parties and occasions of sponsored entertainment do not take on a value of "scarce" commodity. Pustunich is not a dull town. As much for this as for personal reasons, a single event will never have village-wide attendance. If Juan Puc feels that he would perhaps be "crashing" if he went to Garcia's novena, he knows that there will be plenty more to which he can go with complete ease. Garcia, for his part, will turn no one away and will send out, if necessary (and if funds are available), for additional refreshments. There are, indeed, perhaps a half-dozen men who are very popular companions and who command considerable informal respect. When these individuals or their spouses prepare a party or rosario, attendance is always large and few in the village would feel unwelcome.

Nonkinship interrelationships of relative stability tend to result from proximity or common activity rather than other, more intrinsic identification characteristics capable of developing an "us-them" orientation. Co-participants in the Maya harvest ritual tend to be neighbors. Storekeepers tend to be patronized by people who live close by, and their patronage is maintained by the granting of credit. As the four stores have ice coolers of beer and soft drinks, they are natural congregation places, and each store owner attracts a more or less constant core of individuals who spend considerable time lounging and conversing. Perhaps the one exception to the lack of important cliques is the present mayor-shopkeeper and a handful of ex-mayors and village officials (certainly not all available past officials). They spend much time together grumbling and gesticulating. When possible, they foster rumors detrimental to the school teacher.

Within the past dozen years, however, a number of unprecedented avenues for group formation and interaction have been developing. Committees and baseball involve far larger permanent groupings for common purpose than any past activities. In this lack of precedent the new activities do not compete, either conceptually or in terms of time and personnel, with "traditional" interactive foci.

It is nonetheless possible to see a nascent in-group identification attaching itself to participation in team and committee and extending beyond concerns immediately related to sport or civic matters. The baseball team makes a collective gala entrance to the dance floor at Carnival time. Such group behavior, like the team itself, is un-precedented. Team members, it will be recalled, are young, flushed with sports success, and are among the most widely traveled of villagers. They are popular, and insofar as many are married and are fathers they are full members of the "adult" community. As the coach is also the innovative local school teacher, players are among the most active in committee and communal work. With increasing frequency, the teacher is effectively utilizing the team for political action, propagandizing projects and town office candidates. (See Chapter 9.) The team thus represents a developing lobby and political party, as well as a permanent and influential core of innovatively receptive milperos.

A further source of concentrated sentiment lies in the core of continuously active committee members and volunteers for teacher-sponsored communal projects. Here, a growing self-identity as "cooperators" (as opposed to "noncooperators") is setting them apart from villagers who prefer to be "left alone." Though still far from faction-forming in scope, antipathy is beginning to extend beyond the meeting room.

Pustunicheños view participation in village affairs in much the same way as they view dyadic interaction. This embraces an attitude of "is it convenient for me?" with "what's in it for me?" implicit. A correlative factor is the identity of the others who may be participating in the event.

There is no single social, economic, or religious occasion on which all or nearly all villagers cooperate or in which most participate. While almost all village men yearly participate in some group event (novena, Maya ritual, communal project), no single one involves a simple majority of the eligible, available adults.

While in no way antagonistic toward benefits which others may gain through hard work, Pustunicheños tend to balk at donating their own labor to projects that produce proportionally more result for others. Large-scale cooperative efforts are still quite new (see Chapter 9) and many villagers still distrust such village-directed action. They further refuse to invest more time or cash at present for substantial savings later, and some still refuse to understand that the more who share in the cost of a venture, the less the cost to each.

Typical of these various attitudes is the reaction of Pustunich to the potable water system installed some five years ago with state aid. Prior to the installation of a motorized pump and corner hydrants, villagers hauled water from individual solar wells up to twenty-five meters in depth. Only a few had windmills or winches. The installation involved five hydrants set at corners within a two-block radius of the town square and pumphouse. The system, which included an elaborate, terraced, white-stuccoed pumphouse with steps and built-in planter boxes, was inaugurated with much fanfare. Forty-eight families today use the water-pump system and together form the "Potable Water Association." Each member pays $3 monthly for the right to use the hydrants; the funds pay for gasoline, some slight maintenance, and the salary of a part-time pump attendant. As anyone in Pustunich with knowledge of motor maintenance owns a vehicle and is thus wealthy or well-off and would *not* work for wages, the pump attendant generally knows little about motor care. Breakdowns are frequent.

Initially, some thirty family heads cooperated in laying the pipeline, and all lived within the hydrant area or close to it. There was grumbling, later, when additional families, who lived within the area but had not cooperated in laying the pipe, requested membership. It was only with difficulty that the teacher convinced the old members that monthly costs for all would decrease if the new petitioners were allowed to join. The new group was accepted, though many old users grumbled that "they just sat around to see if the thing would work and when they saw it did, and that we had done all the labor, they now want in with none of the responsibility."

Still, a number of families within the hydrant-area and most who lived adjacent to or outside of it refused to join. Most stated that it was inconvenient to walk a block or two for water. Some two years following the installation, however, water delivery was terminated daily at 6:00 P.M. as it was discovered that many found it was not too inconvenient to walk to the hydrants after dark for surreptitious pail filling.

From time to time, the Potable Water Association has found it necessary to close the pump entirely when the number of users in arrears on monthly payments falls above twenty or twenty-five (that is, 50 percent). As payment for pumped water goes, Pustunich is inexpensive (Dzan charges its users $7 monthly). Whenever such a shutdown occurred, those who had paid grumbled that the "many shouldn't suffer from the laxity of a few," while those in arrears complained of the high cost of water. Each such shutdown has inevitably meant the loss of one or two members in arrears and one or two who had paid on time.

Excerpt from field notes, November 1963:

The town pump broke down again and a $1,000 repair job is needed. This is the fourth breakdown in a year and a half, the others costing from $150 to $600, and the expense was split among water users. But $1,000 is apparently another thing. Many want to back out, as repairing it means a $25 assessment from each family.

A meeting was held, and only thirty of the forty-eight consented (after brow-beating from the teacher, Alonso) to do their part. Alonso estimates that eventually, forty will probably agree to pay up. In the meantime, the new machine parts have been ordered and those who signed up will pay their shares in two or three weekly installments. Alonso is bitter over the water problem. He feels that as the people are getting it so cheaply anyhow, they *can* afford to put in their shares for fixing the pump. Some who *haven't* signed up again even have tubing (at considerable expense) connected right into their houses!

In July and August of 1964, the teacher solicited the Community Development Foundation for aid in extending the tubing and hydrants so as to include even more blocks. The $1,000 breakdown had lowered the number of original users to only thirty-two, and thirty new users worked at dynamiting canals and laying pipe.

Excerpt from field notes, August 3, 1964:

Tonight there was another assembly about potable water. The town owes $240 before the remaining parts of the new, extended tubing system can be delivered. Present at the meeting was a hydraulic engineer from Oxkutzkab. He suggested that by charging the new users only $8 apiece, the $240 could be raised easily. The new users balked, claiming that they had worked hard enough laying the pipe. They countered with a suggestion that *all* of the users—both old and new—should split the cost. The old users in turn balked at this, saying that the new pipe wasn't for them and that they'd paid enough in the past years just keeping the system going. The matter was solved when the comisario suggested that the town sell surplus U.S. government foodstuffs (received after the drought of last summer). Only two raised points as to the illegality of this move. All left happily.

Individually, Pustunicheños are slow to give of their time and money to village projects. The average villager will seldom donate time unless he knows that others will do likewise. For the extension of the new potable water tubing, those who would directly benefit and who had pledged labor did not appear with picks until the teacher and butcher (who both lived in the extension area) began work on their portions. (See Chapter 9.) Those with more money give proportionally less than their poorer fellows. Each year at fiesta time, the storekeeper-mayor sells 140 cases of soft drinks and does not donate a cent to the Betterment Committee. During the year of study, the Pro-Electrification Committee obtained a ruling from Ticul limiting the quantity of soda that the mayor could sell, so that the committee itself could set up a concession and make some profit. The mayor swiftly retaliated by charging the town for use of his truck during fiesta preparations—a service which he had previously donated.

Typical of the attitude of the wealthy toward town projects is that of the rich storekeeper Clem Perez toward electrification of the town by the state government. He is against it. It would mean loss of a lucrative generator and battery-rental business. Nevertheless, public opinion forced him to make a donation toward the $15,000 required by the state for electrification. Don Clem pledged $500—but insisted that it be paid at $30 monthly.

Pustunicheños are not necessarily suspicious of cooperative labor or public projects. Indeed, fagina and guardia are known elements of the fairly recent past. Fagina, however, has been voluntary since the socialist Yucatec government some forty years ago effectively ended the power of the hacienda and plantation and attempted to foster the growth of local electorates. Today, failure to participate in village-level projects may elicit grumbling from those who do donate their time—but little else. There are no fines or cash levies in lieu of labor. Eligibility for, and participation in, fagina are no longer criteria of village membership. Participation today is desirable but not required. The teacher constantly complains that noncooperation is a direct blow against the town. Communal projects themselves have undergone transition. Earlier faginal duties were predominantly maintenance-oriented; today's projects explicitly involve "progress" and "growth." The committees of betterment and electrification constantly require cooperation and donations for unprecedented communal works.

Pustunicheños, it must be stressed, do identify with the town's image. They have nothing against a view of the pueblo as progressive and modern. Modernity is a general notion, however, and the image of modernity need be no more than a facade.

The state government itself fosters the importance of image over substance. The town's central well is old and its water, like water in all village wells, is contaminated with amoeba and other microorganisms. The state government could more cheaply have drilled a new deep well down to the clean water level and topped it with a simple functional pump house. Instead it chose to put a motor over the existing well and house the motor and pump in an ostentatious round edifice of stucco tiers, built-in flower boxes, and broad curved stairs. The highly visible plaza pumphouse is now a source of village pride. It is therefore easier to attract volunteer labor for projects of "symbolic" or seminal importance than for subsequent expansion or maintenance. Far more men cooperated in building the showpiece pumphouse than joined the Water Association later. Far more presently cooperate in fund raising and plaza post-hole digging for the anticipated electric line from Merida than will eventually aid in extending lines down the side streets or actually bring electricity into their own homes. The Pustunicheño is at ease with his life-style and the image of his village. Once he has paid lip service to the water pipes and electric poles of modernity, he loses interest. Those who continue to "cooperate" invariably do so for personal advantage rather than for the joy of interaction or the greater village good.

NOTES

1. See Eric R. Wolf, "Types of Latin American Peasantry: A Preliminary Discussion." *American Anthropologist* 57 (1955): 452-471.

2. George M. Foster, "Cofradia and Compadrazgo in Spain and Spanish America." *Southwestern Journal of Anthropology* 9 (1953): 1-28. Benjamin D. Paul, Ritual Kinship (unpublished Ph.D. dissertation, Department of Anthropology, University of Chicago, 1942). Sidney Mintz and Eric R. Wolf, "Ritual Co-Parenthood." *Southwestern Journal of Anthropology* 6 (1950): 341-368. Iwao Ishino, "The Oyabun-Kobun: A Japanese Ritual Kinship Institution." *American Anthropologist* 55 (1953): 695-707. Irwin Press, "The Incidence of Compadrazgo Among Puerto Ricans in Chicago." *Social and Economic Studies* 12 (1963): 475-480.

3. John Gillin, *Moche: A Peruvian Coastal Community* (Washington: Smithsonian Institution, Institute of Social Anthropology, Publication #3, 1947).

4. E. H. Spicer, *Pascua, A Yaqui Village in Arizona* (Chicago: University of Chicago Press, 1940).

5. Alfonso Villa Rojas, *The Maya of East Central Quintana Roo* (Washington: Carnegie Institute of Washington Publication No. 559, 1945).

9

Political Organization

The Official Setup

As a legally constituted pueblo, Pustunich has maintained the following offices since the Revolution: comisario (mayor); secretary; treasurer; vocal. All officials serve for three-year periods and cannot be reelected. Officials ideally are elected by popular vote.

As an ejidal community, Pustunich has also maintained an ejidal comisario and ejidal treasurer. As a town within the federal jurisdiction, Pustunich also has a "president" who presides over the *liga* (federal voting body) within the town. Both liga and ejidal officials are federal representatives, responsible directly to federal government offices in nearby Ticul. These local and federal officials complete the roster of "required" personnel.

Traditionally, the comisario has not been freely elected. Rather, the president of Ticul has had the tacit perquisite of naming the comisarios in his *municipio* (county). Should more than one individual have aspired to village office, their backers attempted to gain favor with the president through gifts, visits, and favors. On election night, the president appeared in town as the official presiding election officer. Following nomination of the chosen candidate, he immediately closed the nominations. On occasion, the backers of the chosen candidate encouraged a generally unpopular villager to run against their man, to provide an appearance of democratic procedure.

Today, as in the past, it is preferred that the comisario be a man who will spend most of his time in town, so as to handle any matters that might arise. As much for this as for reasons of general prestige and courtship of the municipal president, comisarios have tended to be men of greater wealth than most, with businesses or interests that require much time spent in the village. However, there have been comisarios of the pure milpero category.

Favoritism and self-enrichment are expected of the comisario. Looking back fifteen years, older villagers recount incident after incident of graft and corruption.

The functions of the comisario have been limited to titular representation of the village, granting of permissions for use of village resources, and adjudication of minor quarrels. Any major litigations or crimes have gone directly before the district court in Ticul. The comisario has not been expected to innovate or lead the village in public works with frequency. Nor has he been an innovator, except in cases of necessary maintenance or emergency repair.

Two field note excerpts suggest the range of the comisario's judicial capacity (also see Chapter 5):

November 18, 1963: Tonight, Avila, the comisario, held a "Justicia," and gave permission for two men to construct a new street. The two are brothers-in-law sharing one solar. One claimed that cattle constantly entered the solar. He suggested that two meters be lopped off his, and two meters off his brother-in-law's section, down the middle of the solar, so as to create a street which would then be walled with stones. This suggestion was accepted, and they came to Avila for approval. He gave it. Discussion was lively, and entirely in Maya.

After the justicia, I asked Avila about his last major case. This occurred several months ago when two young Ticulenos stole some cattle in Pustunich. They were apprehended and thrown into the Pustunich jail for several hours. They were subsequently fined by Avila and released. Fines generally involve labor for the town or "donation" by the defendant of lime and other building materials for town use.

May 31: There was a novena this evening followed by a dance in front of Avila's store, to mark the end of the Month of Mary. During the dance, two boys fought and one hit the other in the stomach. The victim fell down, gasping for air. Avila placed the fourteen-year-old aggressor in jail for several minutes while the fathers were sent for. Both boys were punished by being given the chore of digging ten cargas each of sascab. Avila says that if one of the fathers had told his son not to comply he would have locked *him* up on the spot for obstructing justice and fined *him* twenty-five cargas. Luckily, both fathers agreed to the mutual punishment. Avila says he made the punishment severe for the following reason: several days ago a few men were chasing a horse in the plaza. Upon galloping over the concrete basketball court, the horse stumbled. It struck its head and immediately died. A hard fall, reasoned Avila, could have killed one of the boys too. And if this had happened while Avila "just stood around watching," the father of the dead boy could blame him—" and rightly, too." So, he stopped the fight (which was on the same concrete) and sentenced the boys.

The comisario and his staff have figured little in the lives of the average villager. Ejidal land rights have been negotiated directly with the ejidal representative. As most can write, and as the town secretary has usually been no more literate than others, letters have been personal matters. All business and liquor permits, bicycle licenses, and notarizations have been obtained from the proper state or federal offices in Ticul. Even in cases of disagreement between two villagers, consultation with the comisario has not been mandatory. A justice of the peace is available in Ticul, and only where two litigants agree to accept the comisario's arbitration has he been consulted on any matter. This is not to state that many comisarios have been men of low prestige, whose opinions were of little value. To the contrary. In all cases, men of considerable popularity have been put forth as candidates. It has always been the personality of the man, however, rather than the office, which subsequently dictated the extent of his influence or the frequency of his consultations.

In the past, without a strong formal leadership, it was difficult to organize Pustunicheños for communal works. Since the revolution, fagina had become less frequent and essentially voluntary in nature. In no instance were all villagers involved in any single project, and frequent truancies would create little more than grumbles. *Guardia* (the institution of maintaining a rotating group of men in town for police, repair, and messenger duty) had long since been abandoned.

Few in Pustunich took an active interest in village improvement or current affairs, and these few represented small factions surrounding or supporting past, present, or potential comisarios. Today, villagers compare the situation of fifteen and twenty years ago to the present state of affairs in nearby Dzan. "There is no unification of purpose in Dzan," comments the present school teacher. "At present, Dzan is trying to roof the comisaria, fix the plaza, fix the school and improve the road to Ticul. Each project has its own backers and each is underway but incomplete. There's the mayor and his group versus the teacher and his group versus others versus others."

The Teachers: A New Type of Village Role

Since the earliest recorded dealings between Pustunich and Ticul (in 1588), Pustunich has been an independent entity. Pustunich is not a suburb of Ticul, regardless of proximity and political dominance. "Political dominance" is relative. A generation ago Ticul named Pustunich comisarios, paid their $30 monthly salary, and contributed $120 monthly for maintenance of a village policeman. Yet beyond this, Pustunich had to provide all other services and monies. Ticul took little interest in Pustunich's internal affairs beyond the very personal dealings that affected the pockets of comisario and president. The everyday decisions regarding policing, maintenance, minor quarrels, fiestas, fines, and permissions were overwhemingly village-autonomous.

The major intrusion into Pustunich affairs was related to the famous August Fiesta in honor of the village patroness, the Virgin Assumption. Though totally planned and managed by Pustunich, the municipal president each year confiscated the entire proceeds of the public events of the fiesta, claiming that "Pustunich was not yet ready to manage its own affairs." All villagers agree that the comisario would receive a kickback from these confiscated funds, perhaps as high as 20 percent. Thus the village government was denied its major potential source of income. Villagers neither expected nor received many benefits from Pustunich as a corporate political entity. Pustunich, to them, was a cultural entity, giving to each dweller a host of socioeconomic identities, a choice of wives or husbands, and the use of lands for the making of milpa. Politics were suspect and unimportant. Most prestige was claimed by good hunters, hard-working individuals, and those with henequen lands and successful businesses. The few teachers in Pustunich were federal appointees from other Mexican states or other areas of Yucatan who lived in the "more civilized" Ticul and left the village soon after school hours each day. Aside from organizing a "Fathers of the Family" committee for the school, as required by the federal school board, they did not lead, nor were they expected to.

One of the teachers had seen promise in a local boy, Carlos Perez. Perez' father was a successful milpero with five strapping sons, ranging in age from fifteen to twenty-five, upon whom he could count for milpa aid. The elder Perez' own father, a robust man of sixty, was also able to put in a full day's work. Carlos' great-grandfather, still able to gather firewood and undertake light harvesting at almost eighty years, was an additional help.

A public high school had been constructed in Ticul. The Pustunich teacher persuaded both Carlos and his father that it would be to the boy's advantage to continue his schooling. The father was willing—and perhaps more important, able—to part with Carlos' economic contribution, and so the boy went on with his studies. Before he had completed his secondary schooling, a federal normal school was opened in the southeastern portion of the state. Carlos, who had begun wearing catrin clothing in high school, went to the normal school as a full-time catrin dresser. Upon receiving his degree, he interned for several years in small towns around the state. As a federal teacher, he was essentially under control of the government with respect to assignment. Following his internship, he petitioned the federal school board for permission to teach in Pustunich. As the request for a small-village post was unusual (the majority petitioned for city or large-town posts), his request was granted. He returned to Pustunich in 1954, married an old sweetheart from another well-to-do milpero family, and settled down in his father's solar.

What villagers initially saw in Perez was a unique combination of qualities. He was a teacher, and thus learned, the first professional in the town's history. It was with pride that Pustunicheños addressed him fondly as "Prof." He represented the federal government. He spoke fluent, florid Spanish with no tell-tale Maya inflection. He always dressed as a catrin, wore shoes and socks, and owned a suit and several ties. No other male in Pustunich was a full-time catrin. Perez was worldly; he knew foreign customs and the names of many foreign places. His wife prepared pancakes for an occasional breakfast. Like the doctor in Ticul (though at no cost) he dispensed penicillin injections and medicines. For a wage-earning villager he earned an unprecedented income. He talked of betterment and change and could rattle off the many heroes and goals of the Revolution.

On the other hand, Perez was still the same boy who had once labored in the milpa with his father and brothers. Indeed, on occasion, he would still help the family with harvest needs. He had numerous cousins and uncles in the village, all of whom were milperos and mestizos in dress. He still spoke a good Maya and knew the terms of address. His own father was one of only two conservative old men in Pustunich who still wore the Indian apron, an item of dress more common today in the isolated interior of Quintana Roo. His wife, too, was a native Pustunicheña of well-to-do conservative family. Perez actually lived in Pustunich, as no other teacher had done before him. In sum, he was ambiguous: neither a familiar type of insider, nor the usual outsider.

Pustunich at first gave Carlos Perez a unanimously enthusiastic reception. School children reported to their parents that he knew as much as, and probably more than, any other teacher. It was not long after his arrival that Perez suggested the village reroof the ramshackle schoolhouse. It was a novel, though not unreasonable request, considering that the school and its new teacher were still a focal point of village conversation. Parents of school and postschool children volunteered their labor. Shortly thereafter, the teacher raised the necessity of latrines in the school yard and stressed the need for sanitary facilities handy to the younger grades. Again response was quick.

Some months later, at a regular town meeting called by the mayor, Carlos suggested that the town clean up and weed the plaza. As the annual fiesta was still months off, the suggestion, unrelated to the school, was viewed as more novel than any of the teacher's preceding ideas. Several dozen villagers volunteered their labor. As both school and plaza did look better following the communal labor, many also donated time when the teacher successfully applied for state economic aid for construction of another school building and a schoolyard stage. He subsequently formed several committees ("Fathers of the Family," "Mothers of the Family") whose function was the planning of school programs and application of pressure on parents who frequently kept children out of school. However, it was not long before these committees began discussions concerning nonschool projects, the town's future, and the role villagers could play in it.

Up to this point the mayor, his clique of cronies and several ex-mayors, and the majority of townspeople viewed the teacher in a disinterested, though not negative, manner. Though response to any one of the teacher's projects had never involved more than several dozens of villagers, this in itself was innovative and certainly no less of a response than ever greeted a sporadic faginal maintenance project of past mayors. With the formation of the "Fathers" and "Mothers" committees, however, the mayor and his close group of perhaps a half dozen began to take another look at the teacher. The first open rupture occurred when Perez, in a most surprising move, petitioned the state government for Pustunich's right to retain the proceeds of its own annual fiesta. Perez tells what followed:

> True liberty came to Pustunich only after I came—in 1955. At the same time, the last cacique was president of Ticul. So when I petitioned for permission to keep the fiesta profits, the presidente accused me of being a bad influence—of inciting the people to rebellion against society and authority. Well, my friends said I should bring a lawyer to the trial, but I said no. I was prepared to defend myself. I had been taught in normal school that a teacher must aid the community—not ask if every little thing was "good" for the community. A school is a coordinating agency, for leading the pueblo to betterment. Well, luckily, the head of justice for the State was *my* old normal school prof! I won the case.

> Before me, the town was very quiet and hard working, but afraid of authority. It didn't participate in any outside politics. It knew nothing of world affairs. Only what went on in the town itself was of importance to the people.

> Well, *I* was the first professional man Pustunich ever produced! Not another teacher, or engineer or what have you in *all* its history. *I* did it!

With the fiesta monies (often in excess of $4,000), more improvements could be planned, and projects came with increasing frequency. Perez then formed a Committee of Civic, Moral, and Material Betterment to guard and spend the substantial fiesta monies that constituted a bonanza increment to town funds. With these funds, and with materials obtained through further applications to the state, Perez asked villagers to construct a cement basketball court-dance floor in a corner of the plaza. Shortly thereafter, he proposed a project for modernizing the town's water supply by providing a motorized pump for the plaza well. Each such project was allocated to a special committee of volunteers that appointed its own officers (with suggestions from the teacher). Funds were allocated by the increasingly powerful Betterment Committee. More projects, now, were directed toward nonschool than school-oriented "needs." Far more open meetings were now being called by Perez than by the mayor.

Though the notion of committees was new and associated with larger, more modern towns, few Pustunicheños were sure that the teacher did not have the "right" to introduce them. Furthermore, as Perez did not occupy a role of traditional distrust, there arose no consensus as to the legitimacy of his leadership or motives. The overall ambiguity of the teacher's behavior is visible in the variety of ways in which he was viewed. A minority tended to see him as operating within traditional limits of power, and these individuals consistently fostered or abetted rumors of how the teacher pocketed immense sums from his many projects. Few in this group donated labor for Perez' projects. Others embraced this view, considering it a natural thing for those in positions of leadership, yet tempered it with statements such as: "So long as he gets improvements done, I don't care if he makes a little on the side. After all, his time's worth something." Still others refused to accept any view but that of the teacher as a purely apolitical, selfless, altruistic force, paving the way toward village fame, betterment, modernization. The mayor and his clique, on the other hand, refused to legitimize Carlos Perez' position of leadership by complaining of his abuse of it. Rather, they viewed Carlos as a dishonest upstart, encroaching upon traditional duties of the mayor's office.

As mayors traditionally called few public meetings, the mayor himself called but few. More and more, the maintenance or repair that might have constituted a reason for mayoral action was anticipated by the teacher who held his own meetings. Such assemblies soon became weekly occurrences, announced by the bell at the village office.

Through Perez' influence, and largely because of his example, his wife's younger brother went on to high and normal schools and, after several years of apprenticeship, returned to teach in the village school. Like his older brother-in-law, the new teacher was from a very conservative mestizo family of means. He, too, had three strong brothers to help the father with milpa labor. The father had once been a wealthier man, and the prestige of having a professor as son was not the least of the factors that influenced his decision.

Alonso Gomez, the younger teacher, also combined a number of "inside" and "outside" characteristics. He returned to Pustunich with a catrin wife from a larger town. It was known that she used a diaphragm and contraceptive jelly so as not to have children. From time to time he received leftist literature in the mails. Gomez moved into a thatched hut in a corner of his father's large, plaza-fronting lot.

Between them, Perez and Gomez could boast of having two of the most conservative peasant fathers in Pustunich. Both parents wore the apron which even then was out of style in all but the most conservative and isolated areas of Yucatan. Both fathers were milperos of considerable acreage. Both had raised many strong sons to the milpa. Both were popular, respected men who had each served time as village comisario and left office with little bad feelings behind them. Both actively participated in Maya ritual and were also known as *muy catolico*. Their sons reaped the benefits of their traditional family backgrounds. While unique professionals, they were at the same time unquestionably Pustunich boys. Moreover, the leadership which they provided was nonpolitical, thus avoiding the onus of occupying traditional foci of distrust.[1]

Together, the teachers fomented project upon project. Soon, no village meeting was conducted without them, as indeed without their projects there would have been little reason for meeting. The comisario's presence was unnecessary, his permission or approval neither sought nor required, and he and his clique increasingly began to boycott town meetings.

When Perez had been a teacher in Pustunich for six years, he was appointed to the federal school board of Yucatan. He was one of only twelve men between federal teachers and the state's school chief. (There was also a separate Yucatan State School Board, with separate state normal school.) The position resulted from his contacts in Merida, his enviable record in Pustunich, and the fact of his representing a small, peasant village. Not least important were his polished manners and "smooth" Spanish. He moved to Merida with the pride of his pueblo accompanying him. His younger brother-in-law, Gomez, became head of the school.

The New System Gains Strength

Gomez broadened the base of outside aid by applying to federal and private as well as state agencies. The motorized well was renovated and pipes were laid to extend water beyond the plaza. A down payment and application were made for town electrification. The Community Development Foundation in Merida was contacted and aid obtained for the building of latrines. Streets were leveled, and a Monument to the Republic was raised. A new economic focus appeared—irrigated citrus groves—as a direct result of Gomez' application to the federal government. "Potable Water," "Pro-Electrification," "Infant Protection," "Fiesta Organization," "Sports," and a host of other committees appeared.

The degree of competition between the growing committee system and traditional politics was unclear. True, the new system controlled a body of largely unprecedented activities and expenditures. While mayors rarely or never called regular meetings and led the village in innovative, rather than merely maintenance, projects, there was no overall consensus as to whether the motorized central water supply, basketball court, electrification, etc., should not really have been under control of the mayor and town treasurer. Similarly, the treasurer had never been responsible for fiesta income in that Ticul expropriated it. Now that Pustunich did control these funds, it was unclear as to whether the Betterment Committee was competing with the treasurer. Indeed, the committee controlled vastly more resources than the town treasury. In fact, few in town could name the latest elected treasurer. Even distinguished visitors to Pustunich came because the teacher—Gomez in the village or Perez from his Merida office—invited them. On such occasions the podium was always shared by mayor and teacher, as it was uncertain which was the "real" host.

At the same time, the rights and duties of town officials had remained largely unchanged. As before, the ejidal comisario was in charge of milpa "approval" and government loans, and the treasurer managed the fines levied by the mayor. The mayor was still the only authority on matters of permits and misdemeanors and the only mediator and judge in cases of minor torts. He remained the political figurehead of the town, obliged to present himself at rallies in Ticul. When asked to whom they would go for advice, many villagers still named both town and ejidal comisarios. Why? "Because they are the officials." When asked to name the most "powerful" man in Pustunich, most villagers responded with "Clemente Perez" because of his wealth. Fitting into no familiar role configuration, the teacher's importance to Pustunich was difficult to define and verbalize.

The corrupt practices of those in formal office were as unchanged as traditional duties. Only two years ago, for example, Artemio Caeh was ejidal comisario. When the time came to submit to the ejidal bank a list of those applying for small loans, about eighty-five names were noted. Artemio took the list to the bank in Ticul and returned with fifty-six approvals. A number of these were of men who still owed money to the ejidal bank and who by law were ineligible to receive further loans. Among those who had been refused loans were some debtless young men who typified the officially preferred, first-time applications. The teacher, Gomez, saw the list and questioned Artemio about it. Artemio suggested that they meet later that same week, for a visit to the ejidal bank in Ticul, to clear the matter. Gomez, however, went the following day. He discovered that the ejidal bank itself did not usually take the time to make individual loan approvals, but instead relied on the judgment of the various village ejidal comisarios. Artemio had merely handed in the list with fifty-six names suggested. Gomez' subsequent investigation among ejiditarios revealed that Artemio had recommended only those who had paid a 20 to 30 peso bribe. His fellow villagers had thought this "normal" procedure and neither held it against him nor thought it proper to inform on him.

The present mayor, Avila, was no less an "operator." In 1963 alone, it is claimed that he: (1) sold a piece of public irrigation land *twice*; (2) sold horsemeat as hamburger. (His butcher business was closed when the teacher—Avila's first cousin, in fact—informed Ticul authorities. Avila denied the charge, yet ceased selling "hamburger"); (3) was found on numerous occasions gambling—a misdemeanor punishable in Pustunich by fine;* (4) accepted a bribe for permitting a Ticuleño to fence off a public access milpa path.

As ambiguous as the teachers' general role identity was, they were themselves too visible to escape speculation. Indeed, as they acquired more influence in the community and as their behavior became more predictable, the teachers' personal stake in their works came into

---

*I myself once stumbled upon Avila and a group of his cronies playing cards for high stakes in an abandoned irrigation tank outside the village.

question. It was not until after Perez' departure for Merida that comments began. More recently, they have become quite overt. "The August Fiesta is Carlos Perez' show," commented one villager.

> He comes here for about fifteen days and organizes it. He works day and night, supposedly for nothing. But of course he diverts some of the money into his own pocket. And rightly so, for he has a right to earn his daily salary if he leaves his Merida job and works here for "nothing." However, he may take too much. *He* handles the money, gives the Junta de Mejoras (Betterment Committee) $1,000 or so for them to work on all year and then he pockets the rest. When we built the theater in the school yard, for example, Professor Carlos claimed the cost was $5,000. *He* did all the paying and he had the fiesta money, so who could prove him wrong? But all the material was donated! I myself did fagina for it and gave 100 big stones which I dug. Others gave too. Don Polo Guerrero gave 1,000 small stones and I helped him. People brought one, two or three cargas of *cal*. At the most—but the *most*—the stage could only have cost $2,000. He must have pocketed the rest. We'd like to see some more betterments in the square, not the school yard. Alonso is following in the footsteps of his brother-in-law—trying to make a good name. Well, this is O.K. As long as the betterments are done. Also, a man who plays up his accomplishments in Pustunich and whose name is known in the state because of this—it's good, because he can get favors for Pustunich.

Several also say that Gomez himself was pocketing up to $40,000 on the extension of potable water tubing. This was an absurd assumption, actually, as materials and food, not money, were given by the state and Community Development Foundation for the project. Even so, these same individuals are frequent workers on his projects. The truth of these allegations is of far less importance than the slowly, yet clearly, shifting identity of the teachers. Their innovative behavior is being accepted by villagers as "normal," and their leadership role is becoming institutionalized.

Merger of the teacher's role with that of more traditional leadership expectations was approached when Professor Gomez' name was proposed for comisario. It happened just prior to the 1960 elections, when he was complaining of one candidate who had sent a turkey to the president of Ticul. Some townsmen suggested that Gomez himself run. He refused, noting that his cousin, the shopkeeper Avila, had expressed an interest in running. "Well, let him be your secretary," his backers rejoined. Gomez suggested that they reverse the ticket, running Avila as comisario and himself as secretary. This was dutifully accepted and formal nomination made.

Three years before, Gomez had created the Sports Committee, a group of adults for organization and promotion of sports events. The Sports Committee of 1960 consisted of the five most popular men in Pustunich. All were milperos and of comfortable though not high income; at least two were constantly on call as communal hunt leaders. All were known as progressive men. All had served as major sponsors of Maya ceremonials.

The baseball players numbered some thirty-five young men representing the first- and second-string teams. They ranged in age from sixteen to thirty-three, and at least half were married. Following his nomination, Gomez utilized the sports organization to propagandize the Avila-Gomez ticket. "On election night," he recalls, "the sentiments of the people won." The vote was ninety-six to sixteen in favor of him and Avila. As usual, no women voted, though all were eligible. Of the ninety-six who voted for Avila, at least ten were minors who by Mexican law were ineligible to vote. It was typical of Pustunich that less than one-fourth of the eligible voters voted, even though the teacher's candidacy had made the election an unusual, interesting one.

Avila, the new comisario, was a man of mixed popularity. The onus of theft hung over him. He was particularly close with a conservative group of ex-comisarios and town officers. At the time of his election, he had recently constructed, at considerable expense, a modern masonry house on the main road, which he hoped would someday become the home of his son who was an automobile mechanic in Merida. In the meantime, the house would serve as a bar. Public sentiment, organized and led by Professor Gomez, was against the comisario's being a bar-owner. Avila closed down and began his term of office with animosity toward his cousin the secretary. The animosity was not lessened when Gomez subsequently forced a halt to Avila's clandestine sales of horsemeat as hamburger.

Not long after his election Gomez resigned his position as town secretary. Officially he resigned because of conflicts in time commitment between his duties as secretary and director-teacher of the school. Complaints had been heard that Gomez was spending too much of his time away from the school. Others, however, claim that the teacher resigned because he couldn't "get along" with Avila and didn't like the way he handled his job as comisario. "He used the excuse of time conflict so as not to cast aspersions on Avila," says one informant. "Alonso [Gomez] is an educated, delicate man." In reality, Gomez was not sure he wanted his general position so closely identified with traditional leadership roles. As an independent teacher he had had more freedom of action. He could not maintain his activities and make any criticisms without appearing to stab his own running mate in the back.

It was after his resignation that Alonso Gomez denounced Avila's horsemeat business. Now that he had actually been a public official and was closely associated with the politics he had always condemned, the professor's condemnation of Avila was especially vehement. "I'm ashamed to say that he's my first cousin," said Gomez publicly. The day following the incident of the public-land fencing, the chairman of the sports group called for a village meeting and proposed Avila's impeachment. This would not have been suggested without the teacher's approval.

The impeachment was not without additional stimulus. In an unprecedented move, Ticul had recently begun impeachment proceedings against the municipal president who was accused of blatantly enriching himself at public expense, showing gross favoritism, and obstructing progress wherever progress did not also involve a kickback for himself.

The major charges against Avila were primarily those of "abuse of power." Informally, the major reasons were attributable to Avila's "great ego," his inability to take either suggestion or criticism, and his hot temper. A typical incident (from field notes, Nov. 1963):

On Sunday, during a baseball game, a stranger drove into town on his motorcycle and rode it across the basketball court, which is forbidden. Generally, this means a fine of up to $5. The town secretary (who had assumed the job upon Alonso's resignation) called the stranger inside the comisaria to discuss the violation. Avila, who had done nothing up to this moment, began shouting at the secretary in front of the large baseball crowd: "There's only one comisario in this town and I'M IT." He continued the harangue with gross language.

Regardless of the popularity of the sports group, they had not reckoned with Pustunich's apathy toward political matters. Though the president of Ticul was himself stripped of office, Avila continued. Most villagers reasoned that an election was due within a year, anyway, and thus no formal impeachment meeting was convened.

It was during this period that the new committee system and the professor enjoyed greatest influence. The mayor began to ignore the teacher and to boycott the frequent town meetings. Earlier, Gomez had engineered Avila's appointment as treasurer of the important Betterment Committee. This had been done with the hope of "rehabilitating" Avila and "making him take a more active role in community improvement." It rankled Avila that he exerted far more influence as committee member than as mayor of the town itself. He was at that time chairman of only one committee—"Infant Protection." It became clear to villagers and outsiders alike that the teacher, not the mayor, had the power to commit the village to a course of action and could be counted upon to deliver the promised approval or number of bodies. Thus the state board of electrification dealt with the teacher, not Avila. Alonso Gomez, not Avila, made the personal appeal for more village aid when the governor of Yucatan visited Pustunich. Gomez, not Avila, was consulted by ejidal authorities following large-scale milpa damage by the cattle of a nearby ranch. The traditional comisario, in short, was virtually isolated from the new activities and expectations.

Final Developments: Some Old and New Expectations

By the time the next elections rolled around, Gomez was ready. He ran, and, with the campaign help of the prestigious baseball team, won handily, thereby integrating fully both old and new systems. Almost simultaneously, the first formal complaint against either him or his brother-in-law Perez was lodged in a major Yucatec daily newspaper by now ex-mayor Avila and his close cronies.

The locus of the new leadership within the role of the old was convenient, ending the ambiguity with which both insiders and outsiders had viewed the teacher and his growing influence. So convenient was the situation, in fact, that the teacher was reelected mayor at the following election—a wholly unconstitutional act in Mexico. "I bowed to the people's will," he shrugged when questioned about it.

The integration of the two systems is one of personnel rather than structure, however. Alonso Gomez is the force behind the committee system, the initiator of most projects, the man with the formal Spanish, the typewriter, and the contacts in Merida. When Gomez leaves the office, these functions will go with him.

At present, the teacher and the now powerful Betterment Committee develop each new project and allocate it and its funds to a committee. Where no committee exists, a new one is formed. Though the teacher has much influence, he has no power over village actions. The Betterment Committee is swayed by the teacher, yet ultimately chooses its own members. As a result, several quite conservative villagers are members, and its chairman is a crony of ex-mayor Avila. The chairman, Pedro Cahuich, in fact opposes electrification, claiming the village can never raise the $33,000 required as a down payment. He accuses the teacher of trying to become a "big man" like his brother-in-law by getting the village electrified. Gomez retorts that Cahuich is opposed because he has a "woman on the side" and couldn't "go on 'night-birding' if the streets were well lit."

The significance of present committee membership lies precisely in its representativeness. It has not crystalized into a body of clearly divergent villagers, "progressive" versus "conservative," or "Alonso's men" versus "Avila's." The committees began over a decade ago with prestige and have retained it. They allow village men to participate in decision making with far less onus of corruption and antisocial motivation than accompanies encumbency in traditional political roles. It is not as accurate to view the new and old systems as competing with one another as to say, simply, that one has left the other behind, relatively unchanged. As new village needs are now automatically and efficiently handled by the committee system, traditional political behavior is effectively "locked in" and, in many respects, protected from directly disruptive influence. Since most villagers have participated in committee activities at some time (albeit on projects promising immediate benefit to themselves), the new form of participation represents an updated return to the fagina of a half-century ago. Just as participation in fagina was a mark of village membership, committee membership or labor donation today is evidence of identification with the community. All participate indirectly and knowingly through the many committee fundraising schemes. At least several times a month a dance or sporting event is held, with admission and refreshment proceeds going to the treasury of one committee or another. Never in the history of Pustunich has the town offered so many opportunities for diversion. There is now less need to go outside the village for fun. The results are a decrease in dependency upon outside recreative resources and the potential for an increase in endogamous matings—both "conservative" elements.

The changes in the village have not gone unnoticed. Ticul treats Pustunich with increased respect. When the town asks for extra bus service during the fiesta season, Ticul swiftly grants the permits. The county seat can no longer bully the village with impunity. The frequent scathing letters sent by teacher-mayor Gomez to the Yucatec daily newspapers (based in Merida and statewide in circulation) far outweigh the small advantages which municipal officials might obtain from intimidation of the small town. With increasing confidence in its dealings with outside legal and official entities, Pustunich is increasingly sophisticated in its dealings with others. Ejidal comisarios have learned that cattlemen who pay for the right to graze their animals in the village ejido are more reluctant to pay high damages when their animals enter a milpa and destroy crops. Following a recent court decision (the teacher presented Pustunich ejiditarios' brief himself, thus superseding even the ejidal comisario) in which substantial cash awards were granted village milperos, nearby cattle owners were so intimidated that many were coaxed into giving substantial donations to the village electrification committee. One large cattleman was heard to say that "the teacher should be machinegunned." Shortly thereafter, a rumor spread among cattlemen that the village milperos were arming themselves with rifles and submachine guns to wipe out the cattle population—and likely the cattlemen as well. In short, the town has become an entity to be reckoned with.

Still, the town is peasant and readily exploitable, looking inward for reasons and objects of ultimate trust. It is apathetic to outside politics. Only a fourth of eligible voters turn out for gubernatorial and national elections. When politicians visit Ticul on their stump through the state, only ex-mayor Avila goes the two miles to hear the candidates. Most outside officials below the governor are still distrusted. Storekeepers must pay $104 for a business stamp, $104 to the Agency of Hacienda, and $36 "for the economy." "We receive nothing in return," comments one storekeeper. "Take the inspectors of merchandise and scales. They come in, flash a badge and extract 'taxes' from you. A bribe. A 'tax' might include $12 for the scale plus $10 more for the inspector's pocket annually. The merchandise inspector may come in to see if you're really selling what you say you are. He opens up a little prepared bag of, say, sugar and says, 'It's sugar . . . that'll be $10.' It's best not to have too much money in the register if you're a small businessman." "Did you know," asks one villager, "that President Kennedy sent $250,000 just to help Pustunich after the 1962 drought? Only $5,000 actually arrived here. The rest went into the pockets of politicos in Mexico and Merida." And government irrigation users, it will be recalled, recently refused to pay their water bill, claiming that the pump inspector had absconded with the previous month's payment.

NOTE

1. For further discussion of role ambiguity and genesis of the teachers' "mandate" to innovate, see Irwin Press, "Ambiguity and Innovation: Implications for the Genesis of the Culture Broker." *American Anthropologist* 71 (1969): 205-217.

10

Religious Organization and Well-Being

The Two Traditions

Pustunich is the inheritor of two "great traditions," to use Redfield's descriptive term for official, outside-generated institutions.[1] Both Maya and Catholic religious traditions have simmered for centuries in the context of local events and needs. The Maya, however, survives only as a "little tradition," nurtured by and responsible to the village alone. Unlike Catholicism, local Maya tradition is dependent upon no outside authority for validation of ritual orthodoxy or for stimulation of ritual continuity. It has survived so long not so much as a reaction against the violent manner in which the Catholic hierarchy conducted the initial conversion, but as a result of the economic base of Yucatec peasants. Slash-and-burn agriculture, with its long-term fallowing, requires extensive lands. Plots have lain scattered at considerable distance from population and colonial administrative centers. Being thus less susceptible to interference from the town-based Catholic hierarchy, Maya ritual has survived in communal and individual-oriented form to meet the continuing needs of a specific and highly stable ecosystem.

The local, "little tradition" of Catholicism is less autonomous. It is overseen by a nonpeasant hierarchy which demands at least outward conformity to an absolute standard of orthodoxy. It also requires that an essential ritual element (the mass) be managed by an appointed specialist who usuall does not reside in a peasant village. These requirements do allow a degree of local control, however. So long as ritual outwardly conforms to official expectations and so long as it consists of other than the mass, no outside direction or participation is needed. For every mass conducted by an outside priest there are dozens of individually sponsored and locally directed rituals.

It must be stressed that nowhere in Yucatan does there exist a civil-religious hierarchy or *cargo* system such as flourishes in the southern highlands of mainland Mexico. Each Yucatec village certainly has its patron saint, and each village attempts to organize an annual fiesta in his or her honor. But there is no cult organization with hierarchy of offices, no *cofradia* to manage an annual round of complex ritual which extensively utilizes physical and economic resources of the village. The cult of saints is a mainland phenomenon. In Yucatan, the cross predominates. Along paths, in roadside shrines, at major corners, and on household altars, the cross is a ubiquitous symbol of devotion to an idea rather than to a personification. Talking crosses (that miraculously transmit the will of God), not specific saints, have led Yucatecans to revolution. Madsen suggests that the cross and crucifixion were interpreted by the Maya as "a new kind of human sacrifice,"[2] one that directly replaced a pre-Colombian tradition.

The bases of Pustunich Catholic ceremonial are rosarios, novenas, masses, and processions, all of which utilize ritual phraseology common to Mexican or Roman Catholic practice in general. "Hail Mary's" and "Our Father's" are the staple of chanters. Here, as opposed to the southern highlands of Mexico, there is no complex, locally originated ritual of drinking, seating arrangements, public feasting, and protocol-laden interaction between hierarchically organized participants. In short, Pustunich Catholicism is more "orthodox" than that of, say, Chiapas and Oaxaca. Relatively independent of economic and political spheres, it is more generalized, less complex, less integrative, less productive of localized identity, and generally less capable of generating high emotion. This is another way of suggesting that Catholic ritual behavior in Pustunich is the less susceptible to disruption and disintegration through changes in it or in other institutions.

At the same time, indigenous ritual is also more "orthodox" than that of most other Mexican areas. The Maya ceremonial form is a nature-oriented ritual performed for community benefit by a specialist who is otherwise structurally undifferentiated from others. As such, it more closely approximates a generalized Amerindian shamanistic tradition wherein the ritual specialist performs both communal (typically for economic well-being) and individual services (for both economic and curative purposes). The Yucatec ritual leader (h-men), however, has no other leadership functions. It must be recalled that for nearly a thousand years Yucatec communities have been cogs within a hierarchically organized state. In Pustunich, political leadership has long been controlled by outside powerholders, either directly or through local deputies. Local ritual specialists have tended to their ritual and healing.

Catholicism

With the exception of a handful of families, all Pustunicheños are nominally Catholic. There is little feeling of closeness with the Catholic hierarchy of supernaturals, however. They are aloof from everyday secular affairs and exhibit little continuing interest in the noncritical events of an individual's life. They sustain themselves, require no earth-produced sustenance, and are approached with candles, repetitious prayer, and the mass. They present little mystery to Pustunicheños. God is the father, Jesus is his son. More to the point, Jesus is God's baby. There is only one image of the adult Christ in Pustunich, although a number of families possess Baby Jesus. The bulk of songs honoring Christ are sung to an eternal "niño Jesus" who never grew up. God or the Virgin Mary may be appealed to in time of stress, but rarely Jesus Christ. Except for an emergency such as illness, the Catholic supernatural hierarchy is rarely called upon. The daily uses of God's name are highly routinized. "*Si Dios quiere*" (if God so wills) is a standard modifier of proposed action. It is another way of reflecting upon life's uncertainties. It means "if all goes well."

God, the Virgin (Assumption), Jesus, and the saints are viewed with respect rather than awe, and it would be inconceivable that any villager might ever crawl the length of a church on his or her knees to demonstrate "devotion." When asked why they go to church or sponsor home ritual, Pustunicheños generally answer, "*por costumbre*"—it's a custom, not an obligation.

Though generally anticlerical and little concerned with daily ritual,

Pustunich is concerned with the fate of the soul as outlined by official Catholic dogma. Thus, most have been married by the Church and only the cost of the marriage mass has precluded 100 percent church marriage. Almost all have been baptized, and whenever possible (the Bishop makes a biennial visit to the campo) children are confirmed. Yet, Pustunicheños wear their Catholicism easily. They conduct the majority of their ritual without the priest and view him merely as an element of the mass. They perform novenas when they are able, and are content to begin four days late rather than not at all. Children are baptized and confirmed when convenient for the parents and when sufficient funds are available for the mandatory festival.

Heaven, Purgatory, and Hell are concepts of use to the priest in sermons; they are rarely thought of by villagers. The spirit of the dead is of concern mainly insofar as it could cause the corpse to rise and frighten the mourners. Thus, during a wake, the corpse is bound hand and foot and its jaws tied shut with a cloth. The offerings and prayers of All-Saints Day are for the souls of the departed, while the formal hierarchy of saints themselves is of secondary importance.

All ritual terminates with refreshment and, if possible, entertainment. There are always more guests present during the serving of sweets and drinks than during the earlier chanting. Although every family possesses a religious picture and cross or crucifix, home altars are rare. Altars—generally being nothing more than small tables bearing the picture of a saint or a cross—as often as not are cluttered with other household paraphernalia. Few families, moreover, make a practice of regular private home ritual. If a more elaborate and widely attended ritual with refreshments cannot be promoted, the result may be no ritual at all. For this reason there are few privately owned images in the village, though most families own framed prints of favorite saints. Those that do exist tend to be of the Christ Child and are usually inexpensive plastic baby-dolls of the type that can be purchased in any dry-goods store. To own such a doll, however, is to be obligated to provide a procession and elaborate *rosario* (single evening's ritual) during the Christmas season; thus the purchase of Baby Jesus is a public demonstration of recent or long-term economic accumulation. In an analogous vein, the procession of young women to the cemetery (with flowers) is foremost a demonstration for the benefit of single boys and secondarily an act of devotion to the souls of dead aunts or uncles.

Catholic Ritual and Participation

Regular home ritual is virtually nonexistent and, as noted earlier, only a handful of women make a habit of frequent attendance upon the Virgin's image in the village church. Few villagers attend mass in Ticul, and masses are offered in Pustunich on only six or seven days each year, and perhaps more if there are a few local weddings.

Mass is for special occasions. Except for an emergency or life crisis, ritual strictly follows the Catholic calendar. The calendar is dotted with holy days or seasons, only a few of which are of interest to the village as a whole. The remainder—and majority—of rituals are private affairs marking name days. Of all ritual occasions, only Carnival and the last day of fiesta attract even a simple majority of Pustunicheños.

The village church is maintained by an elderly bachelor sexton who lives behind the building in a rotting thatch hut. Along with a dozen older women, he lights daily candles before the image of the Virgin Assumption and recites prayers at the foot of the altar. Only public ritual (occasions of general religious interest) and weddings are performed in the church. The bulk of ritual—name-day novenas, prayers for the dead, and other events of individual or family interest—are home affairs.

Table 4 presents a calendar of those days of ritual importance to the entire village. Of these, only Carnival, Easter, Christmas Day, and the last three days of fiesta are viewed as occasions on which no milpa work need be done. Males may stay home on other days to help wives in preparation for private rosarios.

While major holy days are of interest to all villagers, their associated rituals are almost invariably privately sponsored. Only during month-long celebrations (such as the Months of Mary or Sacred Heart of Jesus) are daily obeisances carried out by an amorphous group of volunteers and faithful. All other limited-period ritual—masses, novenas, major processions, and rosarios (single night recitation-rituals, nine of which constitute a novena)—are the public donations of individuals or small groups whose sponsorship is clear. In addition to the absence of a resident priest, no permanent church-body exists for the purpose of directing and coordinating all or most public ritual and allocating funds for their execution. There are no cults or cofradias.

There are, however, a sexton, an ad hoc group of older women who perform daily ritual in the church, a fiesta-organizing committee, a

Table 4
ANNUAL CATHOLIC RITUAL ROUND

Date	Event	How Celebrated
January 5	"The kings" Day	Children may be given small gifts
February 15	Carnival	Mass, novenas, processions, costume ball, drinking
	Good Friday	Mass
	Easter	Mass
May 1-31	Month of Mary	Processions, *mañanitas,* May flower ritual in church
May 31	Last night of Month of Mary	Novenas end. Processions with large standard, basketball games, beer, dancing, sky rockets
June 1-July 3	Sacred Heart of Jesus month	Garlands in church each night. Sky rockets
June 13	Day of San Antonio of Padua (on this day eastern rains supposed to begin)	Individuals with name-day hold more elaborate novenas
August 6-15	Novenas for Virgin Assumption	
August 12-15	Fiesta	Fiesta and masses (dances, games, bull-fights, concessions, novenas, drinking, *jaranas*)
August 15	Virgin Assumption	High fiesta day. Largest and most lavish mass; best bulls
October 31	All Saints (children)	Rosarios in each house to spirits
November 1-8	All Saints (adults) (*animas chicas*)	of departed
December 15-24	Pre-Christmas Novenas	
December 24	Christmas Eve	Individual rosarios with numerous open houses and several large parties with liquor and record music
December 25	Christmas	Usually, no work on this day

Carnival committee, and a pair of women who frequently hire themselves out as ritual singers for rosarios. The committees have no power over form, personnel, and cost of rituals. In no way can they be compared with groups of *principales* or *cofrades* in southern Mexico. Apart from the sexton, whose duties are predominantly those of maintenance, the two singers are perhaps more than any other Pustunicheños the Catholic ritual specialists. The two women are close friends and through years of practice have developed a style of high-pitched harmony typical of much Mexican religious singing. They charge a nominal fee and will donate their services gratis for funerals or major processions. During the dark early mornings of the Month of Mary they voluntarily sing the *mañanitas*, welcoming the dawn to a guitar accompaniment. Their voices are broadcast to the village by loudspeakers provided free (!) by Don Clem Perez. Such acts have firmly established the women as dedicated specialists whose services are viewed as highly desirable to most ritual. They sit in front at rosarios and walk in the nucleus of women and girls in processions. They are always among the first served at rosario dinners.

The church in Pustunich falls under the jurisdiction of Ticul. Ticul is famous for its massive, Moorish-influenced cathedral. Its priests have accommodated Pustunich's religious needs in varying fashion. Some have visited the village frequently and, as did the predecessor of the present priest, have given freely of their time with no charge for masses beyond that which could be obtained by passing the plate. Others have ignored the pueblo. The present priest is a self-styled "progressive" and proudly demonstrates the chapter of a book in English (an obscure travelogue) which describes his work among the poor in another state. His marriage sermons include far more on the need for latrines and proper dietary practice (stressing vitamin content) than on the sanctity of the bond itself. He rarely dresses in priestly habit on church grounds and spends his evenings on the sacristy veranda drinking Cuba Libres.

The priest has organized a majority of Ticul's shoemakers into a cooperative selling unit which receives better prices than they did formerly from Merida retailers. He has also obtained land near Pustunich for a cooperative cabbage and lettuce farm and has begun a savings and loan bank at the Cathedral. These projects are constantly in need of capital and the priest misses no opportunity to accumulate it. He will not perform a mass unless guaranteed at least $100 in advance. Pustunicheños can understand his need for money, yet complain that all of the co-op benefits remain with Ticul. To villagers, he is a "money grubber" and unpopular.

The priest was replaced shortly before I left the village. His successor was a much younger man. The only story to which Pustunich gave credence was that the priest had blatantly brought his woman to live with him in the Cathedral and had been denounced to Merida clerical authorities by his own mother. In truth, he had been spectacularly promoted to a new, modernistic church in an upper-class neighborhood of Merida.

Village views of the present priest merely reflect an anticlerical attitude of long standing. The position of the mass itself reflects an ambivalence. It is reserved for a select number of days on the official religious calendar and is not part of daily ritual practice. It is a special event, and its presence marks an occasion as important. On important occasions, however, the mass is also associated with other ritual elements such as rosarios, processions, sky-rockets, entertainment, and clothing for the image. As such, the mass is only one of a number of items which must be paid for; and it is paid for by an individual, representing himself rather than the community. The mass is viewed as a necessary but insufficient part of the overall ritual complex. The bullfights, gay processions and fireworks, concessions, drinking, and dances of the Fiesta Week are at least as important. Certainly they are anticipated with greater fervor.

Name-day rosarios, which occupy a single night, are the most numerous and cheapest ritual form. They are highly personal events and are rarely sponsored by more than a single individual. A major exception is the day of San Antonio of Padua (June 13), which is of general importance in the milpa calendar and on which several individuals (who share the date as a name day) may collaborate in sponsoring ritual and festivities. Novenas involve nine nights of rosarios and cost roughly nine times as much. A rosario consists of one or more hours of "Hail Mary's," "Our Father's," and associated songs in front of a home altar. The altar, a cloth-covered kitchen table specially decorated with flowers, bears a cross, picture of the sponsor's saint, and candles.

Close friends and kin are specifically invited to participate, and it is usual that several others will also attend without invitation. Most rosarios involve no more than a dozen women. All, however, conclude with refreshments. The lavishness of the spread depends upon the financial resources of the sponsor. Some villagers offer large annual novenas famous for after-ritual parties consisting of liquor and a host of appetizers. Such occasions are well attended. The altar-room may be

crowded with several dozen women while husbands mill in the solar
where brandy and Coke are dispensed from a bucket.

Excerpt from field notes, December 8, 1964:

This evening there was a mass bought by Eucaria Colli. It was in
honor of the Virgin Conception, her patroness, and a prelude to
Christmas. Padre Pineda officiated for only $100 and immediately
left for Ticul in a fancy car.

After the mass, everyone joined a procession to 'Caria's house with
candles and singing. 'Caria herself carried a doll-sized image of
Baby Jesus on a cushion, followed by Fernando Chan and two other
teenagers bearing tiny images of the Three Wise Men. At Eucaria's
house Coleman lanterns were strung around, chairs were set up in
the solar, and a rented loud-speaker system was blaring rock 'n roll.
In the solar was a lovely altar consisting of a table arched over with
palm leaves and illuminated by candles. On the table was a steplike
affair providing different levels on which were placed bunches of
flowers. Incense burned in a cup at the foot of the steps.

Upon arriving, one group prayed outside the door of 'Caria's house
and asked *posada*, symbolizing the Request for Room at the Inn. A
group inside the house responded with songs, but couldn't get the
door open (it was stuck). The posada group hurried around to the
back door where they were admitted. Then all the women who
accompanied the procession entered the house and began fifteen
misterias (three whole "novena services") which lasted for over
one-and-a-half hours. Men milled around outside, drinking. After
the service, the music began again and dancing and refreshments
lasted until well past midnight.

Doña Eucaria gives a mass and novena each year on this, her saint's
day. Perhaps 100 persons were present tonight, including some
forty men.

Rosarios and novenas for ritual days of general interest are elaborate
and typically sponsored by two or more families. Church decorations are
more ornate, while processions require sky-rockets and many candles for

the marchers. The more marchers there are, the more successful the procession. The core consists of sponsors, their family, kindred, and close friends. It is hoped and expected that many others will join along the way. Younger people participate in processions whenever possible, as it is an excellent opportunity for displaying finery, conversing, joking, jostling, and courting under cover of the crowd.

Major Ceremonial

A fiesta "novena" (actually rosario, but Pustunicheños refer to them as "novenas") is the most expensive form of ritual, as new clothes must be purchased for the image of the Virgin Assumption, and each novena group is expected to re-dress the image for its own procession. The Virgin's permanent gold crown and breast-plates are the property of the church.

It is an honor to sponsor a mass and novena during fiesta. As demand is greater than the available opportunities, each individual or group may sponsor only one event. There are nine evening novenas and morning-after masses—the two being viewed as a unit for sponsoring. Some dates (i.e., the third novena and morning mass, or fifth afternoon mass) are firmly in the hands of particular families or groups who have sponsored them for years and are thus viewed as unavailable for sponsorship by others. For most events, however, there is a three- to five-year waiting list. All sponsoring groups have a major donor, whose name is the primary one associated with sponsorship of the ritual, and most have one or more subsidiary sponsors who contribute lesser sums. As individuals who participate in large groups may contribute as little as $5, most Pustunich families have thus been represented at one time or another in a major fiesta ritual. Whereas women, rather than their husbands, sponsor most nonmajor novenas such as name days, men, not women, are associated with sponsorship of fiesta rituals. As will be discussed later, the August Fiesta is the major focus of male Catholic religious participation. A representative list of sponsoring groups during the fiesta of August 1964 is given in Table 5.

During this single fiesta, thirty-eight nuclear family heads (almost 20 percent of the village total) were major sponsors of important ritual, with several dozens more participating as minor donors. Almost all surnames are represented in the total, as are all economic strata. Major sponsors are

Table 5
FIESTA SPONSORING GROUPS, AUGUST 1964

Novena-Mass, August 6-7

Twelve major sponsors contributing $20 to $40 each plus many other *junteros* with $1 to $20 each. This group has sponsored the first novena and mass for over twenty years. The total raised was over $325.

Novena-Mass, August 7-8

Two sponsors only. Miguel Be (sent money from the U.S.A., where he is a brazero) and his grandfather Florentino Moo. Total expenditure, over $125.

Novena-Mass, August 8-9

Two sponsors only. Desiderio Cepeda (brother of the wealthy Manolo) and his neighbor, Celestino Be. This is the first time he has collaborated with Be. Cepeda provided $500 and Be, $100. He has been a major sponsor of Fiesta novenas for five years. For three years before that he donated afternoon masses with three priests participating (at a cost of $100 per priest). This time, they added an evening mass.

SOME COSTS INVOLVED:

2 masses	$150
2 gross sky rockets	68
flowers for church and house	15
musicians for procession and house entertainment	125
two female procession singers	5
horchata (barley water refreshment)	40
candles @ 20¢ each	2.40
candles @ $1 each	4

Novena-Mass, August 9-10

Lorenzo Cua only

Novena-Mass, August 10-11

Sponsored by Evaristo, Santiago, and Elda Mis at a cost of about $180. They maintain that the "right" to this sponsorship has been handed down for over forty years, since their "grandfather's day."

Afternoon Mass, August 12 (First day of Fiesta)

Clemente Perez, Paco Perez, and Ramon Cahuich. The two Perez' are cousins and young Cahuich is a close friend who "asked in." The Perez' have sponsored a mass for the past twelve years. Each of the three contributed about $50 or $60 each.

Novena-Mass, August 12-13

Alonso Gomez, Alfredo Canul, Vincente Mex, and Sabino Ku. All are cronies of Gomez who have collaborated for the past ten years, the last three of which with Gomez. Gomez donated the largest share—$80. The rest, $50 each.

Afternoon Mass, August 14

Francisco and Guadencio Punab plus Jose Palermo from Ticul. The Punab brothers have given masses for over twenty years. They have collaborated with friend Palermo for the past three. Each gave $60.

Novena-Mass, August 14-15

Seven major sponsors, donating $25 each, plus three minor sponsors giving $10, $15, and $20, respectively. Half are cousins and brothers-in-law; the rest, friends.

Afternoon Mass, August 15

This is the major mass of the year. Sponsored solely by Manolo Cepeda, the rico.

generally only too happy to accept minor collaboration, as the result is more spectacular and the names of lesser donors are either unknown to or soon forgotten by the general public. It stypical of wealthy Clem Perez to make only a partial expenditure, just as it is typical of Manolo Cepeda— who resides outside of town and interacts little with other villagers—to make a substantial, though isolated, contribution. It is of further interest that teacher Gomez began to sponsor at about the same time his brother-in-law Carlos Perez left Pustunich for the Federal Teacher's Board in Merida.

Lorenzo Cua is the only solo novena-mass sponsor. Cua's cattle herd has been increasing and he is rated by some villagers as having moved into the second highest economic category. Villagers know that Cua is not *very* wealthy. His sponsorship earns him prestige, yet in that it is viewed as religious devotion, he is spared the necessity of having to donate equally large sums to secular projects such as electrification.

In addition to providing an opportunity for mild ritual display, fiesta provides income for the town's treasury. It is a major moneymaking proposition and the town's principal source of revenue. At present Pustunich is attempting to pay off a down payment on village electrification, in anticipation of power lines which the government is extending east from Ticul. The Fiesta Organizing Committee overlooks no avenue of potential profit. Almost every square meter of the plaza acquires a cash value. The bull ring area is laid out with geometric perfection and divided into a number of pie-shaped wedges. Each wedge is leased to an entrepreneur at a fixed price for the three bullfight days. The lessee must erect his portion of the stand (which consists of two stories with thatched roof) and keep his bullring wedge free of debris. He charges any admission price he wishes; regardless of attendance then, the Fiesta Committee is assured of a return in advance. Similarly, the committee rents out portions of the plaza for food, amusement, and trinket stalls. Milk-bottle toss, shooting galleries, peg and ring games, *empanada* and soft drink stands form a tight semi-circle between the ring and the basketball court. The court becomes a dance floor during the last three evenings and as much as 10 pesos (half a day's wage) admission will be charged on the final night. All other areas of the plaza are taken up by the tables and chairs of the temporary town bar, run by the committee and staffed with hired villagers.

Fiesta is also enjoyable. It has a reputation as one of the best local productions in Yucatan, and tourists or pilgrims come from many kilometers away. Village streets become crowded and noisy. In the afternoons and evenings there are processions with attractive youngsters, loud sky-rockets, and favorite sacred songs. After dark, one may crowd around the basketball court, illuminated by Clem Perez' rented lights, while Fermin Gonzalez or Hernan Ek and his band play for a packed floor of dancing couples. Half of the dance partners are pairs of girls, for the boys are often too shy to display their interests so publicly. As the mid-August fiesta generally coincides with the ripening of the first corn, it is an especially relaxed time in Pustunich. Cash is beginning to come in, small luxurious tastes (for special sweets, transistor radios, etc.) can be indulged, and relations with one's kin are being fortified with exchanges of sweet fresh-corn *atole*. Relatives from other towns and children residing elsewhere make their annual visit and the year's crop of new babies is admired by kin who had not yet seen them. Friends visit one another's houses and, being generally inexperienced at heavy drinking, get drunk, become maudlin—though rarely violent—weep, bare their conscience, sing, and collapse in one another's arms.

If homage to the Virgin Assumption is overshadowed by economic and recreational aspects of the annual fiesta, Lent (whose passing is barely noticed) is totally submerged by the processions and secular carnival which precede it. Carnival is an exhilarating two-day affair with costume contests and jarana dancing. It, too, is a moneymaker, with bar and dancing managed by a Carnival Committee.

The costume displays, as with fiesta mass sponsorship, exhibit the openness of association in Pustunich, as well as the villager's delight in viewing—and participating in—good fun. Each night, villagers enter the dance-floor to the accompaniment of orchestra music and the rousing applause and laughter of the crowds. Those in costume may enter individually or as part of a larger group. A highly respected man enters as a bent, gnarled old Maya peasant, face covered with a nylon stocking. Another man draws raucous guffaws as he staggers, legitimately drunk, in blackface, wearing a priest's cassock. Two friends, both adult married milperos, cause near pandemonium as they enter, one in loin cloth with club, the other on a chain in ape's costume cavorting and screeching. The entire first-string baseball team enters in blackface, grass skirts, and bones in their hair, as "cannibals." A newly married couple enters as clowns. The sons of Clem Perez, along with their wives and several cousins, enter en masse in an array of costumes—circus barker, Red Riding Hood, clown, fairy princess. All costumes, excepting the "old

Maya man,'' are rented from a Ticul shop. Following the final grand parade of costumes to the accompaniment of a fanfare by the hired Ticul orchestra, Clem Perez enters the floor in an imaginative garb with padded belly and red nose. He is "Rey Feo" or King Ugly, "king" of the Carnival. The crowd is delighted, for it is totally foreign to Perez' usual solemnity. Because of this incongruity, he is almost always appointed Rey Feo by the Carnival Committee. In Maya (his Spanish is halting at best), he welcomes all, comments on the quality of the event, and proceeds to read the "last will and testament" of "Juan Carnaval," the paper-mache figure who "represents" the event. Later that evening Juan will be cremated. This will is always eagerly awaited, as it satirizes the foibles of various villagers during the past year. To Archangel K'u, who made a fool of himself at fiesta by tripping over a stump and falling upon a laden table, Juan Carnaval leaves "a new pair of feet." To Moises Alejos, who was embroiled in a hassle with some cattle owners over damage to his milpa, Juan gives "some cattle of his own." And so each announcement is met with howls or chuckles. Juan Carnaval, dangling from his gallows, is set afire and those who paid their admission fees may dance to orchestra music till the small hours of the morning, while young men and boys run among the crowd dabbing laundry bluing powder on the faces of old and young alike. No one minds. It is part of Carnival. There is not an eligible girl or boy in the village who does not drop exhausted into the hammock next morning happily blue from head to toe. The prettiest girls require many hair washings to erase the attention of their admirers.

Sex and Participation

In many respects, Pustunich Catholicism is a woman's religion, and the decreasing participation of males during early teen-years is a normal part of their assumption of the adult sex-role. Boys' attendance at the church begins to wane at roughly the same time their milpa activities increase. During teen-age, boys crowd around the church entrance to make wisecracks about the entering girls, yet rarely enter beyond the door. Only women light daily candles before the Virgin Assumption and say regular prayers to her. The sexton is the only male who regularly attends these sessions. It will be recalled that he has never married and is thus viewed as being less of a man.

It is predominantly the older men who enter the church at special ritual occasions. On one Good Friday, for example, nineteen mostly mature and elderly men were viewed inside the church participating in the mass. Sixty-two adult males, however, milled around outside in their best "whites." Thus, they "attend" while avoiding active participation. As it was, less than half the village males were present. Masses are nonetheless special events and attract more men in general than do home rosarios. Indeed, it is extremely rare that any men other than those of the rosario-sponsoring nuclear family inside the house participate in recitations. Even here, the family males seldom enter. They attend to male guests outside, while the women chant a seemingly endless string of "Hail Mary's." The initial planning of rosarios and novenas exhibits a similar division of labor. Women arrange the ritual portion and edible refreshments. Men buy the liquor and serve it.

Only during fiesta—which involves far more elaborate exhibition than any other occasion—do men organize and participate in the Catholic ritual. Not surprisingly, fiesta masses are better attended by males than are masses of other occasions. However, beyond sponsoring individuals and their sons, few other men participate in the novena or procession that follow a fiesta mass. At the same time, a typical fiesta procession contains upwards of a hundred women and girls in their best huipils. Women who join a procession are generally those who would feel welcome at the rosario and refreshment at its destination. Eligible girls simply march in as many processions as possible.

As noted earlier, most other aspects of the fiesta are male-dominated. The Fiesta Committee is male and elected at a regular village meeting of males. Its overall duty is organization, not ritual supervision. It grants permission for novenas, masses, and concessions. Similarly, the all-male Carnival Committee hires an orchestra, chooses between those who wish to provide masses, and controls the sale of beer and hard liquor.

Protestants

Pustunicheños frequently use the term *Christian* synonymously with "civilized" or "human." Although most Christians are Catholics, they need not be. In that Catholic ritual is either individually sponsored or largely recreative, it is not focal to village identity or welfare. Thus the presence of non-Catholics is not a threat. Indeed, of several Protestants in

Pustunich, one is the mayor himself. In addition to his own family, Mayor Avila's ne'er-do-well brother Julio, his wife, and one other family are Protestant. Avila was a Catholic until he married Josefina Cepeda of Oxkutzkab, a catrina and Protestant. Josefina insisted that Avila convert and that their children be raised as Protestant and catrin. Except for their youngest son, whom Avila maintains as a mestizo for help in store and milpa, Josefina's wishes were met. All practice the new faith. "Practice" in this instance means sporadic trips to Ticul's Protestant Temple. There is little, however, that Avila has had to give up. Though ostensibly a Protestant, he scarcely participates less in overt Catholic ritual than most other mature village males. He has felt guilty over his conversion, however, and on several occasions, when his wife has gone to Ticul on an errand, he has been sighted stealing into the church to light a candle before the Virgin. As a Protestant, Avila thus performs an act of Catholic ritual seldom indulged in by other village men.

Avila's Protestant brother Julio is a jolly man, married to a very fat and jolly woman. Both are well liked by other villagers. They live on and tend the gardens and henequen seedbeds of absentee henequen landlord Jesus Ribero. They are quite poor. They rarely walk the mile to the village center. As do the formal Catholics, the few Protestants take what they want from their religion and leave the rest. They like the promise of salvation and the revival singing to accordion accompaniment. Still, they drink and smoke. Each year on Don Julio's birthday, a Ticul preacher is invited to the poor man's home for a service and refreshment. Don Julio's wife invariably caps the meal with a cigarette.

Pustunich views its Protestants with disinterest. The village is, above all, pragmatic. When a noted Protestant faith healer set up his tent in a town some thirty miles from Pustunich, no less than twenty Catholic villagers made the pilgrimage for a cure.

The Maya Sphere

Overlap between Maya and Catholic ritual is strictly a one-way street. Local Catholic ceremonial reflects few, if any, Maya elements, while the latter is shot-through with Catholic forms. According to Cocom, the h-men, harvest ritual is for "giving thanks to God." The supernatural guardians of the milpa are controlled by Saint Michael the Archangel. The Maya ritual altar itself contains a cross and incense. In the chanting of the h-men one hears frequent reference to "Santo Cristo," the "Espiritu Santo," "Santa Maria Virgin," and "Dios Padre." These are intermingled with the purely native names of the *K'us* who guard the bush—Yun Ah Canul, Yum Ah Itzab, Kiri'ch K'u, and Xtanyolche'.

While there is much formal overlap, there is little coincidence of function or professional personnel. The Catholic ritual follows a calendar imposed by the outside Church hierarchy and is largely independent of natural events. Maya ceremonial, on the other hand, is autonomous (under local control) and almost exclusively reflects and supplements important secular activities relating to land, weather, and crops.

The Maya ritual year begins in April and May, with individual offerings in the fields prior to cutting the bush on a new milpa. (Most villagers work a one-year field and open a new tract each year.) Several weeks later, an offering should be made prior to burning. Some time in May the h-men performs the communal cha chaac ritual—the only all-village ceremonial of the year—which ensures rain. During the summer no ritual need be performed. In late July and August, as the crops ripen, first-corn and first-bean offerings may be made by individual milperos. Then, in September, groups of farmers may hire the h-men for *uhai col* rituals of general harvest thanks. Between September and April, no Maya ritual is performed. During particularly dry summers, milperos who have been lax in offering harvest thanks during the past several years may call in the h-men for a belated ritual, just in case the drought may have been caused by angry milpa deities. It is also felt that wells and solares (backyards) are under supernatural protection. A new well can be "guaranteed" with a *uhai chen* ritual, led by the h-men. Ideally, solares should be protected by performance of *uhai solar*, again under direction of the h-men. These are relatively expensive, however. Whereas a number of farmers may share the expense of a general harvest ritual, wells and backyards are of concern to the owner alone. Thus, uhai chen or uhai solar are unlikely to be performed unless the home owner feels pressed by bad luck or wishes to display his Maya orthodoxy, community membership, and ability to afford the ritual. The only uhai solar of the past several years was sponsored by rich Manolo Cepeda, a loner who, it may be recalled, also was the only solo sponsor of a mass during fiesta.

That Maya supernaturals exert control over natural phenomena is neither overly questioned nor granted. "It is said" that they exist. But why take chances? All milperos know how to perform the simpler *premisias* or field ritual. No special incantations are required, though some will say a "Hail Mary." It's not much trouble to set a bowl of *zacá* (gruel of corn not soaked in limewater) in the milpa prior to burning a new patch of bush. For such minimal effort, the supernatural "owners" of the bush, if they *do* happen to exist, will not mind its destruction. Similarly, it is easy to offer the milpa guardians a thanks-offering of new atole, following harvest of the first ripe ears of corn. Even cha chaac requires little economic outlay per capita and offers a good afternoon of feasting and interaction. Thus, it is a rare male who is not involved in at least one Maya ritual every several years.

In truth, the milpero is less familiar with the theological contents and *raison d'être* of the Maya ritual than with the Catholic. He knows little of the milpa deities beyond their number and certainly knows very few, if any, of their names. Nor are more than a few villagers familiar with magical or ritual phrases for the propitiation of Maya deities.

Specialists and Participants

The full Maya pantheon is known to only three individuals in Pustunich. Foremost among them is Venancio Cocom, descendant of the Cocoms of Mayapan. He is the village h-men, the Maya priest, a wizened man in his mid-sixties, a poor man who makes milpa and dresses in whites. Only Cocom officiates at cha chaac. He is also the most frequently chosen leader of uhai col—the harvest thanksgiving ritual. The Curanderos Belem also have much knowledge of bush and milpa beings and frequently officiate at uhai col.

The Maya specialists, however, occupy no position of general leadership which derives from their curative and ritual expertise. Whatever the influence the brothers Belem have exerted in village affairs can be attributed to their wealth alone. Justo Belem has twice run for mayor. Lacking both local support and the Ticul president's trust, he lost soundly. He was elected president of the area Orange Grower's Association because of his showplace groves, not his ability to influence the ancient balams. Venancio Cocom has never held village office nor is his counsel sought for anything but healing or ritual. When he participates in a communal hunt he is only one among many. Leadership is vested in the most experienced, and generally charismatic, huntsman, not in Cocom with his knowledge of bush spirits and their whims.

If females dominate Catholic ritual, males totally control the Maya.

Neither priest nor participant may be female and no woman is allowed close to an altar. Most Maya ritual is milpa ritual and milpa is the work of men. It is not that Maya ceremonial functions as a secret society. To the contrary, men tell their wives of the ritual and its contents, and women prepare and consume a portion of the key ritual offerings (albeit at a good distance from the altar). The reason women are excluded is that they can harm the ritual by their presence. Similarly, women can unknowingly harm the making of lime. For this reason a piece of feminine attire is placed in the lime pyre as a *contra*—a preventive device against the chance arrival of a female close to the fire. The cha chaac and uhai col offering is a *pib*, or corn cake consisting of twelve layers interspersed with calabash seed paste. Women shape the individual layer patties. The men, however, add the elements which make the pib different from a mass of thick tortillas. They smear calabash seed paste between each layer and make the four indented holes (representing the four directions and their "winds") on top of the completed pib into which more paste and *balche*-bark infusion are added. The men then wrap each pib in juano leaves to be placed in an underground oven beyond the altar. Men prepare all other foods for the ritual. They clean and dice onions, tomatoes, and carrots, and disjoint the chickens, turkeys, and pork for the rich offering stew. They cook it in large pots or buckets. Later, the baked pibs are added to the stew and all present, from the youngest boy at the altar-foot to the youngest girl among the women at the other side of the solar, must partake of it. Thus, though the ritual itself is a male activity, women play an essential part in its preparation and conclusion.

Like the mass, the Maya ritual is elaborate, involving incense-passes, the raising and lowering of various offerings, spilling of offerings beneath and around the altar, mixing of offerings, and other specific movements to the accompaniment of an almost inaudible and constant chanting by the h-men.

Unlike the mass, however, there is no direct audience participation during the ritual itself, which is performed by the h-men and one or two volunteer assistants. The men in attendance participate, rather, by preparing the soup and pibs and partaking of them afterwards to close the ritual. The ritual is strictly the work of the h-men and several assistants who wave the censer and pour a bowl or two of offering upon the grounds in certain directions. The h-men chants in a very low voice while the audience sits on the ground a few yards distant and smokes, gossips, and looks about. Few pay attention for more than a few minutes at a time. Few hear a word of the muted chanting. Small boys run and jostle. The gossip of adults begins with the cutting of onions and continues through the ritual and eating of the rich *xiach* (soup).

Like the Catholic ritual, the Maya does not attract all or almost all potential participants. Nonetheless, more males attend the preplanting cha chaac than any other ritual, Catholic or Maya. Most cha chaacs attract 100 to 150 men, or close to half the nuclear family heads in Pustunich. Others may be working or at the milpa and may contribute varying sums of money for which they receive a prorated number of ritual pibs later. By eating the pib they partake of the grace obtained through the ritual. Even nonmilperos such as storekeeper Clem Perez and the teacher Gomez frequently donate to the cha chaac and are carefully listed in the book of associates for subsequent distribution of pibs.

Regardless of attendance, few exhibit enthusiastic belief in the efficacy of the Maya ritual. Roberto Ek, the secretary to the water office in Oxkutzkab and also ejidal comisario, and Desiderio Gomez, the teacher's younger milpero brother, say that cha chaac does nothing— "it's only a custom. It would rain or not rain regardless of whether it were performed. Many people go because it's a custom and everyone eats well—a fine meal." Though both of these young men rarely attend Maya ritual, they are *not* representative of their age mates, most of whom do participate frequently. This is not to say that others do not hold similar views of the efficacy of cha chaac. However, the "fine meal," male camaraderie, and abundant gossip are attractive, and there is always the chance that the ritual will do some good. Few in Pustunich will give an unhesitating "yes" or "no" to the question of the cha chaac's efficacy. Most prefer to answer "who knows?" and attend with some regularity.

Supernatural Forces

In a similar manner the village is at ease with the lesser spirits and supernatural beings of the locale. All know of the *xtabay*—the female who resides in the ceibo tree and one of the local cactuses and who may lure men to their ends. Familiar, too, are the *alux*—the helpers (usually made of clay) constructed years ago by h-menob or witches to do their evil bidding. Both xtabay and alux can perform mischief and some in Pustunich have had experience with them. Objects may disappear mysteriously from a house or milpa hut. It is said that many years ago h-menob bent on evil made implements of clay in the form of little humans. They would go into the bush and do evil for the h-menob. The h-menob have all died out now and some of the clay men are still running around in the bush and the knowledge of how to stop them is lost. They may steal shoes of men working in the monte, or blow out their candles. When they're not working, the aluxes sleep in caves or lime pits. They can be killed by covering them with dirt as they sleep and then dousing them with water.

Pustunicheños know of these beings but pay little heed to the stories. Once, when the ethnographer brought many little cactuses from the monte to decorate his solar, several villagers jokingly pointed out that they were of the type which contained xtabays. No one appeared worried. Villagers regularly find anthropomorphic forms of clay near the ruins of classic Maya temples in their milpas. They eagerly pick them up and bring them back to town as curios—to be placed in their houses or to be given to friends. They are not buried and watered-down first.

Pustunicheños are not generally afraid of the dark. They keep late hours and walk down dark streets and bush paths. Night is a time for relaxed strolls, gossiping, and town meetings. If hunting lamps are available, night becomes the favored time to hunt and patrol the blackened bush. Often, hunters sit for hours by a known deer path in the pitch-darkness of the deep bush, listening optimistically—not apprehensively—for every tell-tale rustle.

In terms of its effect upon men, the supernatural concerns Pustunich far more in retrospect than in prospect. Few in the village take precautions against, or exhibit much fear of, aluxes, xtabays, winds, or witches. They all know of these phenomena, however, and should an unfortunate or inexplicable event occur they may consider the possibility that such a force was responsible. Few events, however, are viewed as inexplicable by the villagers. Illness comes from weakness of the organism, a "psychological shock," overwork, or lack of caution. Very few incidents of illness have been associated with witchcraft in Pustunich and none has occurred within the past seven or eight years. Accidents are caused by lack of caution, clumsiness, or stupidity.

Infants and children are more susceptible to impersonal winds, shocks, and the power of other persons than are adults. When a child is born it must be kept from winds for nine days, during which neither mother nor infant leaves the house of birth. Following birth, the infant is susceptible to sharp temperature changes and the evil eye for about a year. Evil eye is not common. The most usual form occurs when a mother, carrying her infant, is passed in the street by a pregnant woman. If the latter does not speak to the mother, the child will become ill shortly thereafter, usually manifesting diarrhea by the next morning.

Measles is the only childhood illness which requires interaction with the supernatural. No curer or physician is required. The parents place three gourds of rich chicken soup out under the house eaves for nine days. There is mixed opinion as to whom the soup is for. Some say "the spirits," others infer Catholic deities, still others are not sure at all. The cure is almost always successful—not inconsequentially as a result of the child's daily feeding of the savory potage after the spirit has "partaken" of it. Though measles is cured by supernatural intervention, it is not thought to be *caused* by nonnatural forces.

Susto (magical fright, shock) is very uncommon and not associated with soul loss as in other areas of Mexico. Occasionally it may be diagnosed in retrospect to account for unusual behavior. Typical (of an untypical phenomenon) is the case of the twenty-nine-year-old mentally retarded son of Policarpo Cahuich. He wanders around the village giggling and saying "hi!" to everyone he meets. He dresses himself with difficulty. All in the village treat him kindly, returning his greeting or anticipating it. Adults sharply reprimand any children who attempt to tease the young man. His parents maintain that his condition was caused by an early susto—the child was only two months old when a sky-rocket exploded near his hammock. Others in the village comment that the retardation is congenital and that Don Policarpo and his wife try to obscure this by claiming susto. It is interesting that the boy's name, Adelberto, has been forgotten by most villagers, who instead call him "Paquilla"— a feminine designation. Paquilla is one of two young Pustunicheños (the other also somewhat retarded, yet able to do some work) designated as *medio inutiles.*

Most "winds" are viewed as natural forces. They are things which exist and which can be avoided. If contacted, one will fall ill. They are largely impersonal forces, having no consciousness, and are viewed as malignant air currents or simple temperature gradients. Many attribute minor gastric disturbances or muscle aches to having "gone outside while sweating on a cool day—especially after ironing or making tortillas." Few in Pustunich have suffered from the effects of a "sent" wind. It is known, however, that witches and h-menob can send winds at their enemies. Paco Trujillo says that five years ago his little son, Manuel, had a fit on the street. They took him to Venancio Cocom, the h-men, and Don Ven diagnosed a "wind." However, the wind was not directed at the boy. Cocom figured that the wind had been sent by some h-men (unspecified) to attack another and that little Manuel had simply passed through it while it was doing its work. The cure took four weeks, during which time Manuel had attacks "every Tuesday and Friday."* The cure involved prayers and little yellow crosses which were painted on Manuel's forehead, stomach, palms, and insteps. The cure cost Paco $40.

Witchcraft is known in Pustunich, though very few have personally experienced it. Witches (*brujos*), it is generally held, do not witch on their own behalves. They are paid specialists, performing for clients. They may use snakes, hummingbirds' hearts, and scorpions for their potions, and they can transform themselves into various animal forms.

Excerpt from field notes, July 1964:

Edilberto Perez, one of the town's most respected men, says that his mother was once witched. The witch sneaked into the house and painted her bread blue, so she couldn't eat it. It was in the form of a small animal. It also played with her genitals. She became very pale and went to a h-men in Dzan and offered to pay him if he'd rid her of this. The h-men took a quarter kilo of tiny *hoholi* seeds and went to her house. There he dropped the seeds around the entire periphery. When the witch's animal again came he couldn't enter the house until he had picked up every last seed. While the animal was doing this, the h-men caught it with a noose on the end of a stick. He took it to Dzan with him. I asked Edilberto what his mother had told him the h-men did with the animal. "Who knows?"

Both Mrs. Ordoñez [one of the town's two professional Catholic ritual singers] and her daughter claim to have been victims of witchcraft. Mrs. O. refused to be explicit but said that a neighbor woman had sent something at her, as she was hated by this woman. She claims to have spent over 1,000 pesos on doctors before going to a h-men for a final cure.

---

*Tuesday and Friday are special days in Spain and Latin America, frequently associated with certain saints or propitious events. Looking back over a distance of five years, these are the days Paco associates with his son's illness.

There have been no recent cases of witchcraft, and everyone agrees that, currently, there is no witch in Pustunich. There are, however, witches in other towns—probably Chicam and Mani. No one, furthermore, categorically denies that there are witches in Ticul, Dzan, Yotholin, Sacalum, or Oxkutzkab. There has been some joking gossip about Doña Eucaria Ek, the aged hag who resided on the main road through Pustunich until her recent death. No one, however, took the gossip seriously and teen-aged boys spent many enjoyable hours playing practical jokes on her—with no apparent fear of reprisals other than the eagerly awaited shrieks and invective.

Witchcraft is an interesting, though very infrequent, topic of conversation and does not inspire fear or anxiety. The curandero Torcuato Belem proudly tells of his uncle, a Cocom, who was a "legitimate witch." He killed his own mother through witchcraft, boasts the nephew: "My uncle had horns and a tail," says he, reminiscing. "All of the Cocoms were witches. Nine of my uncles died of witchcraft sent by other witches—it was a witch war." Regardless of the likelihood that this disclosure was a "put-on" for the ethnographer's benefit, it indicates a lack of concern about witchcraft and the stigma of association with, or blood relationship to, witches. Such joking references would be unthinkable in other areas of Mexico, particularly Chiapas.

Illness

Most illness is due to natural cause. "Winds" which cause illness when one has abruptly left a warm place for a colder are impersonal, natural phenomena, a result of simple lack of caution. If one has been making tortillas over a hot fire, it is best to wait about ten minutes before going outside if one wishes to avoid headaches and nausea. Like most other peoples of Mexico, Pustunicheños distinguish many foods as "hot" and "cold."[3] The curanderos know more such distinctions than do most villagers, who concern themselves with the "hotness" of chicken, orange juice, or coffee mainly when confronted with illness, and even here "hot" and "cold" categories may be ignored. These distinctions are becoming less important and the division of foods by actual temperature is of more daily importance. One can eat heated foods immediately after cold, that is, below room temperature, but should wait an hour or two after eating hot foods before eating cold. Otherwise, as even the teacher Gomez maintains, one "can get stomach trouble."

When illness strikes, the first response is almost invariably home remedies and/or patent medicines. It's cheaper than a visit to a curer or physician. All village families know the more common herbs and their use. Furthermore, all are familiar with aspirin, antacids, and other nonprescription drugs. Every village store stocks these (see Appendix I). In general, there is a greater tendency toward use of patent medicines than herbs at the first sign of discomfort.

For fever, acute or lingering symptoms, a specialist is approached. There are two practicing curanderos in the village itself, plus a h-men, who is generally patronized by older patients. They cure through use of herbs, recitation, bloodletting, and exotic acts. A second alternative is the graduate M.D., of which there are three in Ticul. The physicians cure by use of injections and prescriptions. A third alternative is the school teacher, who is trained to administer injections of penicillin.

In cases of accident or high fever, the Ticul M.D. is almost invariably approached. Where infants are involved, the trip to Ticul may be made at the first sign, assumed or actual, of a rise in temperature. Fever— particularly in children—is viewed as potentially dangerous and as something which the doctor with his injections is especially equipped to handle. Most patients feel slighted unless given an injection, and the doctors give them out wholesale ("to keep the peasants coming back," admitted one). One doctor uses such explanations as "weak" or "thin" blood in describing illnesses to *campesinos*. "This way," he comments, "they understand me. If *we* won't satisfy them, they'll just go back to using curanderos." Thus the patient receives both the desired injection and an explanation which he can understand.

As a regular part of normal-school curriculum, the teacher learned first aid and the dispensing of injections. Gomez has made it clear that he is to be approached only in cases of emergency. Still, he is put upon by many who, through a desire to save money, wait too long with symptoms which ordinarily are taken to the M.D. During a recent flu epidemic, storekeeper Clemente was carried in a feverish delirium to the teacher's home for an injection which could have been postponed the five minutes it takes to reach Ticul. Once the teacher began giving out penicillin injections for flu patients, dozens who might have gone to the doctor in Ticul came to him for treatment.

Symptoms which do not involve fever are far more likely to be immediately treated at home. If the symptoms persist and cause considerable discomfort, yet are other than familiar rheumatic pains, the patient may eventually patronize the doctor in Ticul. While most Pustunicheños have been treated by the curanderos, there is no wholesale use of their services. Villagers pay more calls to M.D.s than to curanderos over a year's period, even though curanderos charge less than the combined physician-prescription fee. Lower fees do attract villagers, however, in cases of symptoms which cause continuous, though not severe, discomfort, and in cases, such as rheumatic, arthritic, and "low back" pains, which most agree cannot really be permanently cured by the physician. Complaints which unambiguously fall within the curandero's competence are those of psychiatric origin (strange, unusual behavior) and suspected attack by witch or wind (symptoms being lethargy, head pain, and diarrhea, among others). Regardless of fever or discomfort, those rare cases wherein the family has reason to believe witchcraft was operative are taken directly to the curandero. Fees for such cures are higher than for mundane organic complaints, probably because the curandero is not competing with the physician for jurisdiction over the case. Local curanderos reflect the attitude of the times. Witchcraft is not an important element in village life and will not be diagnosed unless the patient himself has indicated a suspicion or a "preference." Most diagnoses made by curanderos are those of impersonal "winds" which attack the body. Cure entails administration of one type of herb to exorcise the wind and others to alleviate specific symptoms caused by it.

The town's three curers are general-purpose practitioners. They treat everything but accidents. Arthritis, obesity, sorcery, and winds all fall within the scope of their practice. As such, they hardly fit Adams and Rubel's dichotomy of Meso-American curanderos as either (a) "limited practitioner or specialist who concerns himself with particular situations" or (b) "socio-ritual curer who, while utilizing techniques of the specialist, is also concerned closely with the socio-psychological side of illness."[4] Pustunich's curers deal with both the mundane and the psychological, attributing cause of illness to microbe as readily as magic. Their techniques vary from the spectacular to the commonplace, and points between. Literate and better read than most villagers on modern concepts of illness, they are quick to recognize the physician's superiority in treating common infectious diseases which are readily susceptible to antibiotic treatment. They compete best with the physician in more ambiguous or uncertain areas—lingering symptoms, chronic or self-inflicted problems (obesity), and psychological aberrance. In this sense, they are an adjunct to, rather than competitor of, modern medicine.

The two curanderos and the h-men differ considerably in their stylistic presentation to both public and patient. Torcuato Belem is by far the most famous of the three. He exudes confidence and displays his wealth in his new masonry waiting room, his car, and his wives. His specialty is witchcraft and obesity, and his methods are spectacular. He frequently utilizes the fowl-technique, wherein a chicken placed over the patient's head attracts the evil and dies as a sign of cure. In another method, Torcuato drops spools of brightly colored thread from the rafters onto the patient's prone body, and with the proper incantations the evil passes from the body up the threads to the spools which are then disposed of. He has a miraculous *sacstum*—small sphere of clear glass with an imperfection at its center (not unlike a child's marble)—with which he can diagnose patients at a distance.

Torcuato's younger brother Justo presents himself as a specialist in psychosomatic illness. Unlike either Torcuato or the h-men he is likely to prescribe Equanil, Aralen, or phenobarbital, all of which he sells in his general store, and diagnose a case as "psychic shock." He will use bloodletting more frequently than his colleagues. Justo is an astute businessman and almost fanatic in his pursuit of neatness. Both his store and orange grove are neat. A jar or tube is seldom out of place in the tiled store, nor is a stone or weed to be seen under his straight-rowed orange trees. He takes little for granted. "I won't accept a patient I don't think I can cure," he confides. "Especially if they have a high fever, I'll send them off to the M.D. If they die, let *him* take the blame." Belief in the evil eye and winds, he continues, is not related to whether they do or don't exist. "Some believe in it and some don't. Frankly, at the base of it, whether some guy believes in it or not depends simply on whether his parents believed in it."

Cocom, the h-men, might be termed the purist among the three. His methods usually involve herbs and prayers, many of which are familiar to the patient. His patients are generally older people. Unlike the Belems, whose clientele and incomes are largely derived from non-Pustunicheños, Cocom treats villagers almost exclusively. Because his father (also a h-men) lived in a time when the *real* was almost as common as the peso, he insists on following his father's tradition of charging his patients in reales (hypothetical value: 12 1/2¢) but "accepting" payment in the peso equivalent. Often, he hands the patient some reales, which the patient immediately returns in symbolic traditional payment.

Pustunich is at ease with both "inside" and "outside" medical practice. The continuing compartmentalization of symptoms into doctor-specific and curandero-specific precludes active competition between the two and development of conflicting world views to accommodate one or the other. Patient preferences for the two types of practice today represent a continuum. Justo Belem, in examining a list of all village males, points out roughly 10 to 15 percent who patronize physicians only and a similar number who take their ills to curanderos exclusively. The majority—70 to 80 percent—fall somewhere in between. Indeed, the lessening dependence upon local curers has, in fact, freed curers for the far more lucrative "foreign" clientele. The high-paying patients from Merida and Campeche allow the brothers Belem to prosper and thus maintain their traditional trades within (and available to) the village.

Conclusions

Eric Wolf suggests that two levels of religious practice and explanation operate in peasant society. One is that of the peasant himself, concerned with mundane, highly personal events. The second is that of the specialist, concerned with the esoteric and with higher-order meanings. "It is not," says Wolf, "that the peasant is ideologically uncreative; he is limited in his creativity by his concentration upon the first order of business, which is to come to terms with his ecosystem and his fellow-men."[5] In Pustunich, such first- and second-order concerns also serve as foci for two distinct systems of ritual. One, the Catholic, is a general-purpose religious system, introspective and esoteric in the sense that its ritual functions largely to celebrate the supernatural hierarchy and to produce diffuse rewards. Its wealth of symbols is ultimately controlled and interpretable by a hierarchy of outside, nonpeasant specialists. Regardless of its minimal use of priests and maximal reliance upon local ritual organization, Catholic ritual in Pustunich exhibits few local embellishments at odds with the "great tradition" of Mexican Catholicism. The village feels itself to be closely linked to the national religion, and contact with the Church neither threatens nor influences local behavior.

The other ritual system, the Maya, coincides with "the first order of business." True, there was once an outside Maya hierarchy which controlled ritual and symbol and which acted in the general welfare for diffuse or higher-order purposes. These latter functions have long since passed into Catholic hands, leaving behind a ritual of limited purpose. Its specialists are local peasants, its symbolism less remote from interpretation. Its ritual is devoted to supplementing the relationship between specific economic techniques and the local environment. It is thus no less secure an element of village life than is milpa. The Maya ritual system faces no competition from the Catholic, exhibits no overlap in supervisory roles, and looks to no outside referent for reinforcement.

It should again be stressed that ritual specialists have never exercised general leadership in the village. Compartmentalization of ritual and secular authority has been the rule since long before the conquest. What little secular leadership has been required in Pustunich has come from batabs, caciques, and comisarios imported or appointed by outside powerholders. Today, local indigenous specialists concentrate wholly upon major Maya ritual. Minor ritual is strictly an individual concern. Outside specialists (priests) control only the major Catholic rituals. At the same time, such ritual is organized by local secular committees under a mandate from other local secular committees. "Traditional" political behavior, for its part, falls to local secular officials beholden to outside secular authority.

The compartmentalization of Catholic and Maya ritual finds an analogy in the relationship between folk and modern health practice. Symptoms are fairly well differentiatable as either physician- or curer-specific, and a majority of villagers make some use of both. Although such compartmentalization unquestionably reflects a weakening of folk medical practice, it also serves to slow down the process of change by lessening direct conflict between the two systems. Furthermore, the very openness of the community undermines the bases of certain socioritual illness beliefs common elsewhere in Mexico. Pustunich views the world as essentially nonthreatening. The pie, furthermore, is *not* limited in size. Social mobility or economic accumulation is not threatening. Thus the weakness of witchcraft and envy syndromes which, by contrast, are characteristic of Chiapan and Oaxacan Maya groups.

Between the Catholic Church and indigenous Maya ritual, or modern medicine and generalized Mexican folk-medical practice, Pustunicheños find solutions specific to most problems which lie beyond the average individual's control. The village is at ease with both the natural and supernatural, and with both inside- and outside-oriented mechanisms for dealing with them.

NOTES

1. Robert Redfield, "The Social Organization of Tradition." *The Far Eastern Quarterly* 15 (1955): 13-21.

2. William Madsen, "Religious Syncretism." In Robert Wauchope and Manning Nash, eds., *Handbook of Middle American Indians*, Vol. 6 (Austin: University of Texas Press, 1967), p. 386.

3. For a thorough discussion of typical Yucatec hot-cold foods, see Robert Redfield and Alfonso Villa Rojas, *Chan Kom: A Maya Village* (Washington: Carnegie Institute of Washington, Publication No. 448, 1934). Also, Robert Redfield, *The Folk Culture of Yucatan* (Chicago: University of Chicago Press, 1941), p. 343.

4. Richard N. Adams and A. J. Rubel, "Sickness and Social Relations." In Robert Wauchope and Manning Nash, eds., *Handbook of Middle American Indians*, Vol. 6 (Austin: University of Texas Press, 1967), p. 349. For a more thorough discussion and criticism of Latin American curer style, see Irwin Press, "The Urban Curandero." *American Anthropologist* 73 (1971): 741-756.

5. Eric R. Wolf, *Peasants* (Englewood Cliffs, N.J.: Prentice-Hall, 1966), p. 103.

11

In Retrospect: A Society of Parts

Wolf has noted that "what goes on in Gopalpur, India, or Alcala de la Sierra in Spain cannot be explained in terms of that village alone; the explanation must include considerations both of the outside forces impinging on these villages and of the reactions of villagers to these forces."[1] In a circular fashion, the reactions to previous forces determine the reception of future ones and each such interaction permanently modifies behavior and expectations. "Inside" and "outside" become relative concepts, as dependent upon historical perspective as upon geographic origin for differentiation. Thus new concepts of female dress compete with "traditional" views that formal attire should consist in the tiered terno (a local development) and three-inch high-heeled pumps (an "outside" item in vogue since movies and magazines began entering the village many decades ago). To Pustunicheños, the terno and high-heeled pumps are traditional items and "go together" just as sandals or store-bought flats go with the everyday huipil.

It was, in fact, a more recently introduced item which allowed realization of an older borrowed value. The cement basketball court dance floor made use of high heels practical for the first time. Similarly, like the desire for high heels, the desirability of catrin status is nothing new.

The example set by the teacher and the fairly recent availability of higher schools is simply encouraging the realization of a much older mobility value. It should be noted that most of Pustunich's catrins are becoming teachers, thus bypassing any blue collar stage in upward mobility. Indeed, the town's catrins are far better educated than Mexico's ladino (catrin) population in general. The catrin value, though of outside origin, is as much a part of Pustunich as is milpa. It is what contributes to the makeup of a part-society. Similarly, conquest, conversion, rebellion, revolution, the Church, plantation system, and outside political entities have all contributed to the creation of a unique local orientation against which present pressures, both from within and without, are perceived and evaluated.

Benedict's concept of continuity and discontinuity in socialization[2] can be profitably applied to the historic passage of a whole community into the modern era. Pustunich was not thrust unprepared into the present by the opening of a new road. As noted earlier, it has had the opportunity to pick and choose what it would—or more realistically, *could*—of new items as they appeared. Corn mills, movies, and radios were adopted locally almost as soon as they became available. Catrins, on the other hand, appeared only when it became feasible. Thus many aspects of technological and sociological "modernity" have been part of Pustunich's youth, just as many of these aspects have themselves "grown up" along with the village. In perceptually keepin g up with many of these, and in adopting some, Pustunich has felt itself to be at least somewhat modern. There is little cultural paranoia in the sense of an introverted, conscious protectiveness of the way of life.

Outside phenomena in themselves need not threaten conservatism or, for that matter, structural equilibrium. Wage labor, accompanied in Pustunich by a secure traditional economic base, has meant more stability and security than would be possible through milpa alone. The new committee system sponsors so many social and sporting events that it has become far less necessary for villagers to go to Ticul or elsewhere for recreation and "escape." Furthermore, in the process of building up committee participation, Pustunich has essentially reincarnated the long defunct *fagina* (communal labor) of a half century past, and at the same time has built up an unprecedented pride and identification with the little community.

Aside from the provenience of values or behavior, what of the social structure itself? To what extent can it accommodate—or retard— change?

In patrilineal bands, to be an encumbent of one role is to be an encumbent, almost automatically, of all available roles. Personnel who "manage" one institution are generally those who manage all others. To a lesser extent, tribal and corporate clan societies exhibit similar structures. Kinship, economic, ritual, and political roles are frequently ascribed by birth. Thus what the individual does in any capacity cannot usually escape the view of others and, indeed, directly affects them. In simpler societies, moreover, institutions (as well as personnel) tend to be functionally dependent upon one another to some degree. For example, economic well-being is often tied to ritual practice, ritual practice to familial identity (ancestor worship, inheritance of spirit guardians, gerontocratic control of supernatural). Shift in one institution implies some repercussion in others.

In peasant Pustunich, few institutions are critically dependent upon others. Thus while mestizo status is inextricably bound with milpa labor, catrin identity is not dependent upon any particular economic activity. At most, it is negatively associated with milpa. Similarly, while Maya ritual is totally bound to economic activity, the Catholic is not. Milpa work groups are strongly, but not completely, tied to kinship identity. Political behavior is independent of almost everything. The more village-encompassing types of ritual are not family-related, while the more restricted in personnel (harvest *uahi col* or name-day novenas) are. The uahi col, in fact, is dependent upon family ties only to the extent that kin happen to be milpa partners. As with mestizo status, sex role identity is dependent upon economic activity within the village, but not without. White collar work, specifically teaching, is independent of sex identity. The dependence of sex role identification upon ritual participation is strong at certain life-periods only.

The result is a potential for change in one institution without automatic and possibly dysfunctional repercussions in others. Thus the milpa group tends to be derived from the nuclear family, but is not inevitably synonymous with it. If the creation of a catrin son later deprives the father of a milpa partner, he can readily find other partners. It will be recalled that there is but a 1:1 return on milpa labor. To thus add another member to a milpa group does not diminish or improve the return of the "charter" members. Protestantism may claim certain villagers without either severing their ties to milpa ritual or depriving them of major sources of interaction with their fellows. Indeed, the new committee system offers even more interactive and recreative opportunities each month than does the Catholic novena schedule. The committee system itself could grow largely because of isolation (and the isolation of traditional political behavior) from other institutional spheres. Pustunich is theoretically less susceptible to the large-scale "domino" shifts which could potentially occur within other Meso-American peasant communities with civil-religious hierarchies, cargo systems, or economic-leveling, envidia-witchcraft complexes.

Institutional integration is nonetheless sufficient to foster a conscious conservatism. Villagers are quite aware that henequen zone towns which make no milpa have virtually lost the Maya ritual. That henequen towns of similar size maintain up to a half-dozen thriving cantinas, while Pustunich has—and needs—none, is similarly not lost on the villagers. Pustunicheños, as mentioned earlier, know that catrins cannot remain in the town, and that to ensure mobility for all one's children is to doom one's own way of life. Parents thus purposely maintain one or two children of both sexes as mestizos to ensure that traditional milpa and house needs will be met in the future. In so doing they are clearly raising a new generation of "traditional" Pustunicheños. As improving medical care and normal population growth could conceivably cause some pressure within the next generation or two, the creation and banishment of selected catrin children may prove quite *functional*.

It should be stressed that mobility *is* possible in Yucatan. Catrin (ladino) status is achievable. One needs only shoes, better dress, and a nonmilpa economic identity and, regardless of parentage, one is accepted by local catrins and mestizos alike. While the one has more prestige than the other, there is no extension of the terms to include intangibles such as intrinsic quality of the individual. This class system contrasts sharply with that of other Latin-American regions where the ladino-mestizo (or indio) dichotomy is far deeper and approaches the caste-like in the impermeability of ladino status. In many communities of Guatemala and southern Mexico it would be virtually impossible for an indio or mestizo parent to create a ladino child. Neither local indios nor ladinos would accept the identity and the parent would be derided.

The presence of both classes in small Meso-American communities is not infrequent, however. Attempts at interclass mobility are usually frustrated and may end in failure and even greater frustration[3] or symptoms of disorientation and anxiety.[4] It follows that such a system is less likely to weather a change without dysfunctional results. Indeed, from a more classical sociological point of view, the system is likely to *generate* dysfunctional change. Merton suggests that deviation results where certain universal goals are attainable only by certain ascribed role encumbents or individuals of very special achievement.[5] The ladino-indio caste system, as well as the civil-religious hierarchy with its postponement of full prestige, make Guatemalan and south Mexican peasantries theoretically susceptible to potentially disruptive innovation.[6]

We have been speaking of institutional integration. In terms of *interpersonal* integration, institutional personnel requirements are diffuse in Pustunich. That is, for no single institutional function is the entire population or even a group of specified, ascribed-role encumbents required. Economic activities are carried out by small groups of varying composition, as are the bulk of ritual activities. Communal works, uahi col ritual, hunts, house movings, private novenas, lime burnings, and town meetings rarely exhibit identical personnel from one occasion to the next. More to the point, validation or potential sanction of the individual's behavior is seldom vested in the community as a whole. The membership of the group which views—and is dependent upon—his economic behavior is not necessarily the same as that of the groups in which his familial, committee-political, or recreational behavior occurs. The structure can thus potentially accommodate individual novel behavior in one institutional context without automatic repercussion in another. In practice, of course, such separation is never absolute. The potential for nondisruptive change is nonetheless present. It should be stressed that while no single activity attracts even a simple majority of villagers, over a year's period most individuals will have participated in at least one such activity with most others. Through these overlapping contacts and shared (if independently pursued) goals Pustunich is knit into an interactive unit—a system.

To view Pustunich in folk-society terms would produce a picture of a community long in the process of losing its social and cultural heritage. It would have to be examined and analyzed not in terms of what it is, but what it might have been and where it is possibly going.

If we, on the other hand, view Pustunich as an entity composed of individuals and parts organized for the continuity of the community itself rather than for the continuity of any particular social structure or cultural complex, we will understand far more about it. From this point of view, we see the community as still vigorous and successful. That is, it provides its members with economic, social, symbolic, and other means for survival and satisfaction in the broadest sense.

The way in which Pustunich provides and manages these means is complex. Integration of institutions and individuals is incomplete. Inside and outside pressures affect different institutions differently and each accommodates or reaches equilibrium in its own way. The manner in which mestizo-catrin shifts are accommodated—by funneling potentially disruptive catrins out of the community—is quite different from the way in which traditional leadership and modern committee leadership coexist. The latter accommodation results from parallel development and utilization of unprecedented (rather than overtly competitive) avenues for expression.

As a point of more than passing interest, it should be noted that Pustunich is not sending its disgruntled failures to add to the crisis of the cities. The catrins it shunts outward are better trained, more sophisticated, and more capable of adding constructively to Yucatec and Mexican society than are simple mestizo milperos who have lost their lands or become disenchanted with the rural life.

In short, this part-society is vigorous and complex. It is not only a successful adaptation to an old process, but is capable of accommodating and contributing constructively to the new.

Excerpt from field notes, July 1964:

Today was warm with a lovely breeze. I walked aimlessly around town, down every back street. As I passed one alley, I saw Pablo Cocom sitting on the dirt, his back to the stone hedge in front of his thatched house, gazing at the juano palms across the path. He was wearing his peasant white under-shirt and a pair of Indian-style shorts in the fashion of his father, the town's only h-men. Feet in deer-skin sandals, hands and toes gnarled from milpa work.

"Hello, Press," he called. "Hello, Cocom. What'r you doing?"
"Just contemplating the afternoon," he replied. Then he asked: "Did you hear about the failure of the wheat crop in Poland? But don't worry, Gringo. They say on the radio that the agronomists have it under control."

NOTES

1. Eric R. Wolf, *Peasants* (Englewood Cliffs, N.J.: Prentice-Hall, 1966), p. 1.

2. Ruth Benedict, "Continuities and Discontinuities in Cultural Conditioning." *Psychiatry* 1 (1938): 161-167.

3. Cf. Melvin Tumin, *Caste in a Peasant Society* (Princeton, N.J.: Princeton University Press, 1952), p. 148.

4. William C. Sayres, "Disorientation and Status Change." *Southwestern Journal of Anthropology* 12 (1956): 79-86.

5. Robert K. Merton, *Social Theory and Social Structure* (Glencoe, Ill.: The Free Press, 1957), p. 145.

6. For a discussion of industrialization, unionization, democratic voting, and a civil-religious system in Guatemala, see Manning Nash, "Machine Age Maya: the Industrialization of a Guatemalan Community." *Memoir of the American Anthropologist* No. 87 (1958).

Appendix I

The Part-Society as Viewed Through the Total of Items Stocked by Pustunich Stores

Groceries

salt
sugar
corn (in grain or dough)
wheat flour
corn flour
rice flour
chocolate patties
rice
beans
bread
noodles
rendered pork fat
oatmeal
coffee (regular and instant)
garlic
barley
chick peas
lime for corn processing

sweet rolls (fresh daily from Ticul)
onions
bouillon cubes and powder
tea (in commercial single packets)
saffron
veganin tablets
pepper
spices (cinnamon, cloves, etc.)
canned peas
canned hot dogs
canned mackerel ("tuna style")
canned powdered milk for babies
sugared, condensed milk (2 sizes)
pickled peppers in bulk cans
olive oil
saltines
salty "cocktail-style" snacks
home-made pickled onions

For the Man

machete blades
shotgun shot (6 calibres, loose)
gun powder
fulminating caps
sand paper
nails (many sizes)

machine oil (for sewing machines)
galvanized wire
whetstones
woven tump lines
Justrite Hunting Lamps
auto-tire sandal soles

For the Woman

thread
bordering thread
combs, straight and curved
Bouquet Soap
Colgate Soap
Camay Soap
Palmolive Soap
steel wool
laundry brushes
bluing
Epsom salts
razor blades
face powder (2 sizes, perfumed)
skin cream
Rosas Venus Soap

Colgate Tooth Paste
Fab (in small boxes)
rough laundry soap
washing soda
measuring tapes
metal snaps
brilliantine
hair pins (open and closed)
cotton pads
straight pins and safety pins
ribbon (15 sizes and colors)
lace
small mirrors
sewing needles (4 sizes)

For the House

kerosene-lamp chimneys
flashlight batteries (2 sizes)
Coleman Lamp generators
Coleman Lamp mantles
kerosene lamp wicks
gasoline
salt shakers
crocheting and knitting needles

kerosene
flashlight bulbs
insecticide (2 brands)
wall brackets
airmail envelopes
plastic spoons
incense

Medicines, Conundrums

aspirin
Mejoral (like Bufferin)
666 Vaporub
Mentholatum
Kelso Vaporub
suppositories
bicarbonate of soda
Penetrating rub
oil tablets
cold tablets
Benadryl syrup (coughs)
Dr. Ross's Pills
Cepacol (sore throats)
rheumatism medicine
acetic acid
hydrogen peroxide
Aralen (for malaria)

terramycin
penicillin (in injectable flasks)
equanil
coderit (a pain killer)
sulfathiazine tablets (2 types)
sulfa powder
Entero Viaform (amoebic specific)
Tedral (a tranquilizer)
Espasmo Cibalgina (anti-diar-rheac)
Proceptol
Pynil
Vaseline (2 kinds)
alcohol
vinegar
bandages
cotton bandage pads

Notions and Miscellaneous

Kleenex paper napkins
cigarettes (7 brands)
matches
balloons, all sizes
erasers
buttons (19 bottles and 6 boxes)
chewing gum
boys' stockings and T-shirts
radio parts and repair service

ball-point pens and refills
school note-tablets
pencils—regular and colored
guitar strings
candles (3 sizes)
sling-shot rubbers and pouches
toothpicks
rubber-bands

Appendix II

Kinship Terminology

From the point of view of culture change, the kinship terminology utilized in Pustunich presents some interesting facets. The system charted below is that given by a fourteen-year-old female informant. While older villagers utilize somewhat more of the Maya terms, the young girl better represents the present and future.

The system is clearly in a state of transition. For many kinsmen, both Spanish and Maya terms are available. Most Maya terms, where dominant over the Spanish, are those for nuclear family members and lineal kin. Terms for collateral and affinal relatives have been the first to undergo change and already indicate total or partial Spanish supremacy, as with "uncle," "aunt," or "nephew" (no Maya terms now known by any villager). Interestingly, dominance of Spanish terms is more visible among collateral than affinal kin. In addition perhaps to reflecting the initial uxorilocal residence common in past centuries, the preservation of specific Maya referents reflects the greater overall importance of affines to adult villagers. One not only has more obligations of reciprocity, hospitality, and aid with them, as compared with collateral relatives, but males more frequently make milpa with affines than collateral kinsmen.

In the charts following, all terms are referential unless specified. Terms are presented in order of frequency of usage. Regardless of the order in which it falls, any term listed is utilized in Pustunich today. Where only a single term—in Spanish—is given, no Maya equivalent is known to villagers. Among older men, more of the Maya terms are utilized as first choices.

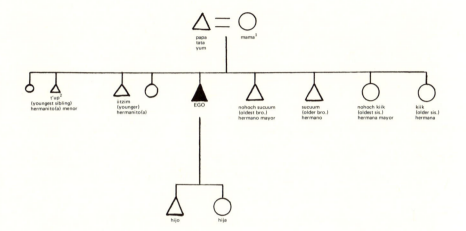

Chart 1 The Nuclear Family

[1]na also means "mother," but of an animal or insect. As such, it is a term of insult.

[2]t'up (youngest sibling) is also a word for baby finger.

SEX-SPECIFIC

uitziim xipal—younger brother

uitziim xchupal—younger sister

inhual—"my child" (used by women only)

inkiik—"my blood" or "my child" (seldom used)

inxipal (ref. to male) or inxchupal (female)—"my child"

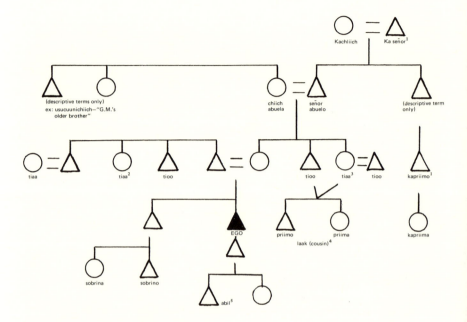

Chart 2 The Extended Family

[1]ka means "second" or "2."

[2]When aunts or uncles are roughly same age as ego, they are addressed by their given names.

[3]Being more specific: uk'iikimama—"mother's elder sister."

[4]laak also refers to relatives in general. inlaako—"my family."

[5]abilxchupal means granddaughter; abilxipal means grandson; inuab il means "my grandchild."

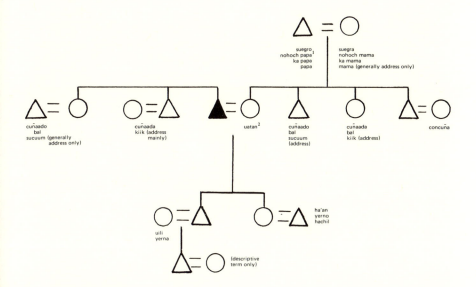

Chart 3 Affines

[1] nohoch means "big" or "great."

[2] cham means "husband." Wife may, in conversation with others, refer to her husband as letí or "that one."

NOTE: ulaakobinuatan means "my wife's siblings" or "my wife's family."

Index